Praise for *Learning LangChain*

With clear explanations and actionable techniques, this is the go-to resource for anyone looking to harness LangChain's power for production-ready generative AI and agents. A must-read for developers aiming to push the boundaries of this platform.

—*Tom Taulli, IT consultant and author of* AI-Assisted Programming

This comprehensive guide on LangChain covers everything from document retrieval and indexing to deploying and monitoring AI agents in production. With engaging examples, intuitive illustrations, and hands-on code, this book made learning LangChain interesting and fun!

—*Rajat K. Goel, senior software engineer, IBM*

This book is a comprehensive LLM guide covering fundamentals to production, packed with technical insights, practical strategies, and robust AI patterns.

—*Gourav Singh Bais, senior data scientist and senior technical content writer, Allianz Services*

Prototyping generative AI apps is easy—shipping them is hard. The strategies and tools in *Learning LangChain* make it possible to turn ideas into modern, production-ready applications.

—*James Spiteri, director of product management for security, Elastic*

Learning LangChain provides a clear path for transforming how you build AI-powered applications. By breaking down flexible architectures and robust checkpointing, it offers a strong foundation for creating reliable, production-ready AI agents at scale.

—*David O'Regan, engineering manager for AI/ML, GitLab*

Learning LangChain helped us skip the boilerplate for debugging and monitoring. The many helpful patterns and tooling insights allowed us to move fast and deploy AI apps with confidence.

—*Chris Focke, chief AI scientist, AppFolio*

Teaching LangChain through clear, actionable examples, this book is a gateway to agentic applications that are as inspiring as Asimov's sci-fi novels.

— *Ilya Meyzin, SVP head of data science, Dun & Bradstreet*

Learning LangChain

Building AI and LLM Applications with
LangChain and LangGraph

Mayo Oshin and Nuno Campos

Learning LangChain

by Mayo Oshin and Nuno Campos

Printed in the United States of America.

Published by O'Reilly Media, Inc., 1005 Gravenstein Highway North, Sebastopol, CA 95472.

O'Reilly books may be purchased for educational, business, or sales promotional use. Online editions are also available for most titles (*http://oreilly.com*). For more information, contact our corporate/institutional sales department: 800-998-9938 or *corporate@oreilly.com*.

Acquisitions Editor: Nicole Butterfield	**Indexer:** Judith McConville
Development Editor: Corbin Collins	**Interior Designer:** David Futato
Production Editor: Clare Laylock	**Cover Designer:** Karen Montgomery
Copyeditor: nSight, Inc.	**Illustrator:** Kate Dullea
Proofreader: Helena Stirling	

February 2025:   First Edition

Revision History for the First Edition

2025-02-13:   First Release

See *http://oreilly.com/catalog/errata.csp?isbn=9781098167288* for release details.

978-1-098-16728-8

[LSI]

Table of Contents

Preface

On November 30, 2022, San Francisco–based firm OpenAI publicly released ChatGPT (*https://oreil.ly/uAnsr*)—the viral AI chatbot that can generate content, answer questions, and solve problems like a human. Within two months of its launch, ChatGPT attracted over 100 million monthly active users (*https://oreil.ly/ATsLe*), the fastest adoption rate of a new consumer technology application (so far). ChatGPT is a chatbot experience powered by an instruction and dialogue-tuned version of OpenAI's GPT-3.5 family of large language models (LLMs). We'll get to definitions of these concepts very shortly.

> Building LLM applications with or without LangChain requires the use of an LLM. In this book we will be making use of the OpenAI API as the LLM provider we use in the code examples (pricing is listed on its platform (*https://oreil.ly/-YYoR*)). One of the benefits of working with LangChain is that you can follow along with all of these examples using either OpenAI or alternative commercial or open source LLM providers.

Three months later, OpenAI released the ChatGPT API (*https://oreil.ly/DwU7R*), giving developers access to the chat and speech-to-text capabilities. This kickstarted an uncountable number of new applications and technical developments under the loose umbrella term of *generative AI*.

Before we define generative AI and LLMs, let's touch on the concept of *machine learning* (ML). Some computer *algorithms* (imagine a repeatable recipe for achievement of some predefined task, such as sorting a deck of cards) are directly written by a software engineer. Other computer algorithms are instead *learned* from vast amounts of training examples—the job of the software engineer shifts from writing the algorithm itself to writing the training logic that creates the algorithm. A lot of attention in the ML field went into developing algorithms for predicting any number of things, from tomorrow's weather to the most efficient delivery route for an Amazon driver.

With the advent of LLMs and other generative models (such as diffusion models for generating images, which we don't cover in this book), those same ML techniques are now applied to the problem of generating new content, such as a new paragraph of text or drawing, that is at the same time unique and informed by examples in the training data. LLMs in particular are generative models dedicated to generating text.

LLMs have two other differences from previous ML algorithms:

- They are trained on much larger amounts of data; training one of these models from scratch would be very costly.
- They are more versatile.

The same text generation model can be used for summarization, translation, classification, and so forth, whereas previous ML models were usually trained and used for a specific task.

These two differences conspire to make the job of the software engineer shift once more, with increasing amounts of time dedicated to working out how to get an LLM to work for their use case. And that's what LangChain is all about.

By the end of 2023, competing LLMs emerged, including Anthropic's Claude and Google's Bard (later renamed Gemini), providing even wider access to these new capabilities. And subsequently, thousands of successful startups and major enterprises have incorporated generative AI APIs to build applications for various use cases, ranging from customer support chatbots to writing and debugging code.

On October 22, 2022, Harrison Chase published the first commit (*https://oreil.ly/ mCdYZ*) on GitHub for the LangChain open source library. LangChain started from the realization that the most interesting LLM applications needed to use LLMs together with "other sources of computation or knowledge" (*https://oreil.ly/uXiPi*). For instance, you can try to get an LLM to generate the answer to this question:

```
How many balls are left after splitting 1,234 balls evenly among 123 people?
```

You'll likely be disappointed by its math prowess. However, if you pair it up with a calculator function, you can instead instruct the LLM to reword the question into an input that a calculator could handle:

```
1,234 % 123
```

Then you can pass that to a calculator function and get an accurate answer to your original question. LangChain was the first (and, at the time of writing, the largest) library to provide such building blocks and the tooling to reliably combine them into larger applications. Before discussing what it takes to build compelling applications with these new tools, let's get more familiar with LLMs and LangChain.

Brief Primer on LLMs

In layman's terms, LLMs are trained algorithms that receive text input and predict and generate humanlike text output. Essentially, they behave like the familiar auto-complete feature found on many smartphones, but taken to an extreme.

Let's break down the term *large language model*:

- *Large* refers to the size of these models in terms of training data and parameters used during the learning process. For example, OpenAI's GPT-3 model contains 175 billion *parameters*, which were learned from training on 45 terabytes of text data.[1] *Parameters* in a neural network model are made up of the numbers that control the output of each *neuron* and the relative weight of its connections with its neighboring neurons. (Exactly which neurons are connected to which other neurons varies for each neural network architecture and is beyond the scope of this book.)

- *Language model* refers to a computer algorithm trained to receive written text (in English or other languages) and produce output also as written text (in the same language or a different one). These are *neural networks*, a type of ML model which resembles a stylized conception of the human brain, with the final output resulting from the combination of the individual outputs of many simple mathematical functions, called *neurons*, and their interconnections. If many of these neurons are organized in specific ways, with the right training process and the right training data, this produces a model that is capable of interpreting the meaning of individual words and sentences, which makes it possible to use them for generating plausible, readable, written text.

Because of the prevalence of English in the training data, most models are better at English than they are at other languages with a smaller number of speakers. By "better" we mean it is easier to get them to produce desired outputs in English. There are LLMs designed for multilingual output, such as BLOOM (*https://oreil.ly/Nq7w0*), that use a larger proportion of training data in other languages. Curiously, the difference in performance between languages isn't as large as might be expected, even in LLMs trained on a predominantly English training corpus. Researchers have found that LLMs are able to transfer some of their semantic understanding to other languages.[2]

---

1 Tom B. Brown et al., "Language Models Are Few-Shot Learners" (*https://oreil.ly/1qoM6*), arXiv, July 22, 2020.

2 Xiang Zhang et al., "Don't Trust ChatGPT When Your Question Is Not in English: A Study of Multilingual Abilities and Types of LLMs" (*https://oreil.ly/u5Cy1*), Proceedings of the 2023 Conference on Empirical Methods in Natural Language Processing, December 6–10, 2023.

Put together, *large language models* are instances of big, general-purpose language models that are trained on vast amounts of text. In other words, these models have learned from patterns in large datasets of text—books, articles, forums, and other publicly available sources—to perform general text-related tasks. These tasks include text generation, summarization, translation, classification, and more.

Let's say we instruct an LLM to complete the following sentence:

```
The capital of England is _____.
```

The LLM will take that input text and predict the correct output answer as London. This looks like magic, but it's not. Under the hood, the LLM estimates the probability of a sequence of word(s) given a previous sequence of words.

 Technically speaking, the model makes predictions based on tokens, not words. A *token* represents an atomic unit of text. Tokens can represent individual characters, words, subwords, or even larger linguistic units, depending on the specific tokenization approach used. For example, using GPT-3.5's tokenizer (called cl100k), the phrase *good morning dearest friend* would consist of five tokens (*https://oreil.ly/dU83b*) (using _ to show the space character):

Good
> With token ID 19045

_morning
> With token ID 6693

_de
> With token ID 409

arest
> With token ID 15795

_friend
> With token ID 4333

Usually tokenizers are trained with the objective of having the most common words encoded into a single token, for example, the word *morning* is encoded as the token 6693. Less common words, or words in other languages (usually tokenizers are trained on English text), require several tokens to encode them. For example, the word *dearest* is encoded as tokens 409, 15795. One token spans on average four characters of text for common English text, or roughly three quarters of a word.

The driving engine behind LLMs' predictive power is known as the *transformer neural network architecture*.[3] The transformer architecture enables models to handle sequences of data, such as sentences or lines of code, and make predictions about the likeliest next word(s) in the sequence. Transformers are designed to understand the context of each word in a sentence by considering it in relation to every other word. This allows the model to build a comprehensive understanding of the meaning of a sentence, paragraph, and so on (in other words, a sequence of words) as the joint meaning of its parts in relation to each other.

So, when the model sees the sequence of words *the capital of England is*, it makes a prediction based on similar examples it saw during its training. In the model's training corpus the word *England* (or the token(s) that represent it) would have often shown up in sentences in similar places to words like *France, United States, China*. The word *capital* would figure in the training data in many sentences also containing words like *England, France*, and *US*, and words like *London, Paris, Washington*. This repetition during the model's training resulted in the capacity to correctly predict that the next word in the sequence should be *London*.

The instructions and input text you provide to the model is called a *prompt*. Prompting can have a significant impact on the quality of output from the LLM. There are several best practices for *prompt design* or *prompt engineering*, including providing clear and concise instructions with contextual examples, which we discuss later in this book. Before we go further into prompting, let's look at some different types of LLMs available for you to use.

The base type, from which all the others derive, is commonly known as a *pretrained LLM*: it has been trained on very large amounts of text (found on the internet and in books, newspapers, code, video transcripts, and so forth) in a self-supervised fashion. This means that—unlike in supervised ML, where prior to training the researcher needs to assemble a dataset of pairs of *input* to *expected output*—for LLMs those pairs are inferred from the training data. In fact, the only feasible way to use datasets that are so large is to assemble those pairs from the training data automatically. Two techniques to do this involve having the model do the following:

Predict the next word
> Remove the last word from each sentence in the training data, and that yields a pair of *input* and *expected output*, such as *The capital of England is ___* and *London*.

---

3 For more information, see Ashish Vaswani et al., "Attention Is All You Need " (*https://oreil.ly/Frtul*), arXiv, June 12, 2017.

Predict a missing word
> Similarly, if you take each sentence and omit a word from the middle, you now have other pairs of input and expected output, such as *The ___ of England is London* and *capital.*

These models are quite difficult to use as is, they require you to prime the response with a suitable prefix. For instance, if you want to know the capital of England, you might get a response by prompting the model with *The capital of England is*, but not with the more natural *What is the capital of England?*

Instruction-Tuned LLMs

Researchers (*https://oreil.ly/lP6hr*) have made pretrained LLMs easier to use by further training (additional training applied on top of the long and costly training described in the previous section), also known as *fine-tuning* them on the following:

Task-specific datasets
> These are datasets of pairs of questions/answers manually assembled by researchers, providing examples of desirable responses to common questions that end users might prompt the model with. For example, the dataset might contain the following pair: *Q: What is the capital of England? A: The capital of England is London.* Unlike the pretraining datasets, these are manually assembled, so they are by necessity much smaller:

Reinforcement learning from human feedback (RLHF)
> Through the use of RLHF methods (*https://oreil.ly/lrlAK*), those manually assembled datasets are augmented with user feedback received on output produced by the model. For example, user A preferred *The capital of England is London* to *London is the capital of England* as an answer to the earlier question.

Instruction-tuning has been key to broadening the number of people who can build applications with LLMs, as they can now be prompted with *instructions*, often in the form of questions such as, *What is the capital of England?*, as opposed to *The capital of England is.*

Dialogue-Tuned LLMs

Models tailored for dialogue or chat purposes are a further enhancement (*https://oreil.ly/1DxW6*) of instruction-tuned LLMs. Different providers of LLMs use different techniques, so this is not necessarily true of all *chat models*, but usually this is done via the following:

Dialogue datasets
> The manually assembled *fine-tuning* datasets are extended to include more examples of multiturn dialogue interactions, that is, sequences of prompt-reply pairs.

Chat format

The input and output formats of the model are given a layer of structure over freeform text, which divides text into parts associated with a role (and optionally other metadata like a name). Usually, the roles available are *system* (for instructions and framing of the task), *user* (the actual task or question), and *assistant* (for the outputs of the model). This method evolved from early prompt engineering techniques (*https://oreil.ly/dINx0*) and makes it easier to tailor the model's output while making it harder for models to confuse user input with instructions. Confusing user input with prior instructions is also known as *jailbreaking*, which can, for instance, lead to carefully crafted prompts, possibly including trade secrets, being exposed to end users.

Fine-Tuned LLMs

Fine-tuned LLMs are created by taking base LLMs and further training them on a proprietary dataset for a specific task. Technically, instruction-tuned and dialogue-tuned LLMs are fine-tuned LLMs, but the term "fine-tuned LLM" is usually used to describe LLMs that are tuned by the developer for their specific task. For example, a model can be fine-tuned to accurately extract the sentiment, risk factors, and key financial figures from a public company's annual report. Usually, fine-tuned models have improved performance on the chosen task at the expense of a loss of generality. That is, they become less capable of answering queries on unrelated tasks.

Throughout the rest of this book, when we use the term *LLM*, we mean instruction-tuned LLMs, and for *chat model* we mean dialogue-instructed LLMs, as defined earlier in this section. These should be your workhorses when using LLMs—the first tools you reach for when starting a new LLM application.

Now let's quickly discuss some common LLM prompting techniques before diving into LangChain.

Brief Primer on Prompting

As we touched on earlier, the main task of the software engineer working with LLMs is not to train an LLM, or even to fine-tune one (usually), but rather to take an existing LLM and work out how to get it to accomplish the task you need for your application. There are commercial providers of LLMs, like OpenAI, Anthropic, and Google, as well as open source LLMs (Llama (*https://oreil.ly/ld3Fu*), Gemma (*https://oreil.ly/RGKfi*), and others), released free-of-charge for others to build upon. Adapting an existing LLM for your task is called *prompt engineering*.

Many prompting techniques have been developed in the past two years, and in a broad sense, this is a book about how to do prompt engineering with LangChain—how to use LangChain to get LLMs to do what you have in mind. But before we get into LangChain proper, it helps to go over some of these techniques first (and we apologize in advance if your favorite prompting technique (*https://oreil.ly/8uGK_*) isn't listed here; there are too many to cover).

To follow along with this section we recommend copying these prompts to the OpenAI Playground to try them yourself:

1. Create an account for the OpenAI API at *http://platform.openai.com*, which will let you use OpenAI LLMs programmatically, that is, using the API from your Python or JavaScript code. It will also give you access to the OpenAI Playground, where you can experiment with prompts from your web browser.

2. If necessary, add payment details for your new OpenAI account. OpenAI is a commercial provider of LLMs and charges a fee for each time you use their models through OpenAI's API or through Playground. You can find the latest pricing on their website (*https://oreil.ly/MiKRD*). Over the past two years, the price for using OpenAI's models has come down significantly as new capabilities and optimizations are introduced.

3. Head on over to the OpenAI Playground (*https://oreil.ly/rxiAG*) and you're ready to try out the following prompts for yourself. We'll make use of the OpenAI API throughout this book.

4. Once you've navigated to the Playground, you will see a panel of presets on the right side of the screen, including your model of choice. If you look further down the panel, you will see Temperature under the "Model configuration" title. Move the Temperature toggle from middle to left until the number shows 0.00. Essentially, temperature controls the randomness of LLM output. The lower the temperature, the more deterministic the model output.

Now on to the prompts!

Zero-Shot Prompting

The first and most straightforward prompting technique consists of simply instructing the LLM to perform the desired task:

```
How old was the 30th president of the United States when his wife's mother died?
```

This is typically what you should try first, and it will usually work for simple questions, especially when the answer to it was likely present in some of the training data. If we prompt OpenAI's gpt-3.5-turbo with the preceding prompt, the following is returned:

```
The 30th president of the United States, Calvin Coolidge, was 48 years old when his wife's mother passed away in 1926.
```

You may get a different result from what we get. There is an element of randomness to how LLMs generate responses, and OpenAI may have updated the model by the time you try it.

While the model did correctly identify the 30th president, the answer isn't quite right. Often you'll have to iterate on prompts and responses to get a reliable system. The next sections expand on how.

Chain-of-Thought

A very useful iteration is to further instruct the model to take the time to *think* (*https://oreil.ly/8xWcs*). This technique has been found to increase performance on a variety of tasks. Curiously, a more recent paper[4] suggests that this technique can also reduce LLM performance on tasks where thinking reduces human performance. Called chain-of-thought (CoT) prompting, this is usually done by prepending the prompt with instructions for the LLM to describe how it could arrive at the answer:

```
Think step by step.

How old was the 30th president of the United States when his wife's mother died?
```

And now let's see what the same model produces for this new prompt:

```
1. First, find out who the 30th president of the United States was. This can be
done by researching a list of US presidents or by searching for "30th president
of the United States" online. You will find that the 30th president was Calvin
Coolidge.

2. Next, find out the year when Calvin Coolidge was the president. This can also
be found by researching online or in a history book. You will find that he was
the president from 1923-1929.

3. Now, you need to determine the year when Calvin Coolidge's wife's mother died.
This can be done by researching the life and death of his wife, Grace Goodhue
Coolidge. You will find that she lived from 1879-1957.

4. Calculate the age of Calvin Coolidge's wife's mother when she died. She was
78 years old.

5. Determine the age of Calvin Coolidge when his wife's mother died. Subtract
the year of his birth, 1872, from the year his mother-in-law died, 1957. This
means that Calvin Coolidge was 85 years old when his wife's mother passed away.
```

---

4 Ryan Liu et al. "Mind Your Step (by Step): Chain-of-Thought Can Reduce Performance on Tasks Where Thinking Makes Humans Worse" (*https://oreil.ly/UHFp9*), arXiv, November 8, 2024.

Notice how the only change in the prompt was the addition of Think step by step, and how much of a difference that made in the model's output. Now the model outputs a sequence of steps you could go through when trying to answer this question. Unfortunately, while the steps are very reasonable, the final output is still incorrect, given it got some facts wrong, namely it listed the wrong birth and death years for President Coolidge's wife's mother. Let's see how to improve on this.

Retrieval-Augmented Generation

Retrieval-augmented generation (RAG) consists of finding relevant pieces of text, also known as *context*, such as facts you'd find in an encyclopedia and including that context in the prompt. The RAG technique can (and in real applications should) be combined with CoT, but for simplicity we'll use these techniques one at a time here. Here's the prompt including RAG:

```
Context:

- Calvin Coolidge (born John Calvin Coolidge Jr.; /ˈkuːlɪdʒ/; July 4, 1872 -
January 5, 1933) was an American attorney and politician who served as the
30th president of the United States from 1923 to 1929.

- Grace Anna Coolidge (née Goodhue; January 3, 1879 - July 8, 1957) was the
wife of the 30th president of the United States, Calvin Coolidge.

- Grace Anna Goodhue was born on January 3, 1879, in Burlington, Vermont, the
only child of Andrew Issachar Goodhue and Lemira Barrett Goodhue.

- Lemira A. Goodhue (Barrett) ; Birthdate: April 26, 1849 ; Birthplace:
Burlington, Chittenden County, VT, United States ; Death: October 24, 1929.

How old was the 30th president of the United States when his wife's mother died?
```

And the output from the model:

```
The 30th president of the United States, Calvin Coolidge, was 54 years old when
his wife's mother, Lemira A. Goodhue, died on October 24, 1929.
```

Now we're a lot closer to the correct answer, but as we touched on earlier, LLMs aren't great at out-of-the-box math. In this case, the final result of 54 years old is off by 3. Let's see how we can improve on this.

Tool Calling

The *tool calling* technique consists of prepending the prompt with a list of external functions the LLM can make use of, along with descriptions of what each is good for and instructions on how to signal in the output that it *wants* to use one (or more) of these functions. Finally, you—the developer of the application—should parse the output and call the appropriate functions. Here's one way to do this:

```
Tools:

- calculator: This tool accepts math expressions and returns their result.

- search: This tool accepts search engine queries and returns the first search
result.

If you want to use tools to arrive at the answer, output the list of tools and
inputs in CSV format, with this header row `tool,input`.

How old was the 30th president of the United States when his wife's mother died?
```

And this is the output you might get:

```
tool,input

calculator,2023-1892

search,"What age was Calvin Coolidge when his mother-in-law died?"
```

While the LLM correctly followed the output format instructions, the tools and inputs selected aren't the most appropriate for this question. This gets at one of the most important things to keep in mind when prompting LLMs: *each prompting technique is most useful when used in combination with (some of) the others*. For instance, here we could improve on this by combining tool calling, chain-of-thought, and RAG into a prompt that uses all three. Let's see what that looks like:

```
Context:

- Calvin Coolidge (born John Calvin Coolidge Jr.; /ˈkuːlɪdʒ/; July 4, 1872 –
January 5, 1933) was an American attorney and politician who served as the 30th
president of the United States from 1923 to 1929.

- Grace Anna Coolidge (née Goodhue; January 3, 1879 – July 8, 1957) was the wife
of the 30th president of the United States, Calvin Coolidge.

- Grace Anna Goodhue was born on January 3, 1879, in Burlington, Vermont, the
only child of Andrew Issachar Goodhue and Lemira Barrett Goodhue.

- Lemira A. Goodhue (Barrett) ; Birthdate: April 26, 1849 ; Birthplace:
Burlington, Chittenden County, VT, United States ; Death: October 24, 1929.

Tools:

- calculator: This tool accepts math expressions and returns their result.

If you want to use tools to arrive at the answer, output the list of tools and
inputs in CSV format, with this header row `tool,input`.

Think step by step.

How old was the 30th president of the United States when his wife's mother died?
```

And with this prompt, maybe after a few tries, we might get this output:

```
tool,input

calculator,1929 - 1872
```

If we parse that CSV output, and have a calculator function execute the operation 1929 - 1872, we finally get the right answer: 57 years.

As per the previous example, by combining RAG with chain-of-thought and tool calling, you can retrieve the most relevant data to ground your model's output, then guide it step by step to ensure it uses that context effectively.

Few-Shot Prompting

Finally, we come to another very useful prompting technique: *few-shot prompting*. This consists of providing the LLM with examples of other questions and the correct answers, which enables the LLM to *learn* how to perform a new task without going through additional training or fine-tuning. When compared to fine-tuning, few-shot prompting is more flexible—you can do it on the fly at query time—but less powerful, and you might achieve better performance with fine-tuning. That said, you should usually always try few-shot prompting before fine-tuning:

Static few-shot prompting
> The most basic version of few-shot prompting is to assemble a predetermined list of a small number of examples that you include in the prompt.

Dynamic few-shot prompting
> If you assemble a dataset of many examples, you can instead pick the most relevant examples for each new query.

The next section covers using LangChain to build applications using LLMs and these prompting techniques.

LangChain and Why It's Important

LangChain was one of the earliest open source libraries to provide LLM and prompting building blocks and the tooling to reliably combine them into larger applications. As of writing, LangChain has amassed over 28 million monthly downloads (*https:// oreil.ly/8OKbf*), 99,000 GitHub stars (*https://oreil.ly/bF5pc*), and the largest developer community in generative AI (72,000+ strong (*https://oreil.ly/PNWL3*)). It has enabled software engineers who don't have an ML background to utilize the power of LLMs to build a variety of apps, ranging from AI chatbots to AI agents that can reason and take action responsibly.

LangChain builds on the idea stressed in the preceding section: that prompting techniques are most useful when used together. To make that easier, LangChain provides simple *abstractions* for each major prompting technique. By abstraction we mean Python and JavaScript functions and classes that encapsulate the ideas of those techniques into easy-to-use wrappers. These abstractions are designed to play well together and to be combined into a larger LLM application.

First of all, LangChain provides integrations with the major LLM providers, both commercial (OpenAI (*https://oreil.ly/TTLXA*), Anthropic (*https://oreil.ly/O4UXw*), Google (*https://oreil.ly/12g3Z*), and more) and open source (Llama (*https://oreil.ly/5WA Vi*), Gemma (*https://oreil.ly/-40Ne*), and others). These integrations share a common interface, making it very easy to try out new LLMs as they're announced and letting you avoid being locked-in to a single provider. We'll use these in Chapter 1.

LangChain also provides *prompt template* abstractions, which enable you to reuse prompts more than once, separating static text in the prompt from placeholders that will be different for each time you send it to the LLM to get a completion generated. We'll talk more about these also in Chapter 1. LangChain prompts can also be stored in the LangChain Hub for sharing with teammates.

LangChain contains many integrations with third-party services (such as Google Sheets, Wolfram Alpha, Zapier, just to name a few) exposed as *tools*, which is a standard interface for functions to be used in the tool-calling technique.

For RAG, LangChain provides integrations with the major *embedding models* (language models designed to output a numeric representation, the *embedding*, of the meaning of a sentence, paragraph, and so on), *vector stores* (databases dedicated to storing embeddings), and *vector indexes* (regular databases with vector-storing capabilities). You'll learn a lot more about these in Chapters 2 and 3.

For CoT, LangChain (through the LangGraph library) provides *agent* abstractions that combine chain-of-thought reasoning and tool calling, first popularized by the ReAct paper (*https://oreil.ly/27BIC*). This enables building LLM applications that do the following:

1. Reason about the steps to take.
2. Translate those steps into external tool calls.
3. Receive the output of those tool calls.
4. Repeat until the task is accomplished.

We cover these in Chapters 5 through 8.

For chatbot use cases, it becomes useful to keep track of previous interactions and use them when generating the response to a future interaction. This is called *memory*, and Chapter 4 discusses using it in LangChain.

Finally, LangChain provides the tools to compose these building blocks into cohesive applications. Chapters 1 through 6 talk more about this.

In addition to this library, LangChain provides LangSmith (*https://oreil.ly/geRgx*)—a platform to help debug, test, deploy, and monitor AI workflows—and LangGraph Platform—a platform for deploying and scaling LangGraph agents. We cover these in Chapters 9 and 10.

What to Expect from This Book

With this book, we hope to convey the excitement and possibility of adding LLMs to your software engineering toolbelt.

We got into programming because we like building things, getting to the end of a project, looking at the final product and realizing there's something new out there, and we built it. Programming with LLMs is so exciting to us because it expands the set of things we can build, it makes previously hard things easy (for example, extracting relevant numbers from a long text) and previously impossible things possible—try building an automated assistant a year ago and you end up with the *phone tree hell* we all know and love from calling up customer support numbers.

Now with LLMs and LangChain, you can actually build pleasant assistants (or myriad other applications) that chat with you and understand your intent to a very reasonable degree. The difference is night and day! If that sounds exciting to you (as it does to us) then you've come to the right place.

In this Preface, we've given you a refresher on what makes LLMs tick and why exactly that gives you "thing-building" superpowers. Having these very large ML models that understand language and can output answers written in conversational English (or some other language) gives you a *programmable* (through prompt engineering), versatile language-generation tool. By the end of the book, we hope you'll see just how powerful that can be.

We'll begin with an AI chatbot customized by, for the most part, plain English instructions. That alone should be an eye-opener: you can now "program" part of the behavior of your application without code.

Then comes the next capability: giving your chatbot access to your own documents, which takes it from a generic assistant to one that's knowledgeable about any area of human knowledge for which you can find a library of written text. This will allow you to have the chatbot answer questions or summarize documents you wrote, for instance.

After that, we'll make the chatbot remember your previous conversations. This will improve it in two ways: It will feel a lot more natural to have a conversation with a chatbot that remembers what you have previously chatted about, and over time the chatbot can be personalized to the preferences of each of its users individually.

Next, we'll use chain-of-thought and tool-calling techniques to give the chatbot the ability to plan and act on those plans, iteratively. This will enable it to work toward more complicated requests, such as writing a research report about a subject of your choice.

As you use your chatbot for more complicated tasks, you'll feel the need to give it the tools to collaborate with you. This encompasses both giving you the ability to interrupt or authorize actions before they are taken, as well as providing the chatbot with the ability to ask for more information or clarification before acting.

Finally, we'll show you how to deploy your chatbot to production and discuss what you need to consider before and after taking that step, including latency, reliability, and security. Then we'll show you how to monitor your chatbot in production and continue to improve it as it is used.

Along the way, we'll teach you the ins and outs of each of these techniques, so that when you finish the book, you will have truly added a new tool (or two) to your software engineering toolbelt.

Conventions Used in This Book

The following typographical conventions are used in this book:

Italic

Indicates new terms, URLs, email addresses, filenames, and file extensions.

`Constant width`

Used for program listings, as well as within paragraphs to refer to program elements such as variable or function names, databases, data types, environment variables, statements, and keywords.

This element signifies a tip or suggestion.

This element signifies a general note.

Using Code Examples

Supplemental material (code examples, exercises, etc.) is available for download at *https://oreil.ly/supp-LearningLangChain*.

If you have a technical question or a problem using the code examples, please send email to *support@oreilly.com*.

This book is here to help you get your job done. In general, if example code is offered with this book, you may use it in your programs and documentation. You do not need to contact us for permission unless you're reproducing a significant portion of the code. For example, writing a program that uses several chunks of code from this book does not require permission. Selling or distributing examples from O'Reilly books does require permission. Answering a question by citing this book and quoting example code does not require permission. Incorporating a significant amount of example code from this book into your product's documentation does require permission.

We appreciate, but generally do not require, attribution. An attribution usually includes the title, author, publisher, and ISBN. For example: "*Learning LangChain* by Mayo Oshin and Nuno Campos (O'Reilly). Copyright 2025 Olumayowa "Mayo" Olufemi Oshin, 978-1-098-16728-8."

If you feel your use of code examples falls outside fair use or the permission given above, feel free to contact us at *permissions@oreilly.com*.

O'Reilly Online Learning

 For more than 40 years, *O'Reilly Media* has provided technology and business training, knowledge, and insight to help companies succeed.

Our unique network of experts and innovators share their knowledge and expertise through books, articles, and our online learning platform. O'Reilly's online learning platform gives you on-demand access to live training courses, in-depth learning paths, interactive coding environments, and a vast collection of text and video from O'Reilly and 200+ other publishers. For more information, visit *https://oreilly.com*.

How to Contact Us

Please address comments and questions concerning this book to the publisher:

O'Reilly Media, Inc.
1005 Gravenstein Highway North
Sebastopol, CA 95472
800-889-8969 (in the United States or Canada)
707-827-7019 (international or local)
707-829-0104 (fax)
support@oreilly.com
https://oreilly.com/about/contact.html

We have a web page for this book, where we list errata, examples, and any additional information. You can access this page at *https://oreil.ly/learning-langchain*.

For news and information about our books and courses, visit *https://oreilly.com*.

Find us on LinkedIn: *https://linkedin.com/company/oreilly-media*.

Watch us on YouTube: *https://youtube.com/oreillymedia*.

Acknowledgments

We would like to express our gratitude and appreciation to the reviewers—Rajat Kant Goel, Douglas Bailley, Tom Taulli, Gourav Bais, and Jacob Lee—for providing valuable technical feedback on improving this book.

## CHAPTER 1

LLM Fundamentals with LangChain

The Preface gave you a taste of the power of LLM prompting, where we saw firsthand the impact that different prompting techniques can have on what you get out of LLMs, especially when judiciously combined. The challenge in building good LLM applications is, in fact, in how to effectively construct the prompt sent to the model and process the model's prediction to return an accurate output (see Figure 1-1).

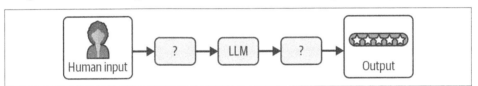

Figure 1-1. The challenge in making LLMs a useful part of your application

If you can solve this problem, you are well on your way to building LLM applications, simple and complex alike. In this chapter, you'll learn more about how LangChain's building blocks map to LLM concepts and how, when combined effectively, they enable you to build LLM applications. But first, the sidebar "Why LangChain?" is a brief primer on why we think it useful to use LangChain to build LLM applications.

Why LangChain?

You can of course build LLM applications without LangChain. The most obvious alternative is to use the software development kit (SDK)—the package exposing the methods of their HTTP API as functions in the programming language of your choice—of the LLM provider you tried first (for example, OpenAI). We think learning LangChain will pay off in the short term and over the long run because of the following factors:

Prebuilt common patterns

LangChain comes with reference implementations of the most common LLM application patterns (we mentioned some of these in the Preface: chain-of-thought, tool calling, and others). This is the quickest way to get started with LLMs and might often be all you need. We'd suggest starting any new application from these and checking whether the results out of the box are good enough for your use case. If not, then see the next item for the other half of the LangChain libraries.

Interchangeable building blocks

These are components that can be easily swapped out for alternatives. Every component (an LLM, chat model, output parser, and so on—more on these shortly) follows a shared specification, which makes your application future-proof. As new capabilities are released by model providers and as your needs change, you can evolve your application without rewriting it each time.

Throughout this book we make use of the following major components in the code examples:

- LLM/chat model: OpenAI
- Embeddings: OpenAI
- Vector store: PGVector

You can swap out each of these for any of the alternatives listed on the following pages:

Chat models

See the LangChain documentation (*https://oreil.ly/8Qlnb*). If you don't want to use OpenAI (a commercial API) we suggest Anthropic (*https://oreil.ly/XdGfD*) as a commercial alternative or Ollama (*https://oreil.ly/eKy6-*) as an open source one.

Embeddings

See the LangChain documentation (*https://oreil.ly/sKpfM*). If you don't want to use OpenAI (a commercial API) we suggest Cohere (*https://oreil.ly/o1D0C*) as a commercial alternative or Ollama (*https://oreil.ly/FarfL*) as an open source one.

Vector stores

See the LangChain documentation (*https://oreil.ly/q3RF1*). If you don't want to use PGVector (an open source extension to the popular SQL database Postgres) we suggest using either Weaviate (*https://oreil.ly/XqlYa*) (a dedicated vector store) or OpenSearch (*https://oreil.ly/1s357*) (vector search features that are part of a popular search database).

This effort goes beyond, for instance, all LLMs having the same methods, with similar arguments and return values. Let's look at the example of chat models and two popular LLM providers, OpenAI and Anthropic. Both have a chat API which receives *chat messages* (loosely defined as objects with a type string and a content string) and returns a new message generated by the model. But if you try to use both models in the same conversation, you'll immediately run into issues, as their chat message formats are subtly incompatible. LangChain abstracts away these differences to enable building applications that are truly independent of a particular provider. For instance, with LangChain, a chatbot conversation where you use both OpenAI and Anthropic models works.

Finally, as you build out your LLM applications with several of these components, we've found it useful to have the *orchestration* capabilities of LangChain:

- All major components are instrumented by the callbacks system for observability (more on this in Chapter 8).
- All major components implement the same interface (more on this toward the end of this chapter).
- Long-running LLM applications can be interrupted, resumed, or retried (more on this in Chapter 6).

Getting Set Up with LangChain

To follow along with the rest of the chapter, and the chapters to come, we recommend setting up LangChain on your computer first.

See the instructions in the Preface regarding setting up an OpenAI account and complete these if you haven't yet. If you prefer using a different LLM provider, see "Why LangChain?" on page 1 for alternatives.

Then head over to the API Keys page (*https://oreil.ly/BKrtV*) on the OpenAI website (after logging in to your OpenAI account), create an API key, and save it—you'll need it soon.

 In this book, we'll show code examples in both Python and Java-Script (JS). LangChain offers the same functionality in both languages, so just pick the one you're most comfortable with and follow the respective code snippets throughout the book (the code examples for each language are equivalent).

First, some setup instructions for readers using Python:

1. Ensure that you have Python installed. See the instructions for your operating system (*https://oreil.ly/20K9l*).
2. Install Jupyter if you want to run the examples in a notebook environment. You can do this by running `pip install notebook` in your terminal.

3. Install the LangChain library by running the following commands in your terminal:

```
pip install langchain langchain-openai langchain-community
pip install langchain-text-splitters langchain-postgres
```

4. Take the OpenAI API key you generated at the beginning of this section and make it available in your terminal environment. You can do this by running the following:

```
export OPENAI_API_KEY=your-key
```

5. Don't forget to replace your-key with the API key you generated previously.

6. Open a Jupyter notebook by running this command:

```
jupyter notebook
```

You're now ready to follow along with the Python code examples.

Here are the instructions for readers using JavaScript:

1. Take the OpenAI API key you generated at the beginning of this section and make it available in your terminal environment. You can do this by running the following:

```
export OPENAI_API_KEY=your-key
```

2. Don't forget to replace your-key with the API key you generated previously.

3. If you want to run the examples as Node.js scripts, install Node by following the instructions (*https://oreil.ly/5gjiO*).

4. Install the LangChain libraries by running the following commands in your terminal:

```
npm install langchain @langchain/openai @langchain/community
npm install @langchain/core pg
```

5. Take each example, save it as a *.js* file and run it with node ./file.js.

Using LLMs in LangChain

To recap, LLMs are the driving engine behind most generative AI applications. LangChain provides two simple interfaces to interact with any LLM API provider:

- Chat models
- LLMs

The LLM interface simply takes a string prompt as input, sends the input to the model provider, and then returns the model prediction as output.

Let's import LangChain's OpenAI LLM wrapper to invoke a model prediction using a simple prompt:

Python

```python
from langchain_openai.llms import OpenAI

model = OpenAI(model="gpt-3.5-turbo")

model.invoke("The sky is")
```

JavaScript

```javascript
import { OpenAI } from "@langchain/openai";

const model = new OpenAI({ model: "gpt-3.5-turbo" });

await model.invoke("The sky is");
```

The output:

```
Blue!
```

 Notice the parameter model passed to OpenAI. This is the most common parameter to configure when using an LLM or chat model, the underlying model to use, as most providers offer several models with different trade-offs in capability and cost (usually larger models are more capable, but also more expensive and slower). See OpenAI's overview (*https://oreil.ly/dM886*) of the models they offer.

Other useful parameters to configure include the following, offered by most providers.

temperature
> This controls the sampling algorithm used to generate output. Lower values produce more predictable outputs (for example, 0.1), while higher values generate more creative, or unexpected, results (such as 0.9). Different tasks will need different values for this parameter. For instance, producing structured output usually benefits from a lower temperature, whereas creative writing tasks do better with a higher value:

max_tokens
> This limits the size (and cost) of the output. A lower value may cause the LLM to stop generating the output before getting to a natural end, so it may appear to have been truncated.

Beyond these, each provider exposes a different set of parameters. We recommend looking at the documentation for the one you choose. For an example, refer to OpenAI's platform (*https://oreil.ly/5O1RW*).

Alternatively, the chat model interface enables back and forth conversations between the user and model. The reason why it's a separate interface is because popular LLM providers like OpenAI differentiate messages sent to and from the model into *user*, *assistant*, and *system* roles (here *role* denotes the type of content the message contains):

System role
> Used for instructions the model should use to answer a user question

User role
> Used for the user's query and any other content produced by the user

Assistant role
> Used for content generated by the model

The chat model's interface makes it easier to configure and manage conversions in your AI chatbot application. Here's an example utilizing LangChain's ChatOpenAI model:

Python

```python
from langchain_openai.chat_models import ChatOpenAI
from langchain_core.messages import HumanMessage

model = ChatOpenAI()
prompt = [HumanMessage("What is the capital of France?")]

model.invoke(prompt)
```

JavaScript

```javascript
import { ChatOpenAI } from '@langchain/openai'
import { HumanMessage } from '@langchain/core/messages'

const model = new ChatOpenAI()
const prompt = [new HumanMessage('What is the capital of France?')]

await model.invoke(prompt)
```

The output:

```
AIMessage(content='The capital of France is Paris.')
```

Instead of a single prompt string, chat models make use of different types of chat message interfaces associated with each role mentioned previously. These include the following:

HumanMessage
> A message sent from the perspective of the human, with the user role

AIMessage
> A message sent from the perspective of the AI that the human is interacting with, with the assistant role

---

SystemMessage
A message setting the instructions the AI should follow, with the system role

ChatMessage
A message allowing for arbitrary setting of role

Let's incorporate a `SystemMessage` instruction in our example:

Python

```python
from langchain_core.messages import HumanMessage, SystemMessage
from langchain_openai.chat_models import ChatOpenAI

model = ChatOpenAI()
system_msg = SystemMessage(
    '''You are a helpful assistant that responds to questions with three
        exclamation marks.'''
)
human_msg = HumanMessage('What is the capital of France?')

model.invoke([system_msg, human_msg])
```

JavaScript

```javascript
import { ChatOpenAI } from "@langchain/openai";
import { HumanMessage, SystemMessage } from "@langchain/core/messages";

const model = new ChatOpenAI();
const prompt = [
  new SystemMessage(
    `You are a helpful assistant that responds to questions with three
      exclamation marks.`,
  ),
  new HumanMessage("What is the capital of France?"),
];

await model.invoke(prompt);
```

The output:

```
AIMessage('Paris!!!')
```

As you can see, the model obeyed the instruction provided in the `SystemMessage` even though it wasn't present in the user's question. This enables you to preconfigure your AI application to respond in a relatively predictable manner based on the user's input.

Making LLM Prompts Reusable

The previous section showed how the `prompt` instruction significantly influences the model's output. Prompts help the model understand context and generate relevant answers to queries.

Here is an example of a detailed prompt:

```
Answer the question based on the context below. If the question cannot be
answered using the information provided, answer with "I don't know".

Context: The most recent advancements in NLP are being driven by Large Language
Models (LLMs). These models outperform their smaller counterparts and have
become invaluable for developers who are creating applications with NLP
capabilities. Developers can tap into these models through Hugging Face's
`transformers` library, or by utilizing OpenAI and Cohere's offerings through
the `openai` and `cohere` libraries, respectively.

Question: Which model providers offer LLMs?

Answer:
```

Although the prompt looks like a simple string, the challenge is figuring out what the text should contain and how it should vary based on the user's input. In this example, the Context and Question values are hardcoded, but what if we wanted to pass these in dynamically?

Fortunately, LangChain provides prompt template interfaces that make it easy to construct prompts with dynamic inputs:

Python

```python
from langchain_core.prompts import PromptTemplate

template = PromptTemplate.from_template("""Answer the question based on the
    context below. If the question cannot be answered using the information
    provided, answer with "I don't know".

Context: {context}

Question: {question}

Answer: """)

template.invoke({
    "context": """The most recent advancements in NLP are being driven by Large
        Language Models (LLMs). These models outperform their smaller
        counterparts and have become invaluable for developers who are creating
        applications with NLP capabilities. Developers can tap into these
        models through Hugging Face's `transformers` library, or by utilizing
        OpenAI and Cohere's offerings through the `openai` and `cohere`
        libraries, respectively.""",
    "question": "Which model providers offer LLMs?"
})
```

JavaScript

```javascript
import { PromptTemplate } from '@langchain/core/prompts'

const template = PromptTemplate.fromTemplate(`Answer the question based on the
  context below. If the question cannot be answered using the information
  provided, answer with "I don't know".

Context: {context}

Question: {question}

Answer: `)

await template.invoke({
  context: `The most recent advancements in NLP are being driven by Large
    Language Models (LLMs). These models outperform their smaller
    counterparts and have become invaluable for developers who are creating
    applications with NLP capabilities. Developers can tap into these models
    through Hugging Face's \`transformers\` library, or by utilizing OpenAI
    and Cohere's offerings through the \`openai\` and \`cohere\` libraries,
    respectively.`,
  question: "Which model providers offer LLMs?"
})
```

The output:

```
StringPromptValue(text='Answer the question based on the context below. If the
  question cannot be answered using the information provided, answer with "I
  don\'t know".\n\nContext: The most recent advancements in NLP are being
  driven by Large Language Models (LLMs). These models outperform their
  smaller counterparts and have become invaluable for developers who are
  creating applications with NLP capabilities. Developers can tap into these
  models through Hugging Face\'s `transformers` library, or by utilizing
  OpenAI and Cohere\'s offerings through the `openai` and `cohere` libraries,
  respectively.\n\nQuestion: Which model providers offer LLMs?\n\nAnswer: ')
```

This example takes the static prompt from the previous block and makes it dynamic. The `template` contains the structure of the final prompt alongside the definition of where the dynamic inputs will be inserted.

As such, the template can be used as a recipe to build multiple static, specific prompts. When you format the prompt with some specific values—in this case, `context` and `question`—you get a static prompt ready to be passed in to an LLM.

As you can see, the `question` argument is passed dynamically via the `invoke` function. By default, LangChain prompts follow Python's `f-string` syntax for defining dynamic parameters—any word surrounded by curly braces, such as {question}, are placeholders for values passed in at runtime. In the previous example, {question} was replaced by "`Which model providers offer LLMs?`"

Let's see how we'd feed this into an LLM OpenAI model using LangChain:

Python

```python
from langchain_openai.llms import OpenAI
from langchain_core.prompts import PromptTemplate

# both `template` and `model` can be reused many times

template = PromptTemplate.from_template("""Answer the question based on the
    context below. If the question cannot be answered using the information
    provided, answer with "I don't know".

Context: {context}

Question: {question}

Answer: """)

model = OpenAI()

# `prompt` and `completion` are the results of using template and model once

prompt = template.invoke({
    "context": """The most recent advancements in NLP are being driven by Large
        Language Models (LLMs). These models outperform their smaller
        counterparts and have become invaluable for developers who are creating
        applications with NLP capabilities. Developers can tap into these
        models through Hugging Face's `transformers` library, or by utilizing
        OpenAI and Cohere's offerings through the `openai` and `cohere`
        libraries, respectively.""",
    "question": "Which model providers offer LLMs?"
})

completion = model.invoke(prompt)
```

JavaScript

```javascript
import { PromptTemplate } from '@langchain/core/prompts'
import { OpenAI } from '@langchain/openai'

const model = new OpenAI()
const template = PromptTemplate.fromTemplate(`Answer the question based on the
    context below. If the question cannot be answered using the information
    provided, answer with "I don't know".

Context: {context}

Question: {question}

Answer: `)

const prompt = await template.invoke({
```

```
    context: `The most recent advancements in NLP are being driven by Large
        Language Models (LLMs). These models outperform their smaller
        counterparts and have become invaluable for developers who are creating
        applications with NLP capabilities. Developers can tap into these models
        through Hugging Face's \`transformers\` library, or by utilizing OpenAI
        and Cohere's offerings through the \`openai\` and \`cohere\` libraries,
        respectively.`,
    question: "Which model providers offer LLMs?"
})

await model.invoke(prompt)
```

The output:

```
Hugging Face's `transformers` library, OpenAI using the `openai` library, and
Cohere using the `cohere` library offer LLMs.
```

If you're looking to build an AI chat application, the ChatPromptTemplate can be used instead to provide dynamic inputs based on the role of the chat message:

Python

```
from langchain_core.prompts import ChatPromptTemplate
template = ChatPromptTemplate.from_messages([
    ('system', '''Answer the question based on the context below. If the
        question cannot be answered using the information provided, answer with
        "I don\'t know".'''),
    ('human', 'Context: {context}'),
    ('human', 'Question: {question}'),
])

template.invoke({
    "context": """The most recent advancements in NLP are being driven by Large
        Language Models (LLMs). These models outperform their smaller
        counterparts and have become invaluable for developers who are creating
        applications with NLP capabilities. Developers can tap into these
        models through Hugging Face's `transformers` library, or by utilizing
        OpenAI and Cohere's offerings through the `openai` and `cohere`
        libraries, respectively.""",
    "question": "Which model providers offer LLMs?"
})
```

JavaScript

```
import { ChatPromptTemplate } from '@langchain/core/prompts'

const template = ChatPromptTemplate.fromMessages([
    ['system', `Answer the question based on the context below. If the question
        cannot be answered using the information provided, answer with "I
        don\'t know".`],
    ['human', 'Context: {context}'],
    ['human', 'Question: {question}'],
])
```

```
await template.invoke({
    context: `The most recent advancements in NLP are being driven by Large
        Language Models (LLMs). These models outperform their smaller
        counterparts and have become invaluable for developers who are creating
        applications with NLP capabilities. Developers can tap into these models
        through Hugging Face's \`transformers\` library, or by utilizing OpenAI
        and Cohere's offerings through the \`openai\` and \`cohere\` libraries,
        respectively.`,
    question: "Which model providers offer LLMs?"
})
```

The output:

```
ChatPromptValue(messages=[SystemMessage(content='Answer the question based on
    the context below. If the question cannot be answered using the information
    provided, answer with "I don\'t know".'), HumanMessage(content="Context:
    The most recent advancements in NLP are being driven by Large Language
    Models (LLMs). These models outperform their smaller counterparts and have
    become invaluable for developers who are creating applications with NLP
    capabilities. Developers can tap into these models through Hugging Face\'s
    `transformers` library, or by utilizing OpenAI and Cohere\'s offerings
    through the `openai` and `cohere` libraries, respectively."), HumanMessage
    (content='Question: Which model providers offer LLMs?')])
```

Notice how the prompt contains instructions in a SystemMessage and two instances
of HumanMessage that contain dynamic context and question variables. You can still
format the template in the same way and get back a static prompt that you can pass to
a large language model for a prediction output:

Python

```
from langchain_openai.chat_models import ChatOpenAI
from langchain_core.prompts import ChatPromptTemplate

# both `template` and `model` can be reused many times

template = ChatPromptTemplate.from_messages([
    ('system', '''Answer the question based on the context below. If the
        question cannot be answered using the information provided, answer
        with "I don\'t know".'''),
    ('human', 'Context: {context}'),
    ('human', 'Question: {question}'),
])

model = ChatOpenAI()

# `prompt` and `completion` are the results of using template and model once

prompt = template.invoke({
    "context": """The most recent advancements in NLP are being driven by
        Large Language Models (LLMs). These models outperform their smaller
        counterparts and have become invaluable for developers who are creating
        applications with NLP capabilities. Developers can tap into these
```

```
        models through Hugging Face's `transformers` library, or by utilizing
        OpenAI and Cohere's offerings through the `openai` and `cohere`
        libraries, respectively.""",
    "question": "Which model providers offer LLMs?"
})

model.invoke(prompt)
```

JavaScript

```
import { ChatPromptTemplate } from '@langchain/core/prompts'
import { ChatOpenAI } from '@langchain/openai'

const model = new ChatOpenAI()
const template = ChatPromptTemplate.fromMessages([
  ['system', `Answer the question based on the context below. If the question
    cannot be answered using the information provided, answer with "I
    don\'t know".`],
  ['human', 'Context: {context}'],
  ['human', 'Question: {question}'],
])

const prompt = await template.invoke({
  context: `The most recent advancements in NLP are being driven by Large
    Language Models (LLMs). These models outperform their smaller
    counterparts and have become invaluable for developers who are creating
    applications with NLP capabilities. Developers can tap into these models
    through Hugging Face's \`transformers\` library, or by utilizing OpenAI
    and Cohere's offerings through the \`openai\` and \`cohere\` libraries,
    respectively.`,
  question: "Which model providers offer LLMs?"
})

await model.invoke(prompt)
```

The output:

```
AIMessage(content="Hugging Face's `transformers` library, OpenAI using the
    `openai` library, and Cohere using the `cohere` library offer LLMs.")
```

Getting Specific Formats out of LLMs

Plain text outputs are useful, but there may be use cases where you need the LLM to
generate a *structured* output—that is, output in a machine-readable format, such as
JSON, XML, CSV, or even in a programming language such as Python or JavaScript.
This is very useful when you intend to hand that output off to some other piece of
code, making an LLM play a part in your larger application.

JSON Output

The most common format to generate with LLMs is JSON. JSON outputs can (for example) be sent over the wire to your frontend code or be saved to a database.

When generating JSON, the first task is to define the schema you want the LLM to respect when producing the output. Then, you should include that schema in the prompt, along with the text you want to use as the source. Let's see an example:

Python

```python
from langchain_openai import ChatOpenAI
from langchain_core.pydantic_v1 import BaseModel

class AnswerWithJustification(BaseModel):
    '''An answer to the user's question along with justification for the
        answer.'''
    answer: str
    '''The answer to the user's question'''
    justification: str
    '''Justification for the answer'''

llm = ChatOpenAI(model="gpt-3.5-turbo", temperature=0)
structured_llm = llm.with_structured_output(AnswerWithJustification)

structured_llm.invoke("""What weighs more, a pound of bricks or a pound
    of feathers""")
```

JavaScript

```javascript
import { ChatOpenAI } from '@langchain/openai'
import { z } from "zod";

const answerSchema = z
  .object({
    answer: z.string().describe("The answer to the user's question"),
    justification: z.string().describe(`Justification for the
      answer`),
  })
  .describe(`An answer to the user's question along with justification for
    the answer.`);

const model = new ChatOpenAI({
  model: "gpt-3.5-turbo",
  temperature: 0,
}).withStructuredOutput(answerSchema)
await model.invoke("What weighs more, a pound of bricks or a pound of feathers")
```

The output:

```
{
    answer: "They weigh the same",
    justification: "Both a pound of bricks and a pound of feathers weigh one pound.
        The weight is the same, but the volu"... 42 more characters
}
```

So, first define a schema. In Python, this is easiest to do with Pydantic (a library used for validating data against schemas). In JS, this is easiest to do with Zod (an equivalent library). The method `with_structured_output` will use that schema for two things:

- The schema will be converted to a `JSONSchema` object (a JSON format used to describe the shape [types, names, descriptions] of JSON data), which will be sent to the LLM. For each LLM, LangChain picks the best method to do this, usually function calling or prompting.

- The schema will also be used to validate the output returned by the LLM before returning it; this ensures the output produced respects the schema you passed in exactly.

Other Machine-Readable Formats with Output Parsers

You can also use an LLM or chat model to produce output in other formats, such as CSV or XML. This is where output parsers come in handy. *Output parsers* are classes that help you structure large language model responses. They serve two functions:

Providing format instructions
    Output parsers can be used to inject some additional instructions in the prompt that will help guide the LLM to output text in the format it knows how to parse.

Validating and parsing output
    The main function is to take the textual output of the LLM or chat model and render it to a more structured format, such as a list, XML, or other format. This can include removing extraneous information, correcting incomplete output, and validating the parsed values.

Here's an example of how an output parser works:

Python

```python
from langchain_core.output_parsers import CommaSeparatedListOutputParser
parser = CommaSeparatedListOutputParser()
items = parser.invoke("apple, banana, cherry")
```

JavaScript

```javascript
import { CommaSeparatedListOutputParser } from '@langchain/core/output_parsers'

const parser = new CommaSeparatedListOutputParser()

await parser.invoke("apple, banana, cherry")
```

The output:

```
['apple', 'banana', 'cherry']
```

LangChain provides a variety of output parsers for various use cases, including CSV, XML, and more. We'll see how to combine output parsers with models and prompts in the next section.

Assembling the Many Pieces of an LLM Application

The key components you've learned about so far are essential building blocks of the LangChain framework. Which brings us to the critical question: How do you combine them effectively to build your LLM application?

Using the Runnable Interface

As you may have noticed, all the code examples used so far utilize a similar interface and the `invoke()` method to generate outputs from the model (or prompt template, or output parser). All components have the following:

- There is a common interface with these methods:
  - `invoke`: transforms a single input into an output
  - `batch`: efficiently transforms multiple inputs into multiple outputs
  - `stream`: streams output from a single input as it's produced
- There are built-in utilities for retries, fallbacks, schemas, and runtime configurability.
- In Python, each of the three methods have `asyncio` equivalents.

As such, all components behave the same way, and the interface learned for one of them applies to all:

Python

```python
from langchain_openai.llms import ChatOpenAI

model = ChatOpenAI()

completion = model.invoke('Hi there!')
# Hi!
```

```
completions = model.batch(['Hi there!', 'Bye!'])
# ['Hi!', 'See you!']

for token in model.stream('Bye!'):
    print(token)
    # Good
    # bye
    # !
```

JavaScript

```
import { ChatOpenAI } from '@langchain/openai'

const model = new ChatOpenAI()

const completion = await model.invoke('Hi there!')
// Hi!

const completions = await model.batch(['Hi there!', 'Bye!'])
// ['Hi!', 'See you!']

for await (const token of await model.stream('Bye!')) {
  console.log(token)
  // Good
  // bye
  // !
}
```

In this example, you see how the three main methods work:

- invoke() takes a single input and returns a single output.
- batch() takes a list of outputs and returns a list of outputs.
- stream() takes a single input and returns an iterator of parts of the output as they become available.

In some cases, where the underlying component doesn't support iterative output, there will be a single part containing all output.

You can combine these components in two ways:

Imperative
    Call your components directly, for example, with model.invoke(...)

Declarative
    Use LangChain Expression Language (LCEL), as covered in an upcoming section

Table 1-1 summarizes their differences, and we'll see each in action next.

Table 1-1. The main differences between imperative and declarative composition.

	Imperative	Declarative
Syntax	All of Python or JavaScript	LCEL
Parallel execution	Python: with threads or coroutines	Automatic
	JavaScript: with `Promise.all`	
Streaming	With yield keyword	Automatic
Async execution	With async functions	Automatic

Imperative Composition

Imperative composition is just a fancy name for writing the code you're used to writing, composing these components into functions and classes. Here's an example combining prompts, models, and output parsers:

Python

```python
from langchain_openai.chat_models import ChatOpenAI
from langchain_core.prompts import ChatPromptTemplate
from langchain_core.runnables import chain

# the building blocks

template = ChatPromptTemplate.from_messages([
    ('system', 'You are a helpful assistant.'),
    ('human', '{question}'),
])

model = ChatOpenAI()

# combine them in a function
# @chain decorator adds the same Runnable interface for any function you write

@chain
def chatbot(values):
    prompt = template.invoke(values)
    return model.invoke(prompt)

# use it

chatbot.invoke({"question": "Which model providers offer LLMs?"})
```

JavaScript

```javascript
import {ChatOpenAI} from '@langchain/openai'
import {ChatPromptTemplate} from '@langchain/core/prompts'
import {RunnableLambda} from '@langchain/core/runnables'

// the building blocks

const template = ChatPromptTemplate.fromMessages([
```

```
    ['system', 'You are a helpful assistant.'],
    ['human', '{question}'],
])

const model = new ChatOpenAI()

// combine them in a function
// RunnableLambda adds the same Runnable interface for any function you write

const chatbot = RunnableLambda.from(async values => {
  const prompt = await template.invoke(values)
  return await model.invoke(prompt)
})

// use it

await chatbot.invoke({
  "question": "Which model providers offer LLMs?"
})
```

The output:

```
AIMessage(content="Hugging Face's `transformers` library, OpenAI using the
    `openai` library, and Cohere using the `cohere` library offer LLMs.")
```

The preceding is a complete example of a chatbot, using a prompt and chat model. As you can see, it uses familiar Python syntax and supports any custom logic you might want to add in that function.

On the other hand, if you want to enable streaming or async support, you'd have to modify your function to support it. For example, streaming support can be added as follows:

Python

```
@chain
def chatbot(values):
    prompt = template.invoke(values)
    for token in model.stream(prompt):
        yield token


for part in chatbot.stream({
    "question": "Which model providers offer LLMs?"
}):
    print(part)
```

JavaScript

```
const chatbot = RunnableLambda.from(async function* (values) {
  const prompt = await template.invoke(values)
  for await (const token of await model.stream(prompt)) {
    yield token
  }
})
```

```
for await (const token of await chatbot.stream({
  "question": "Which model providers offer LLMs?"
})) {
  console.log(token)
}
```

The output:

```
AIMessageChunk(content="Hugging")
AIMessageChunk(content=" Face's")
AIMessageChunk(content=" `transformers`")
...
```

So, either in JS or Python, you can enable streaming for your custom function by yielding the values you want to stream and then calling it with `stream`.

For asynchronous execution, you'd rewrite your function like this:

Python

```
@chain
async def chatbot(values):
    prompt = await template.ainvoke(values)
    return await model.ainvoke(prompt)

await chatbot.ainvoke({"question": "Which model providers offer LLMs?"})
# > AIMessage(content="""Hugging Face's `transformers` library, OpenAI using
    the `openai` library, and Cohere using the `cohere` library offer LLMs.""")
```

This one applies to Python only, as asynchronous execution is the only option in JavaScript.

Declarative Composition

LCEL is a *declarative language* for composing LangChain components. LangChain compiles LCEL compositions to an *optimized execution plan*, with automatic parallelization, streaming, tracing, and async support.

Let's see the same example using LCEL:

Python

```
from langchain_openai.chat_models import ChatOpenAI
from langchain_core.prompts import ChatPromptTemplate

# the building blocks

template = ChatPromptTemplate.from_messages([
    ('system', 'You are a helpful assistant.'),
    ('human', '{question}'),
])
```

```
model = ChatOpenAI()

# combine them with the | operator

chatbot = template | model

# use it

chatbot.invoke({"question": "Which model providers offer LLMs?"})
```

JavaScript

```
import { ChatOpenAI } from '@langchain/openai'
import { ChatPromptTemplate } from '@langchain/core/prompts'
import { RunnableLambda } from '@langchain/core/runnables'

// the building blocks

const template = ChatPromptTemplate.fromMessages([
  ['system', 'You are a helpful assistant.'],
  ['human', '{question}'],
])

const model = new ChatOpenAI()

// combine them in a function

const chatbot = template.pipe(model)

// use it

await chatbot.invoke({
  "question": "Which model providers offer LLMs?"
})
```

The output:

```
AIMessage(content="Hugging Face's `transformers` library, OpenAI using the
    `openai` library, and Cohere using the `cohere` library offer LLMs.")
```

Crucially, the last line is the same between the two examples—that is, you use the function and the LCEL sequence in the same way, with invoke/stream/batch. And in this version, you don't need to do anything else to use streaming:

Python

```
chatbot = template | model

for part in chatbot.stream({
    "question": "Which model providers offer LLMs?"
}):
    print(part)
    # > AIMessageChunk(content="Hugging")
    # > AIMessageChunk(content=" Face's")
```

```
# > AIMessageChunk(content=" `transformers`")
# ...
```

JavaScript

```
const chatbot = template.pipe(model)

for await (const token of await chatbot.stream({
  "question": "Which model providers offer LLMs?"
})) {
  console.log(token)
}
```

And, for Python only, it's the same for using asynchronous methods:

Python

```
chatbot = template | model

await chatbot.ainvoke({
    "question": "Which model providers offer LLMs?"
})
```

Summary

In this chapter, you've learned about the building blocks and key components necessary to build LLM applications using LangChain. LLM applications are essentially a chain consisting of the large language model to make predictions, the prompt instruction(s) to guide the model toward a desired output, and an optional output parser to transform the format of the model's output.

All LangChain components share the same interface with `invoke`, `stream`, and `batch` methods to handle various inputs and outputs. They can either be combined and executed imperatively by calling them directly or declaratively using LCEL.

The imperative approach is useful if you intend to write a lot of custom logic, whereas the declarative approach is useful for simply assembling existing components with limited customization.

In Chapter 2, you'll learn how to provide external data to your AI chatbot as *context* so that you can build an LLM application that enables you to "chat" with your data.

## CHAPTER 2

RAG Part I: Indexing Your Data

In the previous chapter, you learned about the important building blocks used to create an LLM application using LangChain. You also built a simple AI chatbot consisting of a prompt sent to the model and the output generated by the model. But there are major limitations to this simple chatbot.

What if your use case requires knowledge that the model wasn't trained on? For example, let's say you want to use AI to ask questions about a company, but the information is contained in a private PDF or other type of document. While we've seen model providers enriching their training datasets to include more and more of the world's public information (no matter what format it is stored in), two major limitations continue to exist in LLM's knowledge corpus:

Private data

Information that isn't publicly available is, by definition, not included in the training data of LLMs.

Current events

Training an LLM is a costly and time-consuming process that can span multiple years, with data-gathering being one of the first steps. This results in what is called the knowledge cutoff, or a date beyond which the LLM has no knowledge of real-world events; usually this would be the date the training set was finalized. This can be anywhere from a few months to a few years into the past, depending on the model in question.

In either case, the model will most likely hallucinate (find misleading or false information) and respond with inaccurate information. Adapting the prompt won't resolve the issue either because it relies on the model's current knowledge.

The Goal: Picking Relevant Context for LLMs

If the only private/current data you needed for your LLM use case was one to two pages of text, this chapter would be a lot shorter: all you'd need to make that information available to the LLM is to include that entire text in every single prompt you sent to the model.

The challenge in making data available to LLMs is first and foremost a quantity problem. You have more information than can fit in each prompt you send to the LLM. Which small subset of your large collection of text do you include each time you call the model? Or in other words, how do you pick (with the aid of the model) which text is most relevant to answer each question?

In this chapter and the next, you'll learn how to overcome this challenge in two steps:

1. *Indexing* your documents, that is, preprocessing them in a way where your application can easily find the most relevant ones for each question
2. *Retrieving* this external data from the index and using it as *context* for the LLM to generate an accurate output based on your data

This chapter focuses on indexing, the first step, which involves preprocessing your documents into a format that can be understood and searched with LLMs. This technique is called *retrieval-augmented generation* (RAG). But before we begin, let's discuss *why* your documents require preprocessing.

Let's assume you would like to use LLMs to analyze the financial performance and risks in Tesla's 2022 annual report (*https://oreil.ly/Bp51E*), which is stored as text in PDF format. Your goal is to be able to ask a question like "What key risks did Tesla face in 2022?" and get a humanlike response based on context from the risk factors section of the document.

Breaking it down, there are four key steps (shown in Figure 2-1) that you'd need to take in order to achieve this goal:

1. Extract the text from the document.
2. Split the text into manageable chunks.
3. Convert the text into numbers that computers can understand.
4. Store these number representations of your text somewhere that makes it easy and fast to retrieve the relevant sections of your document to answer a given question.

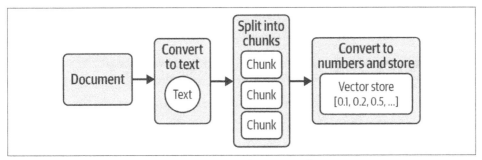

Figure 2-1. Four key steps to preprocess your documents for LLM usage

Figure 2-1 illustrates the flow of this preprocessing and transformation of your documents, a process known as ingestion. *Ingestion* is simply the process of converting your documents into numbers that computers can understand and analyze, and storing them in a special type of database for efficient retrieval. These numbers are formally known as *embeddings*, and this special type of database is known as a *vector store*. Let's look a little more closely at what embeddings are and why they're important, starting with something simpler than LLM-powered embeddings.

Embeddings: Converting Text to Numbers

Embedding refers to representing text as a (long) sequence of numbers. This is a lossy representation—that is, you can't recover the original text from these number sequences, so you usually store both the original text and this numeric representation.

So, why bother? Because you gain the flexibility and power that comes with working with numbers: you can do math on words! Let's see why that's exciting.

Embeddings Before LLMs

Long before LLMs, computer scientists were using embeddings—for instance, to enable full-text search capabilities in websites or to classify emails as spam. Let's see an example:

1. Take these three sentences:
   - What a sunny day.
   - Such bright skies today.
   - I haven't seen a sunny day in weeks.

2. List all unique words in them: *what, a, sunny, day, such, bright,* and so on.

3. For each sentence, go word by word and assign the number 0 if not present, 1 if used once in the sentence, 2 if present twice, and so on.

Table 2-1 shows the result.

Table 2-1. Word embeddings for three sentences

Word	What a sunny day.	Such bright skies today.	I haven't seen a sunny day in weeks.
what	1	0	0
a	1	0	1
sunny	1	0	1
day	1	0	1
such	0	1	0
bright	0	1	0
skies	0	1	0
today	0	1	0
I	0	0	1
haven't	0	0	1
seen	0	0	1
in	0	0	1
weeks	0	0	1

In this model, the embedding for *I haven't seen a sunny day in weeks* is the sequence of numbers *0 1 1 1 0 0 0 0 1 1 1 1 1*. This is called the *bag-of-words* model, and these embeddings are also called *sparse embeddings* (or sparse vectors—*vector* is another word for a sequence of numbers), because a lot of the numbers will be 0. Most English sentences use only a very small subset of all existing English words.

You can successfully use this model for:

Keyword search
> You can find which documents contain a given word or words.

Classification of documents
> You can calculate embeddings for a collection of examples previously labeled as email spam or not spam, average them out, and obtain average word frequencies for each of the classes (spam or not spam). Then, each new document is compared to those averages and classified accordingly.

The limitation here is that the model has no awareness of meaning, only of the actual words used. For instance, the embeddings for *sunny day* and *bright skies* look very different. In fact they have no words in common, even though we know they have similar meaning. Or, in the email classification problem, a would-be spammer can trick the filter by replacing common "spam words" with their synonyms.

In the next section, we'll see how semantic embeddings address this limitation by using numbers to represent the meaning of the text, instead of the exact words found in the text.

LLM-Based Embeddings

We're going to skip over all the ML developments that came in between and jump straight to LLM-based embeddings. Just know that there was a gradual evolution from the simple method outlined in the previous section to the sophisticated method described in this one.

You can think of embedding models as an offshoot from the training process of LLMs. If you remember from the Preface, the LLM training process (learning from vast amounts of written text) enables LLMs to complete a prompt (or input) with the most appropriate continuation (output). This capability stems from an understanding of the meaning of words and sentences in the context of the surrounding text, learned from how words are used together in the training texts. This *understanding* of the meaning (or semantics) of the prompt can be extracted as a numeric representation (or embedding) of the input text, and can be used directly for some very interesting use cases too.

In practice, most embedding models are trained for that purpose alone, following somewhat similar architectures and training processes as LLMs, as that is more efficient and results in higher-quality embeddings.[1]

An *embedding model* then is an algorithm that takes a piece of text and outputs a numerical representation of its meaning—technically, a long list of floating-point (decimal) numbers, usually somewhere between 100 and 2,000 numbers, or *dimensions*. These are also called *dense* embeddings, as opposed to the *sparse* embeddings of the previous section, as here usually all dimensions are different from 0.

 Different models produce different numbers and different sizes of lists. All of these are specific to each model; that is, even if the size of the lists matches, you cannot compare embeddings from different models. Combining embeddings from different models should always be avoided.

Semantic Embeddings Explained

Consider these three words: *lion*, *pet*, and *dog*. Intuitively, which pair of these words share similar characteristics to each other at first glance? The obvious answer is *pet* and *dog*. But computers do not have the ability to tap into this intuition or nuanced understanding of the English language. In order for a computer to differentiate between a lion, pet, or dog, you need to be able to translate them into the language of computers, which is numbers.

---

1 Arvind Neelakantan et al., "Text and Code Embeddings by Contrastive Pre-Training" (*https://oreil.ly/ YOVmh*), arXiv, January 21, 2022.

Figure 2-2 illustrates converting each word into hypothetical number representations that retain their meaning.

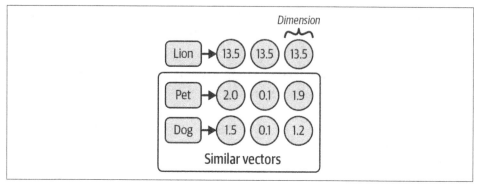

Figure 2-2. Semantic representations of words

Figure 2-2 shows each word alongside its corresponding semantic embedding. Note that the numbers themselves have no particular meaning, but instead the sequences of numbers for two words (or sentences) that are close in meaning should be *closer* than those of unrelated words. As you can see, each number is a *floating-point value*, and each of them represents a semantic *dimension*. Let's see what we mean by *closer*:

If we plot these vectors in a three-dimensional space, it could look like Figure 2-3.

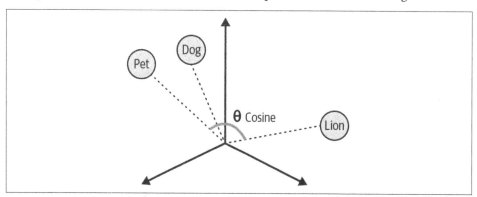

Figure 2-3. Plot of word vectors in a multidimensional space

Figure 2-3 shows the *pet* and *dog* vectors are closer to each other in distance than the *lion* plot. We can also observe that the angles between each plot varies depending on how similar they are. For example, the words *pet* and *lion* have a wider angle between one another than the *pet* and *dog* do, indicating more similarities shared by the latter word pairs. The narrower the angle or shorter the distance between two vectors, the closer their similarities.

One effective way to calculate the degree of similarity between two vectors in a multidimensional space is called cosine similarity. *Cosine similarity* computes the dot product of vectors and divides it by the product of their magnitudes to output a number between –1 and 1, where 0 means the vectors share no correlation, –1 means they are absolutely dissimilar, and 1 means they are absolutely similar. So, in the case of our three words here, the cosine similarity between *pet* and *dog* could be 0.75, but between *pet* and *lion* it might be 0.1.

The ability to convert sentences into embeddings that capture semantic meaning and then perform calculations to find semantic similarities between different sentences enables us to get an LLM to find the most relevant documents to answer questions about a large body of text like our Tesla PDF document. Now that you understand the big picture, let's revisit the first step (indexing) of preprocessing your document.

Other Uses for Embeddings

These sequences of numbers and vectors have a number of interesting properties:

- As you learned earlier, if you think of a vector as describing a point in high-dimensional space, points that are closer together have more similar meanings, so a distance function can be used to measure similarity.

- Groups of points close together can be said to be related; therefore, a clustering algorithm can be used to identify topics (or clusters of points) and classify new inputs into one of those topics.

- If you average out multiple embeddings, the average embedding can be said to represent the overall meaning of that group; that is, you can embed a long document (for instance, this book) by:

  1. Embedding each page separately

  2. Taking the average of the embeddings of all pages as the book embedding

- You can "travel" the "meaning" space by using the elementary math operations of addition and subtraction: for instance, the operation *king – man + woman = queen*. If you take the meaning (or semantic embedding) of *king*, subtract the meaning of *man*, presumably you arrive at the more abstract meaning of *monarch*, at which point, if you add the meaning of *woman*, you've arrived close to the meaning (or embedding) of the word *queen*.

- There are models that can produce embeddings for nontext content, for instance, images, videos, and sounds, in addition to text. This enables, for instance, finding images that are most similar or relevant for a given sentence.

We won't explore all of these attributes in this book, but it's useful to know they can be used for a number of applications (*https://oreil.ly/PU2C8*) such as:

Search
> Finding the most relevant documents for a new query

Clustering
> Given a body of documents, dividing them into groups (for instance, topics)

Classification
> Assigning a new document to a previously identified group or label (for instance, a topic)

Recommendation
> Given a document, surfacing similar documents

Detecting anomalies
> Identifying documents that are very dissimilar from previously seen ones

We hope this leaves you with some intuition that embeddings are quite versatile and can be put to good use in your future projects.

Converting Your Documents into Text

As mentioned at the beginning of the chapter, the first step in preprocessing your document is to convert it to text. In order to achieve this, you would need to build logic to parse and extract the document with minimal loss of quality. Fortunately, LangChain provides *document loaders* that handle the parsing logic and enable you to "load" data from various sources into a Document class that consists of text and associated metadata.

For example, consider a simple *.txt* file. You can simply import a LangChain TextLoader class to extract the text, like this:

Python

```
from langchain_community.document_loaders import TextLoader

loader = TextLoader("./test.txt")
loader.load()
```

JavaScript

```
import { TextLoader } from "langchain/document_loaders/fs/text";

const loader = new TextLoader("./test.txt");

const docs = await loader.load();
```

The output:

```
[Document(page_content='text content \n', metadata={'line_number': 0, 'source':
    './test.txt'})]
```

The previous code block assumes that you have a file named `test.txt` in your current directory. Usage of all LangChain document loaders follows a similar pattern:

1. Start by picking the loader for your type of document from the long list of integrations (*https://oreil.ly/iLJ33*).

2. Create an instance of the loader in question, along with any parameters to configure it, including the location of your documents (usually a filesystem path or web address).

3. Load the documents by calling `load()`, which returns a list of documents ready to pass to the next stage (more on that soon).

Aside from *.txt* files, LangChain provides document loaders for other popular file types including *.csv*, *.json*, and Markdown, alongside integrations with popular platforms such as Slack and Notion.

For example, you can use `WebBaseLoader` to load HTML from web URLs and parse it to text.

Install the beautifulsoup4 package:

```
pip install beautifulsoup4
```

Python

```python
from langchain_community.document_loaders import WebBaseLoader

loader = WebBaseLoader("https://www.langchain.com/")
loader.load()
```

JavaScript

```javascript
// install cheerio: npm install cheerio
import {
  CheerioWebBaseLoader
} from "@langchain/community/document_loaders/web/cheerio";

const loader = new CheerioWebBaseLoader("https://www.langchain.com/");

const docs = await loader.load();
```

In the case of our Tesla PDF use case, we can utilize LangChain's `PDFLoader` to extract text from the PDF document:

Python

```
# install the pdf parsing library
# pip install pypdf

from langchain_community.document_loaders import PyPDFLoader

loader = PyPDFLoader("./test.pdf")
pages = loader.load()
```

JavaScript

```
// install the pdf parsing library: npm install pdf-parse

import { PDFLoader } from "langchain/document_loaders/fs/pdf";

const loader = new PDFLoader("./test.pdf");

const docs = await loader.load();
```

The text has been extracted from the PDF document and stored in the `Document` class. But there's a problem. The loaded document is over 100,000 characters long, so it won't fit into the context window of the vast majority of LLMs or embedding models. In order to overcome this limitation, we need to split the `Document` into manageable chunks of text that we can later convert into embeddings and semantically search, bringing us to the second step (retrieving).

 LLMs and embedding models are designed with a hard limit on the size of input and output tokens they can handle. This limit is usually called *context window*, and usually applies to the combination of input and output; that is, if the context window is 100 (we'll talk about units in a second), and your input measures 90, the output can be at most of length 10. Context windows are usually measured in number of tokens, for instance 8,192 tokens. Tokens, as mentioned in the Preface, are a representation of text as numbers, with each token usually covering between three and four characters of English text.

Splitting Your Text into Chunks

At first glance it may seem straightforward to split a large body of text into chunks, but keeping *semantically* related (related by meaning) chunks of text together is a complex process. To make it easier to split large documents into small, but still meaningful, pieces of text, LangChain provides `RecursiveCharacterTextSplitter`, which does the following:

1. Take a list of separators, in order of importance. By default these are:

    a. The paragraph separator: \n\n

    b. The line separator: \n

    c. The word separator: space character

2. To respect the given chunk size, for instance, 1,000 characters, start by splitting up paragraphs.

3. For any paragraph longer than the desired chunk size, split by the next separator: lines. Continue until all chunks are smaller than the desired length, or there are no additional separators to try.

4. Emit each chunk as a Document, with the metadata of the original document passed in and additional information about the position in the original document.

Let's see an example:

Python

```
from langchain_text_splitters import RecursiveCharacterTextSplitter

loader = TextLoader("./test.txt") # or any other loader
docs = loader.load()

splitter = RecursiveCharacterTextSplitter(
    chunk_size=1000,
    chunk_overlap=200,
)
splitted_docs = splitter.split_documents(docs)
```

JavaScript

```
import { TextLoader } from "langchain/document_loaders/fs/text";
import { RecursiveCharacterTextSplitter } from "@langchain/textsplitters";

const loader = new TextLoader("./test.txt"); // or any other loader
const docs = await loader.load();

const splitter = new RecursiveCharacterTextSplitter({
  chunkSize: 1000,
  chunkOverlap: 200,
});

const splittedDocs = await splitter.splitDocuments(docs)
```

In the preceding code, the documents created by the document loader are split into chunks of 1,000 characters each, with some overlap between chunks of 200 characters to maintain some context. The result is also a list of documents, where each document is up to 1,000 characters in length, split along the natural divisions of written text—paragraphs, new lines and finally, words. This uses the structure of the text to keep each chunk a consistent, readable snippet of text.

RecursiveCharacterTextSplitter can also be used to split code languages and Markdown into semantic chunks. This is done by using keywords specific to each language as the separators, which ensures, for instance, the body of each function is kept in the same chunk, instead of split between several. Usually, as programming languages have more structure than written text, there's less need to use overlap between the chunks. LangChain contains separators for a number of popular languages, such as Python, JS, Markdown, HTML, and many more. Here's an example:

Python

```python
from langchain_text_splitters import (
    Language,
    RecursiveCharacterTextSplitter,
)

PYTHON_CODE = """
def hello_world():
    print("Hello, World!")

# Call the function
hello_world()
"""
python_splitter = RecursiveCharacterTextSplitter.from_language(
    language=Language.PYTHON, chunk_size=50, chunk_overlap=0
)
python_docs = python_splitter.create_documents([PYTHON_CODE])
```

JavaScript

```javascript
import { RecursiveCharacterTextSplitter } from "@langchain/textsplitters";

const PYTHON_CODE = `
def hello_world():
  print("Hello, World!")

# Call the function
hello_world()
`;

const pythonSplitter = RecursiveCharacterTextSplitter.fromLanguage("python", {
  chunkSize: 50,
  chunkOverlap: 0,
});
const pythonDocs = await pythonSplitter.createDocuments([PYTHON_CODE]);
```

The output:

```
[Document(page_content='def hello_world():\n    print("Hello, World!")'),
    Document(page_content='# Call the function\nhello_world()')]
```

Notice how we're still using RecursiveCharacterTextSplitter as before, but now we're creating an instance of it for a specific language, using the from_language method. This one accepts the name of the language, and the usual parameters for chunk size, and so on. Also notice we are now using the method create_documents, which accepts a list of strings, rather than the list of documents we had before. This method is useful when the text you want to split doesn't come from a document loader, so you have only the raw text strings.

You can also use the optional second argument to create_documents in order to pass a list of metadata to associate with each text string. This metadata list should have the same length as the list of strings and will be used to populate the metadata field of each Document returned.

Let's see an example for Markdown text, using the metadata argument as well:

Python

```
markdown_text = """
# LangChain

⚡ Building applications with LLMs through composability ⚡

## Quick Install

```bash
pip install langchain
```

As an open source project in a rapidly developing field, we are extremely open
    to contributions.
"""

md_splitter = RecursiveCharacterTextSplitter.from_language(
    language=Language.MARKDOWN, chunk_size=60, chunk_overlap=0
)
md_docs = md_splitter.create_documents([markdown_text],
    [{"source": "https://www.langchain.com"}])
```

JavaScript

```
const markdownText = `
# LangChain

⚡ Building applications with LLMs through composability ⚡

## Quick Install

\`\`\`bash
pip install langchain
\`\`\`
```

```
As an open source project in a rapidly developing field, we are extremely
  open to contributions.
`;

const mdSplitter = RecursiveCharacterTextSplitter.fromLanguage("markdown", {
  chunkSize: 60,
  chunkOverlap: 0,
});
const mdDocs = await mdSplitter.createDocuments([markdownText],
  [{"source": "https://www.langchain.com"}]);
```

The output:

```
[Document(page_content='# LangChain',
    metadata={"source": "https://www.langchain.com"}),
 Document(page_content='⚡ Building applications with LLMs through composability
    ⚡', metadata={"source": "https://www.langchain.com"}),
 Document(page_content='## Quick Install\n\n```bash',
    metadata={"source": "https://www.langchain.com"}),
 Document(page_content='pip install langchain',
    metadata={"source": "https://www.langchain.com"}),
 Document(page_content='```', metadata={"source": "https://www.langchain.com"}),
 Document(page_content='As an open source project in a rapidly developing field,
    we', metadata={"source": "https://www.langchain.com"}),
 Document(page_content='are extremely open to contributions.',
    metadata={"source": "https://www.langchain.com"})]
```

Notice two things:

- The text is split along the natural stopping points in the Markdown document;
  for instance, the heading goes into one chunk, the line of text under it in a
  separate chunk, and so on.

- The metadata we passed in the second argument is attached to each resulting
  document, which allows you to track, for instance, where the document came
  from and where you can go to see the original.

Generating Text Embeddings

LangChain also has an `Embeddings` class designed to interface with text embedding
models—including OpenAI, Cohere, and Hugging Face—and generate vector representations of text. This class provides two methods: one for embedding documents
and one for embedding a query. The former takes a list of text strings as input, while
the latter takes a single text string.

Here's an example of embedding a document using OpenAI's embedding model (*https://oreil.ly/9tnzQ*):

Python

```python
from langchain_openai import OpenAIEmbeddings

model = OpenAIEmbeddings()

embeddings = model.embed_documents([
    "Hi there!",
    "Oh, hello!",
    "What's your name?",
    "My friends call me World",
    "Hello World!"
])
```

JavaScript

```javascript
import { OpenAIEmbeddings } from "@langchain/openai";

const model = new OpenAIEmbeddings();

const embeddings = await embeddings.embedDocuments([
    "Hi there!",
    "Oh, hello!",
    "What' s your name?",
    "My friends call me World",
    "Hello World!"
]);
```

The output:

```
[
  [
    -0.004845875, 0.004899438, -0.016358767, -0.024475135, -0.017341806,
     0.012571548, -0.019156644, 0.009036391, -0.010227379, -0.026945334,
     0.022861943, 0.010321903, -0.023479493, -0.0066544134, 0.007977734,
    0.0026371893, 0.025206111, -0.012048521, 0.012943339, 0.013094575,
    -0.010580265, -0.003509951, 0.004070787, 0.008639394, -0.020631202,
    ... 1511 more items
  ]
  [
    -0.009446913, -0.013253193, 0.013174579, 0.0057552797, -0.038993083,
     0.0077763423, -0.0260478, -0.0114384955, -0.0022683728, -0.016509168,
     0.041797023, 0.01787183, 0.00552271, -0.0049789557, 0.018146982,
    -0.01542166, 0.033752076, 0.006112323, 0.023872782, -0.016535373,
    -0.006623321, 0.016116094, -0.0061090477, -0.0044155475, -0.016627092,
    ... 1511 more items
  ]
  ... 3 more items
]
```

Notice that you can embed multiple documents at the same time; you should prefer this to embedding them one at a time, as it will be more efficient (due to how these models are constructed). You get back a list containing multiple lists of numbers—each inner list is a vector or embedding, as explained in an earlier section.

Now let's see an end-to-end example using the three capabilities we've seen so far:

- Document loaders, to convert any document to plain text
- Text splitters, to split each large document into many smaller ones
- Embeddings models, to create a numeric representation of the meaning of each split

Here's the code:

Python

```python
from langchain_community.document_loaders import TextLoader
from langchain_text_splitters import RecursiveCharacterTextSplitter
from langchain_openai import OpenAIEmbeddings

## Load the document

loader = TextLoader("./test.txt")
doc = loader.load()

"""
[
    Document(page_content='Document loaders\n\nUse document loaders to load data
        from a source as `Document`\'s. A `Document` is a piece of text\nand
        associated metadata. For example, there are document loaders for
        loading a simple `.txt` file, for loading the text\ncontents of any web
        page, or even for loading a transcript of a YouTube video.\n\nEvery
        document loader exposes two methods:\n1. "Load": load documents from
        the configured source\n2. "Load and split": load documents from the
        configured source and split them using the passed in text
        splitter\n\nThey optionally implement:\n3. "Lazy load": load
        documents into memory lazily\n', metadata={'source': 'test.txt'})
]
"""

## Split the document

text_splitter = RecursiveCharacterTextSplitter(
    chunk_size=1000,
    chunk_overlap=20,
)
chunks = text_splitter.split_documents(doc)

## Generate embeddings
```

```
embeddings_model = OpenAIEmbeddings()
embeddings = embeddings_model.embed_documents(
    [chunk.page_content for chunk in chunks]
)
"""
[[0.0053587136790156364,
 -0.0004999046213924885,
  0.038883671164512634,
 -0.003001077566295862,
 -0.00900818221271038, ...], ...]
"""
```

JavaScript

```
import { TextLoader } from "langchain/document_loaders/fs/text";
import { RecursiveCharacterTextSplitter } from "@langchain/textsplitters";
import { OpenAIEmbeddings } from "@langchain/openai";

// Load the document

const loader = new TextLoader("./test.txt");
const docs = await loader.load();

// Split the document

const splitter = new RecursiveCharacterTextSplitter({
  chunkSize: 1000,
  chunkOverlap: 200,
});
const chunks = await splitter.splitDocuments(docs)

// Generate embeddings

const model = new OpenAIEmbeddings();
await embeddings.embedDocuments(chunks.map(c => c.pageContent));
```

Once you've generated embeddings from your documents, the next step is to store them in a special database known as a vector store.

Storing Embeddings in a Vector Store

Earlier in this chapter, we discussed the cosine similarity calculation to measure the similarity between vectors in a vector space. A vector store is a database designed to store vectors and perform complex calculations, like cosine similarity, efficiently and quickly.

Unlike traditional databases that specialize in storing structured data (such as JSON documents or data conforming to the schema of a relational database), vector stores handle unstructured data, including text and images. Like traditional databases, vector stores are capable of performing create, read, update, delete (CRUD), and search operations.

Vector stores unlock a wide variety of use cases, including scalable applications that utilize AI to answer questions about large documents, as illustrated in Figure 2-4.

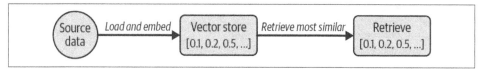

Figure 2-4. Loading, embedding, storing, and retrieving relevant docs from a vector store

Figure 2-4 illustrates how document embeddings are inserted into the vector store and how later, when a query is sent, similar embeddings are retrieved from the vector store.

Currently, there is an abundance of vector store providers to choose from, each specializing in different capabilities. Your selection should depend on the critical requirements of your application, including multitenancy, metadata filtering capabilities, performance, cost, and scalability.

Although vector stores are niche databases built to manage vector data, there are a few disadvantages working with them:

- Most vector stores are relatively new and may not stand the test of time.
- Managing and optimizing vector stores can present a relatively steep learning curve.
- Managing a separate database adds complexity to your application and may drain valuable resources.

Fortunately, vector store capabilities have recently been extended to PostgreSQL (a popular open source relational database) via the `pgvector` extension. This enables you to use the same database you're already familiar with and to power both your transactional tables (for instance your users table) as well as your vector search tables.

Getting Set Up with PGVector

To use Postgres and PGVector you'll need to follow a few setup steps:

1. Ensure you have Docker installed on your computer, following the instructions for your operating system (*https://oreil.ly/Gn28O*).
2. Run the following command in your terminal; it will launch a Postgres instance in your computer running on port 6024:

```
docker run \
    --name pgvector-container \
    -e POSTGRES_USER=langchain \
    -e POSTGRES_PASSWORD=langchain \
    -e POSTGRES_DB=langchain \
    -p 6024:5432 \
    -d pgvector/pgvector:pg16
```

Open your docker dashboard containers and you should see a green running status next to pgvector-container.

3. Save the connection string to use in your code; we'll need it later:

```
postgresql+psycopg://langchain:langchain@localhost:6024/langchain
```

Working with Vector Stores

Picking up where we left off in the previous section on embeddings, now let's see an example of loading, splitting, embedding, and storing a document in PGVector:

Python

```python
# first, pip install langchain-postgres
from langchain_community.document_loaders import TextLoader
from langchain_openai import OpenAIEmbeddings
from langchain_text_splitters import RecursiveCharacterTextSplitter
from langchain_postgres.vectorstores import PGVector
from langchain_core.documents import Document
import uuid

# Load the document, split it into chunks
raw_documents = TextLoader('./test.txt').load()
text_splitter = RecursiveCharacterTextSplitter(chunk_size=1000,
    chunk_overlap=200)
documents = text_splitter.split_documents(raw_documents)

# embed each chunk and insert it into the vector store
embeddings_model = OpenAIEmbeddings()
connection = 'postgresql+psycopg://langchain:langchain@localhost:6024/langchain'
db = PGVector.from_documents(documents, embeddings_model, connection=connection)
```

JavaScript

```javascript
import { TextLoader } from "langchain/document_loaders/fs/text";
import { RecursiveCharacterTextSplitter } from "@langchain/textsplitters";
import { OpenAIEmbeddings } from "@langchain/openai";
import { PGVectorStore } from "@langchain/community/vectorstores/pgvector";
import { v4 as uuidv4 } from 'uuid';

// Load the document, split it into chunks
const loader = new TextLoader("./test.txt");
const raw_docs = await loader.load();
const splitter = new RecursiveCharacterTextSplitter({
  chunkSize: 1000,
```

```
  chunkOverlap: 200,
});
const docs = await splitter.splitDocuments(docs)

// embed each chunk and insert it into the vector store
const embeddings_model = new OpenAIEmbeddings();
const db = await PGVectorStore.fromDocuments(docs, embeddings_model, {
  postgresConnectionOptions: {
    connectionString: 'postgresql://langchain:langchain@localhost:6024/langchain'
  }
})
```

Notice how we reuse the code from the previous sections to first load the documents with the loader and then split them into smaller chunks. Then, we instantiate the embeddings model we want to use—in this case, OpenAI's. Note that you could use any other embeddings model supported by LangChain here.

Next, we have a new line of code, which creates a vector store given documents, the embeddings model, and a connection string. This will do a few things:

- Establish a connection to the Postgres instance running in your computer (see "Getting Set Up with PGVector" on page 40.)

- Run any setup necessary, such as creating tables to hold your documents and vectors, if this is the first time you're running it.

- Create embeddings for each document you passed in, using the model you chose.

- Store the embeddings, the document's metadata, and the document's text content in Postgres, ready to be searched.

Let's see what it looks like to search documents:

Python

```
db.similarity_search("query", k=4)
```

JavaScript

```
await pgvectorStore.similaritySearch("query", 4);
```

This method will find the most relevant documents (which you previously indexed), by following this process:

- The search query—in this case, the word query—will be sent to the embeddings model to retrieve its embedding.

- Then, it will run a query on Postgres to find the N (in this case 4) previously stored embeddings that are most similar to your query.

- Finally, it will fetch the text content and metadata that relates to each of those embeddings.

- The model can now return a list of Document sorted by how similar they are to the query—the most similar first, the second most similar after, and so on.

You can also add more documents to an existing database. Let's see an example:

Python

```python
ids = [str(uuid.uuid4()), str(uuid.uuid4())]
db.add_documents(
    [
        Document(
            page_content="there are cats in the pond",
            metadata={"location": "pond", "topic": "animals"},
        ),
        Document(
            page_content="ducks are also found in the pond",
            metadata={"location": "pond", "topic": "animals"},
        ),
    ],
    ids=ids,
)
```

JavaScript

```javascript
const ids = [uuidv4(), uuidv4()];

await db.addDocuments(
  [
    {
      pageContent: "there are cats in the pond",
      metadata: {location: "pond", topic: "animals"}
    },
    {
      pageContent: "ducks are also found in the pond",
      metadata: {location: "pond", topic: "animals"}
    },
  ],
  {ids}
);
```

The add_documents method we're using here will follow a similar process to fromDocuments:

- Create embeddings for each document you passed in, using the model you chose.
- Store the embeddings, the document's metadata, and the document's text content in Postgres, ready to be searched.

In this example, we are using the optional ids argument to assign identifiers to each document, which allows us to update or delete them later.

Here's an example of the delete operation:

Python

```
db.delete(ids=[1])
```

JavaScript

```
await db.delete({ ids: [ids[1]] })
```

This removes the second document inserted by using its Universally Unique Identifier (UUID). Now let's see how to do this in a more systematic way.

Tracking Changes to Your Documents

One of the key challenges with working with vector stores is working with data that regularly changes, because changes mean re-indexing. And re-indexing can lead to costly recomputations of embeddings and duplications of preexisting content.

Fortunately, LangChain provides an indexing API to make it easy to keep your documents in sync with your vector store. The API utilizes a class (`RecordManager`) to keep track of document writes into the vector store. When indexing content, hashes are computed for each document and the following information is stored in `RecordManager`:

- The document hash (hash of both page content and metadata)
- Write time
- The source ID (each document should include information in its metadata to determine the ultimate source of this document).

In addition, the indexing API provides cleanup modes to help you decide how to delete existing documents in the vector store. For example, If you've made changes to how documents are processed before insertion or if source documents have changed, you may want to remove any existing documents that come from the same source as the new documents being indexed. If some source documents have been deleted, you'll want to delete all existing documents in the vector store and replace them with the re-indexed documents.

The modes are as follows:

- `None` mode does not do any automatic cleanup, allowing the user to manually do cleanup of old content.
- `Incremental` and `full` modes delete previous versions of the content if the content of the source document or derived documents has changed.

- Full mode will additionally delete any documents not included in documents currently being indexed.

Here's an example of the use of the indexing API with Postgres database set up as a record manager:

Python

```python
from langchain.indexes import SQLRecordManager, index
from langchain_postgres.vectorstores import PGVector
from langchain_openai import OpenAIEmbeddings
from langchain.docstore.document import Document

connection = "postgresql+psycopg://langchain:langchain@localhost:6024/langchain"
collection_name = "my_docs"
embeddings_model = OpenAIEmbeddings(model="text-embedding-3-small")
namespace = "my_docs_namespace"

vectorstore = PGVector(
    embeddings=embeddings_model,
    collection_name=collection_name,
    connection=connection,
    use_jsonb=True,
)

record_manager = SQLRecordManager(
    namespace,
    db_url="postgresql+psycopg://langchain:langchain@localhost:6024/langchain",
)

# Create the schema if it doesn't exist
record_manager.create_schema()

# Create documents
docs = [
    Document(page_content='there are cats in the pond', metadata={
        "id": 1, "source": "cats.txt"}),
    Document(page_content='ducks are also found in the pond', metadata={
        "id": 2, "source": "ducks.txt"}),
]

# Index the documents
index_1 = index(
    docs,
    record_manager,
    vectorstore,
    cleanup="incremental",  # prevent duplicate documents
    source_id_key="source",  # use the source field as the source_id
)

print("Index attempt 1:", index_1)
```

```python
# second time you attempt to index, it will not add the documents again
index_2 = index(
    docs,
    record_manager,
    vectorstore,
    cleanup="incremental",
    source_id_key="source",
)

print("Index attempt 2:", index_2)

# If we mutate a document, the new version will be written and all old
# versions sharing the same source will be deleted.

docs[0].page_content = "I just modified this document!"

index_3 = index(
    docs,
    record_manager,
    vectorstore,
    cleanup="incremental",
    source_id_key="source",
)

print("Index attempt 3:", index_3)
```

JavaScript

```javascript
/**
 * 1. Ensure docker is installed and running (https://docs.docker.com/get-docker/)
 * 2. Run the following command to start the postgres container:
 *
 * docker run \
 *   --name pgvector-container \
 *   -e POSTGRES_USER=langchain \
 *   -e POSTGRES_PASSWORD=langchain \
 *   -e POSTGRES_DB=langchain \
 *   -p 6024:5432 \
 *   -d pgvector/pgvector:pg16
 * 3. Use the connection string below for the postgres container
 */

import { PostgresRecordManager } from '@langchain/community/indexes/postgres';
import { index } from 'langchain/indexes';
import { OpenAIEmbeddings } from '@langchain/openai';
import { PGVectorStore } from '@langchain/community/vectorstores/pgvector';
import { v4 as uuidv4 } from 'uuid';

const tableName = 'test_langchain';
const connectionString =
  'postgresql://langchain:langchain@localhost:6024/langchain';
// Load the document, split it into chunks
```

```
const config = {
  postgresConnectionOptions: {
    connectionString,
  },
  tableName: tableName,
  columns: {
    idColumnName: 'id',
    vectorColumnName: 'vector',
    contentColumnName: 'content',
    metadataColumnName: 'metadata',
  },
};

const vectorStore = await PGVectorStore.initialize(
  new OpenAIEmbeddings(),
  config
);

// Create a new record manager
const recordManagerConfig = {
  postgresConnectionOptions: {
    connectionString,
  },
  tableName: 'upsertion_records',
};
const recordManager = new PostgresRecordManager(
  'test_namespace',
  recordManagerConfig
);

// Create the schema if it doesn't exist
await recordManager.createSchema();

const docs = [
  {
    pageContent: 'there are cats in the pond',
    metadata: { id: uuidv4(), source: 'cats.txt' },
  },
  {
    pageContent: 'ducks are also found in the pond',
    metadata: { id: uuidv4(), source: 'ducks.txt' },
  },
];

// the first attempt will index both documents
const index_attempt_1 = await index({
  docsSource: docs,
  recordManager,
  vectorStore,
  options: {
    // prevent duplicate documents by id from being indexed
    cleanup: 'incremental',
```

```
    // the key in the metadata that will be used to identify the document
    sourceIdKey: 'source',
    },
  });

  console.log(index_attempt_1);

  // the second attempt will skip indexing because the identical documents
  // already exist
  const index_attempt_2 = await index({
    docsSource: docs,
    recordManager,
    vectorStore,
    options: {
      cleanup: 'incremental',
      sourceIdKey: 'source',
    },
  });

  console.log(index_attempt_2);

  // If we mutate a document, the new version will be written and all old
  // versions sharing the same source will be deleted.
  docs[0].pageContent = 'I modified the first document content';
  const index_attempt_3 = await index({
    docsSource: docs,
    recordManager,
    vectorStore,
    options: {
      cleanup: 'incremental',
      sourceIdKey: 'source',
    },
  });

  console.log(index_attempt_3);
```

First, you create a record manager, which keeps track of which documents have been indexed before. Then you use the `index` function to synchronize your vector store with the new list of documents. In this example, we're using the incremental mode, so any documents that have the same ID as previous ones will be replaced with the new version.

Indexing Optimization

A basic RAG indexing stage involves naive text splitting and embedding of chunks of a given document. However, this basic approach leads to inconsistent retrieval results and a relatively high occurrence of hallucinations, especially when the data source contains images and tables.

There are various strategies to enhance the accuracy and performance of the indexing stage. We will cover three of them in the next sections: MultiVectorRetriever, RAPTOR, and ColBERT.

MultiVectorRetriever

A document that contains a mixture of text and tables cannot be simply split by text into chunks and embedded as context: the entire table can be easily lost. To solve this problem, we can decouple documents that we want to use for answer synthesis, from a reference that we want to use for the retriever. Figure 2-5 illustrates how.

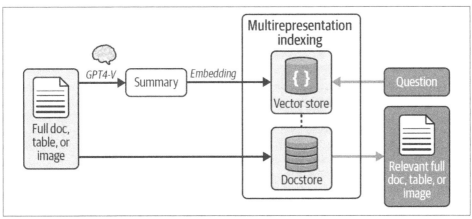

Figure 2-5. Indexing multiple representations of a single document

For example, in the case of a document that contains tables, we can first generate and embed summaries of table elements, ensuring each summary contains an id reference to the full raw table. Next, we store the raw referenced tables in a separate docstore. Finally, when a user's query retrieves a table summary, we pass the entire referenced raw table as context to the final prompt sent to the LLM for answer synthesis. This approach enables us to provide the model with the full context of information required to answer the question.

Here's an example. First, let's use the LLM to generate summaries of the documents:

Python

```
from langchain_community.document_loaders import TextLoader
from langchain_text_splitters import RecursiveCharacterTextSplitter
from langchain_openai import OpenAIEmbeddings
from langchain_postgres.vectorstores import PGVector
from langchain_core.output_parsers import StrOutputParser
from langchain_core.prompts import ChatPromptTemplate
from pydantic import BaseModel
from langchain_core.runnables import RunnablePassthrough
from langchain_openai import ChatOpenAI
```

```python
from langchain_core.documents import Document
from langchain.retrievers.multi_vector import MultiVectorRetriever
from langchain.storage import InMemoryStore
import uuid

connection = "postgresql+psycopg://langchain:langchain@localhost:6024/langchain"
collection_name = "summaries"
embeddings_model = OpenAIEmbeddings()
# Load the document
loader = TextLoader("./test.txt", encoding="utf-8")
docs = loader.load()

print("length of loaded docs: ", len(docs[0].page_content))
# Split the document
splitter = RecursiveCharacterTextSplitter(chunk_size=1000, chunk_overlap=200)
chunks = splitter.split_documents(docs)

# The rest of your code remains the same, starting from:
prompt_text = "Summarize the following document:\n\n{doc}"

prompt = ChatPromptTemplate.from_template(prompt_text)
llm = ChatOpenAI(temperature=0, model="gpt-3.5-turbo")
summarize_chain = {
    "doc": lambda x: x.page_content} | prompt | llm | StrOutputParser()

# batch the chain across the chunks
summaries = summarize_chain.batch(chunks, {"max_concurrency": 5})
```

Next, let's define the vector store and docstore to store the raw summaries and their embeddings:

Python

```python
# The vectorstore to use to index the child chunks
vectorstore = PGVector(
    embeddings=embeddings_model,
    collection_name=collection_name,
    connection=connection,
    use_jsonb=True,
)
# The storage layer for the parent documents
store = InMemoryStore()
id_key = "doc_id"

# indexing the summaries in our vector store, whilst retaining the original
# documents in our document store:
retriever = MultiVectorRetriever(
    vectorstore=vectorstore,
    docstore=store,
    id_key=id_key,
)

# Changed from summaries to chunks since we need same length as docs
```

```python
doc_ids = [str(uuid.uuid4()) for _ in chunks]

# Each summary is linked to the original document by the doc_id
summary_docs = [
    Document(page_content=s, metadata={id_key: doc_ids[i]})
    for i, s in enumerate(summaries)
]

# Add the document summaries to the vector store for similarity search
retriever.vectorstore.add_documents(summary_docs)

# Store the original documents in the document store, linked to their summaries
# via doc_ids
# This allows us to first search summaries efficiently, then fetch the full
# docs when needed
retriever.docstore.mset(list(zip(doc_ids, chunks)))

# vector store retrieves the summaries
sub_docs = retriever.vectorstore.similarity_search(
    "chapter on philosophy", k=2)
```

Finally, let's retrieve the relevant full context document based on a query:

Python

```python
# Whereas the retriever will return the larger source document chunks:
retrieved_docs = retriever.invoke("chapter on philosophy")
```

Here's the full implementation in JavaScript:

JavaScript

```javascript
import * as uuid from 'uuid';
import { MultiVectorRetriever } from 'langchain/retrievers/multi_vector';
import { OpenAIEmbeddings } from '@langchain/openai';
import { RecursiveCharacterTextSplitter } from '@langchain/textsplitters';
import { InMemoryStore } from '@langchain/core/stores';
import { TextLoader } from 'langchain/document_loaders/fs/text';
import { Document } from '@langchain/core/documents';
import { PGVectorStore } from '@langchain/community/vectorstores/pgvector';
import { ChatOpenAI } from '@langchain/openai';
import { PromptTemplate } from '@langchain/core/prompts';
import { RunnableSequence } from '@langchain/core/runnables';
import { StringOutputParser } from '@langchain/core/output_parsers';

const connectionString =
  'postgresql://langchain:langchain@localhost:6024/langchain';
const collectionName = 'summaries';

const textLoader = new TextLoader('./test.txt');
const parentDocuments = await textLoader.load();
const splitter = new RecursiveCharacterTextSplitter({
  chunkSize: 10000,
```

```
  chunkOverlap: 20,
});
const docs = await splitter.splitDocuments(parentDocuments);

const prompt = PromptTemplate.fromTemplate(
  `Summarize the following document:\n\n{doc}`
);

const llm = new ChatOpenAI({ modelName: 'gpt-3.5-turbo' });

const chain = RunnableSequence.from([
  { doc: (doc) => doc.pageContent },
  prompt,
  llm,
  new StringOutputParser(),
]);

// batch summarization chain across the chunks
const summaries = await chain.batch(docs, {
  maxConcurrency: 5,
});

const idKey = 'doc_id';
const docIds = docs.map((_) => uuid.v4());
// create summary docs with metadata linking to the original docs
const summaryDocs = summaries.map((summary, i) => {
  const summaryDoc = new Document({
    pageContent: summary,
    metadata: {
      [idKey]: docIds[i],
    },
  });
  return summaryDoc;
});

// The byteStore to use to store the original chunks
const byteStore = new InMemoryStore();

// vector store for the summaries
const vectorStore = await PGVectorStore.fromDocuments(
  docs,
  new OpenAIEmbeddings(),
  {
    postgresConnectionOptions: {
      connectionString,
    },
  }
);

const retriever = new MultiVectorRetriever({
  vectorstore: vectorStore,
  byteStore,
```

```
    idKey,
});

const keyValuePairs = docs.map((originalDoc, i) => [docIds[i], originalDoc]);

// Use the retriever to add the original chunks to the document store
await retriever.docstore.mset(keyValuePairs);

// Vectorstore alone retrieves the small chunks
const vectorstoreResult = await retriever.vectorstore.similaritySearch(
  'chapter on philosophy',
  2
);
console.log(`summary: ${vectorstoreResult[0].pageContent}`);
console.log(
  `summary retrieved length: ${vectorstoreResult[0].pageContent.length}`
);

// Retriever returns larger chunk result
const retrieverResult = await retriever.invoke('chapter on philosophy');
console.log(
  `multi-vector retrieved chunk length: ${retrieverResult[0].pageContent.length}`
);
```

RAPTOR: Recursive Abstractive Processing for Tree-Organized Retrieval

RAG systems need to handle lower-level questions that reference specific facts found in a single document or higher-level questions that distill ideas that span many documents. Handling both types of questions can be a challenge with typical k-nearest neighbors (k-NN) retrieval over document chunks.

Recursive abstractive processing for tree-organized retrieval (RAPTOR) is an effective strategy that involves creating document summaries that capture higher-level concepts, embedding and clustering those documents, and then summarizing each cluster (*https://oreil.ly/VdIpJ*).[2] This is done recursively, producing a tree of summaries with increasingly high-level concepts. The summaries and initial documents are then indexed together, giving coverage across lower-to-higher-level user questions. Figure 2-6 illustrates.

---

2 Parth Sarthi et al., "RAPTOR: Recursive Abstractive Processing for Tree-Organized Retrieval" (*https://oreil.ly/hS4NB*), arXiv, January 31, 2024. Paper published at ICLR 2024.

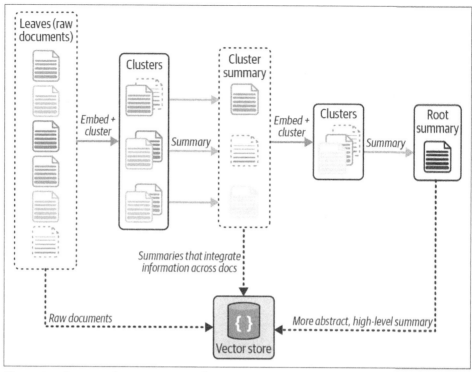

Figure 2-6. Recursively summarizing documents

ColBERT: Optimizing Embeddings

One of the challenges of using embeddings models during the indexing stage is that they compress text into fixed-length (vector) representations that capture the semantic content of the document. Although this compression is useful for retrieval, embedding irrelevant or redundant content may lead to hallucinations in the final LLM output.

One solution to this problem is to do the following:

1. Generate contextual embeddings for each token in the document and query.

2. Calculate and score similarity between each query token and all document tokens.

3. Sum the maximum similarity score of each query embedding to any of the document embeddings to get a score for each document.

This results in a granular and effective embedding approach for better retrieval. Fortunately, the embedding model called ColBERT embodies the solution to this problem.[3]

Here's how we can utilize ColBERT for optimal embedding of our data:

Python

```python
# RAGatouille is a library that makes it simple to use ColBERT
#! pip install -U ragatouille

from ragatouille import RAGPretrainedModel
RAG = RAGPretrainedModel.from_pretrained("colbert-ir/colbertv2.0")

import requests

def get_wikipedia_page(title: str):
    """
    Retrieve the full text content of a Wikipedia page.

    :param title: str - Title of the Wikipedia page.
    :return: str - Full text content of the page as raw string.
    """
    # Wikipedia API endpoint
    URL = "https://en.wikipedia.org/w/api.php"

    # Parameters for the API request
    params = {
        "action": "query",
        "format": "json",
        "titles": title,
        "prop": "extracts",
        "explaintext": True,
    }

    # Custom User-Agent header to comply with Wikipedia's best practices
    headers = {"User-Agent": "RAGatouille_tutorial/0.0.1"}

    response = requests.get(URL, params=params, headers=headers)
    data = response.json()

    # Extracting page content
    page = next(iter(data["query"]["pages"].values()))
    return page["extract"] if "extract" in page else None

full_document = get_wikipedia_page("Hayao_Miyazaki")

## Create an index
```

---

3 Keshav Santhanam et al., "ColBERTv2: Effective and Efficient Retrieval via Lightweight Late Interaction" (*https://oreil.ly/9spW2*), arXiv, December 2, 2021.

```
RAG.index(
    collection=[full_document],
    index_name="Miyazaki-123",
    max_document_length=180,
    split_documents=True,
)

#query
results = RAG.search(query="What animation studio did Miyazaki found?", k=3)
results

#utilize langchain retriever
retriever = RAG.as_langchain_retriever(k=3)
retriever.invoke("What animation studio did Miyazaki found?")
```

By using ColBERT, you can improve the relevancy of retrieved documents used as context by the LLM.

Summary

In this chapter, you've learned how to prepare and preprocess your documents for your LLM application using various LangChain's modules. The document loaders enable you to extract text from your data source, the text splitters help you split your document into semantically similar chunks, and the embeddings models convert your text into vector representations of their meaning.

Separately, vector stores allow you to perform CRUD operations on these embeddings alongside complex calculations to compute semantically similar chunks of text. Finally, indexing optimization strategies enable your AI app to improve the quality of embeddings and perform accurate retrieval of documents that contain semistructured data including tables.

In Chapter 3, you'll learn how to efficiently retrieve the most similar chunks of documents from your vector store based on your query, provide it as context the model can see, and then generate an accurate output.

RAG Part II: Chatting with Your Data

In the previous chapter, you learned how to process your data and create and store embeddings in a vector store. In this chapter, you'll learn how to efficiently retrieve the most relevant embeddings and chunks of documents based on a user's query. This enables you to construct a prompt that contains relevant documents as context, improving the accuracy of the LLM's final output.

This process—which involves embedding a user's query, retrieving similar documents from a data source, and then passing them as context to the prompt sent to the LLM—is formally known as *retrieval-augmented generation* (RAG).

RAG is an essential component of building chat-enabled LLM apps that are accurate, efficient, and up-to-date. In this chapter, you'll progress from basics to advanced strategies to build an effective RAG system for various data sources (such as vector stores and databases) and data structures (structured and unstructured).

But first, let's define RAG and discuss its benefits.

Introducing Retrieval-Augmented Generation

RAG is a technique used to enhance the accuracy of outputs generated by LLMs by providing context from external sources. The term was originally coined in a paper by Meta AI researchers who discovered that RAG-enabled models are more factual and specific than non-RAG models.[1]

---

1 Patrick Lewis et al., "Retrieval-Augmented Generation for Knowledge-Intensive NLP Tasks" (*https://oreil.ly/Qzd2K*), arXiv, April 12, 2021.

Without RAG, the LLM relies solely on its pretrained data, which may be outdated. For example, let's ask ChatGPT a question about a current event and see its response:

Input

```
Which country is the latest winner of the men's FIFA World Cup?
```

Output

```
The most recent FIFA World Cup winner was France, who won the tournament in 2018.
```

The response by the LLM is factually incorrect and outdated. The latest winner at the time of this book's publication is Argentina, who won the World Cup in 2022. While this example question may be trivial, LLM hallucination can have disastrous consequences if its answers are relied upon for fact-checking or important decision making.

To combat this problem, we need to provide the LLM with factual, up-to-date information from which it can formulate an accurate response. Continuing on from the previous example, let's go over to Wikipedia's page for the FIFA World Cup (*https://oreil.ly/LpLOV*), copy the introduction paragraph, and then append it as *context* to our prompt to ChatGPT:

```
Which country is the latest winner of the men's FIFA World Cup?

See context below.

The FIFA World Cup, often called the World Cup, is an international association
football competition among the senior men's national teams of the members of
the Fédération Internationale de Football Association (FIFA), the sport's
global governing body. The tournament has been held every four years since the
inaugural tournament in 1930, with the exception of 1942 and 1946 due to the
Second World War. The reigning champions are Argentina, who won their third
title at the 2022 tournament.
```

Note that the last sentence contains the necessary context the LLM can use to provide an accurate answer. Here's the response from the LLM:

```
The latest winner of the men's FIFA World Cup is Argentina, who won their third
title at the 2022 tournament.
```

Because of the up-to-date additional context provided, the LLM was able to generate an accurate response to the prompt. But copying and pasting relevant information as context isn't practical nor scalable for a production AI application. We need an automated system to fetch relevant information based on a user's query, append it as context to the prompt, and then execute the generation request to the LLM.

Retrieving Relevant Documents

A RAG system for an AI app typically follows three core stages:

Indexing

This stage involves preprocessing the external data source and storing embeddings that represent the data in a vector store where they can be easily retrieved.

Retrieval

This stage involves retrieving the relevant embeddings and data stored in the vector store based on a user's query.

Generation

This stage involves synthesizing the original prompt with the retrieved relevant documents as one final prompt sent to the model for a prediction.

The three basic stages look like Figure 3-1.

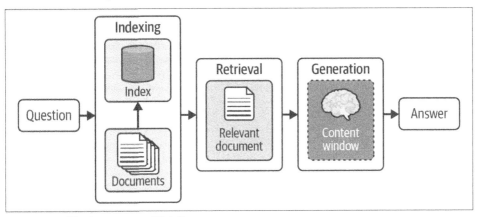

Figure 3-1. The key stages of RAG

The indexing stage of this process was covered extensively in Chapter 2, where you learned how to use document loaders, text splitters, embeddings, and vector stores.

Let's run through an example from scratch again, starting with the indexing stage:

Python

```python
from langchain_community.document_loaders import TextLoader
from langchain_openai import OpenAIEmbeddings
from langchain_text_splitters import RecursiveCharacterTextSplitter
from langchain_postgres.vectorstores import PGVector

# Load the document, split it into chunks
raw_documents = TextLoader('./test.txt').load()
text_splitter = RecursiveCharacterTextSplitter(chunk_size=1000,
    chunk_overlap=200)
documents = text_splitter.split_documents(raw_documents)

# embed each chunk and insert it into the vector store
model = OpenAIEmbeddings()
connection = 'postgresql+psycopg://langchain:langchain@localhost:6024/langchain'
db = PGVector.from_documents(documents, model, connection=connection)
```

JavaScript

```javascript
import { TextLoader } from "langchain/document_loaders/fs/text";
import { RecursiveCharacterTextSplitter } from "@langchain/textsplitters";
import { OpenAIEmbeddings } from "@langchain/openai";
import { PGVectorStore } from "@langchain/community/vectorstores/pgvector";

// Load the document, split it into chunks
const loader = new TextLoader("./test.txt");
const raw_docs = await loader.load();
const splitter = new RecursiveCharacterTextSplitter({
  chunkSize: 1000,
  chunkOverlap: 200,
});
const docs = await splitter.splitDocuments(docs)

// embed each chunk and insert it into the vector store
const model = new OpenAIEmbeddings();
const db = await PGVectorStore.fromDocuments(docs, model, {
  postgresConnectionOptions: {
    connectionString: 'postgresql://langchain:langchain@localhost:6024/langchain'
  }
})
```

Chapter 2 has more details on the indexing stage.

The indexing stage is now complete. In order to execute the retrieval stage, we need to perform similarity search calculations—such as cosine similarity—between the user's query and our stored embeddings, so relevant chunks of our indexed document are retrieved (see Figure 3-2).

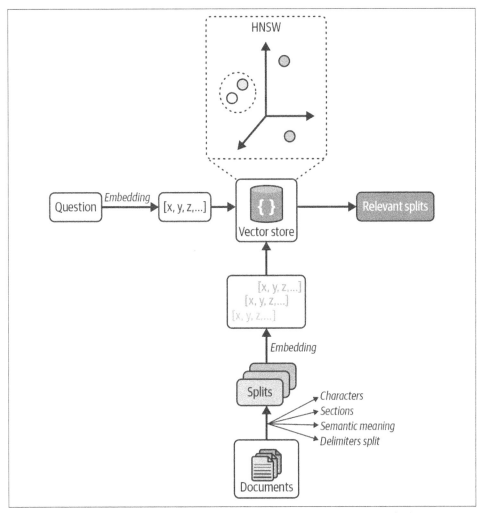

Figure 3-2. An example flow of indexing documents alongside retrieval of relevant documents from a vector store; the Hierarchical Navigable Small World (HNSW) box depicts calculating similarity of documents against the user's query

Figure 3-2 illustrates the steps in the retrieval process:

1. Convert the user's query into embeddings.
2. Calculate the embeddings in the vector store that are most similar to the user's query.
3. Retrieve the relevant document embeddings and their corresponding text chunk.

We can represent these steps programmatically using LangChain as follows:

Python

```
# create retriever
retriever = db.as_retriever()

# fetch relevant documents
docs = retriever.invoke("""Who are the key figures in the ancient greek
    history of philosophy?""")
```

JavaScript

```
// create retriever
const retriever = db.asRetriever()

// fetch relevant documents
const docs = await retriever.invoke(`Who are the key figures in the ancient
    greek history of philosophy?`)
```

Note that we are using a vector store method you haven't seen before: `as_retriever`. This function abstracts the logic of embedding the user's query and the underlying similarity search calculations performed by the vector store to retrieve the relevant documents.

There is also an argument k, which determines the number of relevant documents to fetch from the vector store. For example:

Python

```
# create retriever with k=2
retriever = db.as_retriever(search_kwargs={"k": 2})

# fetch the 2 most relevant documents
docs = retriever.invoke("""Who are the key figures in the ancient greek history
    of philosophy?""")
```

JavaScript

```
// create retriever with k=2
const retriever = db.asRetriever({k: 2})

// fetch the 2 most relevant documents
const docs = await retriever.invoke(`Who are the key figures in the ancient
    greek history of philosophy?`)
```

In this example, the argument k is specified as 2. This tells the vector store to return the two most relevant documents based on the user's query.

It may seem counterintuitive to use a low k value, but retrieving more documents is not always better. The more documents are retrieved, the slower your application will perform, the larger the prompt (and associated cost of generation) will be, and the greater the likelihood of retrieving chunks of text that contain irrelevant information, which will cause the LLM to hallucinate.

Now that we've completed the retrieval stage of the RAG system, let's move on to the final generation stage.

Generating LLM Predictions Using Relevant Documents

Once we've retrieved the relevant documents based on the user's query, the final step is to add them to the original prompt as context and then invoke the model to generate a final output (Figure 3-3).

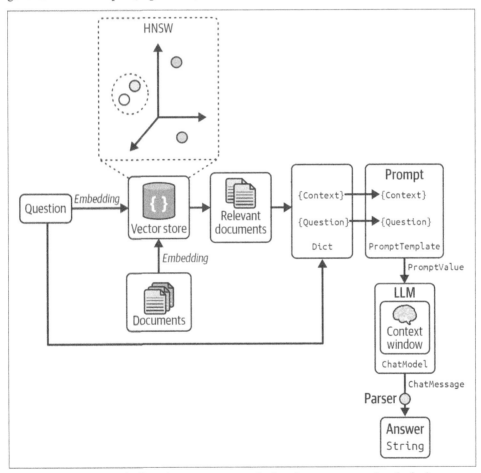

Figure 3-3. An example flow demonstrating indexing documents, retrieval of relevant documents from a vector store, and inclusion of retrieved documents as context in the LLM prompt

Here's a code example continuing on from our previous example:

Python

```python
from langchain_openai import ChatOpenAI
from langchain_core.prompts import ChatPromptTemplate

retriever = db.as_retriever()

prompt = ChatPromptTemplate.from_template("""Answer the question based only on
    the following context:
{context}

Question: {question}
""")

llm = ChatOpenAI(model_name="gpt-3.5-turbo", temperature=0)

chain = prompt | llm

# fetch relevant documents
docs = retriever.get_relevant_documents("""Who are the key figures in the
    ancient greek history of philosophy?""")

# run
chain.invoke({"context": docs,"question": """Who are the key figures in the
    ancient greek history of philosophy?"""})
```

JavaScript

```javascript
import {ChatOpenAI} from '@langchain/openai'
import {ChatPromptTemplate} from '@langchain/core/prompts'

const retriever = db.asRetriever()

const prompt = ChatPromptTemplate.fromTemplate(`Answer the question based only
    on the following context:
{context}

Question: {question}
`)

const llm = new ChatOpenAI({temperature: 0, modelName: 'gpt-3.5-turbo'})

const chain = prompt.pipe(llm)

// fetch relevant documents
const docs = await retriever.invoke(`Who are the key figures in the ancient
    greek history of philosophy?`)

await chain.invoke({context: docs, question: `Who are the key figures in the
    ancient greek history of philosophy?`})
```

Note the following changes:

- We implement dynamic `context` and `question` variables into our prompt, which allows us to define a `ChatPromptTemplate` the model can use to generate a response.
- We define a `ChatOpenAI` interface to act as our LLM. Temperature is set to 0 to eliminate the creativity in outputs from the model.
- We create a chain to compose the prompt and LLM. A reminder: the | operator (or `pipe` method in JS) takes the output of `prompt` and uses it as the input to `llm`.
- We `invoke` the chain passing in the `context` variable (our retrieved relevant docs) and the user's question to generate a final output.

We can encapsulate this retrieval logic in a single function:

Python

```python
from langchain_openai import ChatOpenAI
from langchain_core.prompts import ChatPromptTemplate
from langchain_core.runnables import chain

retriever = db.as_retriever()

prompt = ChatPromptTemplate.from_template("""Answer the question based only on
    the following context:
{context}

Question: {question}
""")

llm = ChatOpenAI(model="gpt-3.5-turbo", temperature=0)

@chain
def qa(input):
    # fetch relevant documents
    docs = retriever.get_relevant_documents(input)
    # format prompt
    formatted = prompt.invoke({"context": docs, "question": input})
    # generate answer
    answer = llm.invoke(formatted)
    return answer

# run
qa.invoke("Who are the key figures in the ancient greek history of philosophy?")
```

JavaScript

```javascript
import {ChatOpenAI} from '@langchain/openai'
import {ChatPromptTemplate} from '@langchain/core/prompts'
import {RunnableLambda} from '@langchain/core/runnables'
```

```
const retriever = db.asRetriever()

const prompt = ChatPromptTemplate.fromTemplate(`Answer the question based only
  on the following context:
{context}

Question: {question}
`)

const llm = new ChatOpenAI({temperature: 0, modelName: 'gpt-3.5-turbo'})

const qa = RunnableLambda.from(async input => {
  // fetch relevant documents
  const docs = await retriever.invoke(input)
  // format prompt
  const formatted = await prompt.invoke({context: docs, question: input})
  // generate answer
  const answer = await llm.invoke(formatted)
  return answer
})

await qa.invoke(`Who are the key figures in the ancient greek history of
  philosophy?`)
```

Notice how we now have a new runnable qa function that can be called with just a question and takes care to first fetch the relevant docs for context, format them into the prompt, and finally generate the answer. In the Python code, the @chain decorator turns the function into a runnable chain. This notion of encapsulating multiple steps into a single function will be key to building interesting apps with LLMs.

You can also return the retrieved documents for further inspection:

Python

```
@chain
def qa(input):
    # fetch relevant documents
    docs = retriever.get_relevant_documents(input)
    # format prompt
    formatted = prompt.invoke({"context": docs, "question": input})
    # generate answer
    answer = llm.invoke(formatted)
    return {"answer": answer, "docs": docs}
```

JavaScript

```
const qa = RunnableLambda.from(async input => {
  // fetch relevant documents
  const docs = await retriever.invoke(input)
  // format prompt
  const formatted = await prompt.invoke({context: docs, question: input})
```

```
    // generate answer
    const answer = await llm.invoke(formatted)
    return {answer, docs}
})
```

Congratulations! You've now built a basic RAG system to power an AI app for personal use.

However, a production-ready AI app used by multiple users requires a more advanced RAG system. In order to build a robust RAG system, we need to answer the following questions effectively:

- How do we handle the variability in the quality of a user's input?
- How do we route queries to retrieve relevant data from a variety of data sources?
- How do we transform natural language to the query language of the target data source?
- How do we optimize our indexing process, i.e., embedding, text splitting?

Next we'll discuss the latest research-backed strategies to answer these questions and build a production-ready RAG system. These strategies can be summarized in Figure 3-4.

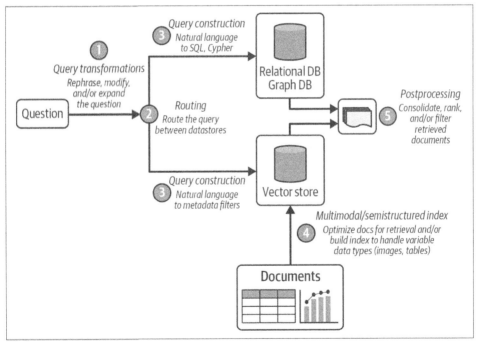

Figure 3-4. Effective strategies to optimize the accuracy of your RAG system

All code blocks in the rest of this chapter use the vector store we set up at the beginning of the chapter.

Query Transformation

One of the major problems with a basic RAG system is that it relies too heavily on the quality of a user's query to generate an accurate output. In a production setting, a user is likely to construct their query in an incomplete, ambiguous, or poorly worded manner that leads to model hallucination.

Query transformation is a subset of strategies designed to modify the user's input to answer the first RAG problem question: How do we handle the variability in the quality of a user's input? Figure 3-5 illustrates the range of query transformation strategies, ranging from those that make a user's input more or less abstract in order to generate an accurate LLM output. The next section begins with a middle ground strategy.

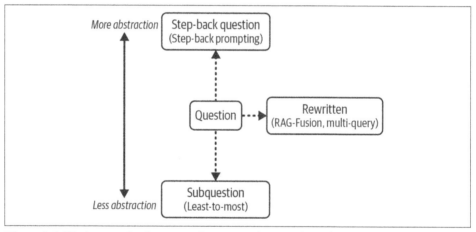

Figure 3-5. Various methods to transform a user's query based on the abstraction level

Rewrite-Retrieve-Read

The Rewrite-Retrieve-Read strategy proposed by a Microsoft Research team simply prompts the LLM to rewrite the user's query before performing retrieval.[2] To illustrate, let's return to the chain we built in the previous section, this time invoked with a poorly worded user query:

---

2 Xinbei Ma et al., "Query Rewriting for Retrieval-Augmented Large Language Models" (*https://oreil.ly/zyw5E*), arXiv, October 23, 2023. Research commissioned by Microsoft Research Asia.

Python

```python
@chain
def qa(input):
    # fetch relevant documents
    docs = retriever.get_relevant_documents(input)
    # format prompt
    formatted = prompt.invoke({"context": docs, "question": input})
    # generate answer
    answer = llm.invoke(formatted)
    return answer

qa.invoke("""Today I woke up and brushed my teeth, then I sat down to read the
    news. But then I forgot the food on the cooker. Who are some key figures in
    the ancient greek history of philosophy?""")
```

JavaScript

```javascript
const qa = RunnableLambda.from(async input => {
  // fetch relevant documents
  const docs = await retriever.invoke(input)
  // format prompt
  const formatted = await prompt.invoke({context: docs, question: input})
  // generate answer
  const answer = await llm.invoke(formatted)
  return answer
})

await qa.invoke(`Today I woke up and brushed my teeth, then I sat down to read
    the news. But then I forgot the food on the cooker. Who are some key figures
    in the ancient greek history of philosophy?`)
```

The output (remember: if you rerun it, your output might be different from this):

```
Based on the given context, there is no information provided.
```

The model failed to answer the question because it was distracted by the irrelevant information provided in the user's query.

Now let's implement the Rewrite-Retrieve-Read prompt:

Python

```python
rewrite_prompt = ChatPromptTemplate.from_template("""Provide a better search
    query for web search engine to answer the given question, end the queries
    with '**'. Question: {x} Answer:""")

def parse_rewriter_output(message):
    return message.content.strip('"').strip("**")

rewriter = rewrite_prompt | llm | parse_rewriter_output

@chain
def qa_rrr(input):
```

```python
    # rewrite the query
    new_query = rewriter.invoke(input)
    # fetch relevant documents
    docs = retriever.get_relevant_documents(new_query)
    # format prompt
    formatted = prompt.invoke({"context": docs, "question": input})
    # generate answer
    answer = llm.invoke(formatted)
    return answer

# run
qa_rrr.invoke("""Today I woke up and brushed my teeth, then I sat down to read
    the news. But then I forgot the food on the cooker. Who are some key
    figures in the ancient greek history of philosophy?""")
```

JavaScript

```javascript
const rewritePrompt = ChatPromptTemplate.fromTemplate(`Provide a better search
    query for web search engine to answer the given question, end the queries
    with '**'. Question: {question} Answer:`)

const rewriter = rewritePrompt.pipe(llm).pipe(message => {
  return message.content.replaceAll('"', '').replaceAll('**')
})

const qa = RunnableLambda.from(async input => {
  const newQuery = await rewriter.invoke({question: input});
  // fetch relevant documents
  const docs = await retriever.invoke(newQuery)
  // format prompt
  const formatted = await prompt.invoke({context: docs, question: input})
  // generate answer
  const answer = await llm.invoke(formatted)
  return answer
})

await qa.invoke(`Today I woke up and brushed my teeth, then I sat down to read
    the news. But then I forgot the food on the cooker. Who are some key
    figures in the ancient greek history of philosophy?`)
```

The output:

```
Based on the given context, some key figures in the ancient greek history of
philosophy include: Themistocles (an Athenian statesman), Pythagoras, and Plato.
```

Notice that we have had an LLM rewrite the user's initial distracted query into a much clearer one, and it is that more focused query that is passed to the retriever to fetch the most relevant documents. Note: this technique can be used with any retrieval method, be that a vector store such as we have here or, for instance, a web search tool. The downside of this approach is that it introduces additional latency into your chain, because now we need to perform two LLM calls in sequence.

Multi-Query Retrieval

A user's single query can be insufficient to capture the full scope of information required to answer the query comprehensively. The multi-query retrieval strategy resolves this problem by instructing an LLM to generate multiple queries based on a user's initial query, executing a parallel retrieval of each query from the data source and then inserting the retrieved results as prompt context to generate a final model output. Figure 3-6 illustrates.

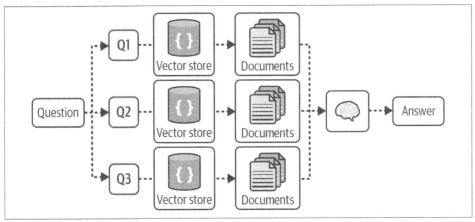

Figure 3-6. Demonstration of the multi-query retrieval strategy

This strategy is particularly useful for use cases where a single question may rely on multiple perspectives to provide a comprehensive answer.

Here's a code example of multi-query retrieval in action:

Python

```
from langchain.prompts import ChatPromptTemplate

perspectives_prompt = ChatPromptTemplate.from_template("""You are an AI language
    model assistant. Your task is to generate five different versions of the
    given user question to retrieve relevant documents from a vector database.
    By generating multiple perspectives on the user question, your goal is to
    help the user overcome some of the limitations of the distance-based
    similarity search. Provide these alternative questions separated by
    newlines. Original question: {question}""")

def parse_queries_output(message):
    return message.content.split('\n')

query_gen = perspectives_prompt | llm | parse_queries_output
```

JavaScript

```javascript
const perspectivesPrompt = ChatPromptTemplate.fromTemplate(`You are an AI
  language model assistant. Your task is to generate five different versions
  of the given user question to retrieve relevant documents from a vector
  database. By generating multiple perspectives on the user question, your
  goal is to help the user overcome some of the limitations of the
  distance-based similarity search. Provide these alternative questions
  separated by newlines. Original question: {question}`)

const queryGen = perspectivesPrompt.pipe(llm).pipe(message => {
  return message.content.split('\n')
})
```

Note that the prompt template is designed to generate variations of questions based on the user's initial query.

Next we take the list of generated queries, retrieve the most relevant docs for each of them in parallel, and then combine to get the unique union of all the retrieved relevant documents:

Python

```python
def get_unique_union(document_lists):
    # Flatten list of lists, and dedupe them
    deduped_docs = {
        doc.page_content: doc
        for sublist in document_lists for doc in sublist
    }
    # return a flat list of unique docs
    return list(deduped_docs.values())

retrieval_chain = query_gen | retriever.batch | get_unique_union
```

JavaScript

```javascript
const retrievalChain = queryGen
  .pipe(retriever.batch.bind(retriever))
  .pipe(documentLists => {
    const dedupedDocs = {}
    documentLists.flat().forEach(doc => {
      dedupedDocs[doc.pageContent] = doc
    })
    return Object.values(dedupedDocs)
  })
```

Because we're retrieving documents from the same retriever with multiple (related) queries, it's likely at least some of them are repeated. Before using them as context to answer the question, we need to deduplicate them, to end up with a single instance of each. Here we dedupe docs by using their content (a string) as the key in a dictionary (or object in JS), because a dictionary can only contain one entry for each key. After we've iterated through all docs, we simply get all the dictionary values, which is now free of duplicates.

Notice our use as well of `.batch`, which runs all generated queries in parallel and returns a list of the results—in this case, a list of lists of documents, which we then flatten and dedupe as described earlier.

This final step is to construct a prompt, including the user's question and combined retrieved relevant documents, and a model interface to generate the prediction:

Python

```python
prompt = ChatPromptTemplate.from_template("""Answer the following question based
    on this context:

{context}

Question: {question}
""")

@chain
def multi_query_qa(input):
    # fetch relevant documents
    docs = retrieval_chain.invoke(input)
    # format prompt
    formatted = prompt.invoke({"context": docs, "question": input})
    # generate answer
    answer = llm.invoke(formatted)
    return answer

# run
multi_query_qa.invoke("""Who are some key figures in the ancient greek history
    of philosophy?""")
```

JavaScript

```javascript
const prompt = ChatPromptTemplate.fromTemplate(`Answer the following
  question based on this context:

{context}

Question: {question}
`)

const multiQueryQa = RunnableLambda.from(async input => {
  // fetch relevant documents
  const docs = await retrievalChain.invoke(input)
  // format prompt
  const formatted = await prompt.invoke({context: docs, question: input})
  // generate answer
  const answer = await llm.invoke(formatted)
  return answer
})
```

```
await multiQueryQa.invoke(`Who are some key figures in the ancient greek
    history of philosophy?`)
```

Notice how this isn't that different from our previous QA chains, as all the new logic for multi-query retrieval is contained in `retrieval_chain`. This is key to making good use of these techniques—implementing each technique as a standalone chain (in this case, `retrieval_chain`), which makes it easy to adopt them and even to combine them.

RAG-Fusion

The RAG-Fusion strategy shares similarities with the multi-query retrieval strategy, except we will apply a final reranking step to all the retrieved documents.[3] This reranking step makes use of the *reciprocal rank fusion* (RRF) algorithm, which involves combining the ranks of different search results to produce a single, unified ranking. By combining ranks from different queries, we pull the most relevant documents to the top of the final list. RRF is well-suited for combining results from queries that might have different scales or distributions of scores.

Let's demonstrate RAG-Fusion in code. First, we craft a prompt similar to the multi-query retrieval strategy to generate a list of queries based on the user query:

Python

```
from langchain.prompts import ChatPromptTemplate
from langchain_openai import ChatOpenAI

prompt_rag_fusion = ChatPromptTemplate.from_template("""You are a helpful
    assistant that generates multiple search queries based on a single input
    query. \n
    Generate multiple search queries related to: {question} \n
    Output (4 queries):""")

def parse_queries_output(message):
    return message.content.split('\n')

llm = ChatOpenAI(temperature=0)

query_gen = prompt_rag_fusion | llm | parse_queries_output
```

JavaScript

```
import {ChatPromptTemplate} from '@langchain/core/prompts';
import {ChatOpenAI} from '@langchain/openai';
```

---

3 Zackary Rackauckas, "RAG-Fusion: A New Take on Retrieval-Augmented Generation" (*https://oreil.ly/k7TTY*), arXiv, February 21, 2024. From the *International Journal on Natural Language Computing*, vol. 13, no. 1 (February 2024).

```
import {RunnableLambda} from '@langchain/core/runnables';

const perspectivesPrompt = ChatPromptTemplate.fromTemplate(`You are a helpful
  assistant that generates multiple search queries based on a single input
  query. \n
  Generate multiple search queries related to: {question} \n
  Output (4 queries):`)

const queryGen = perspectivesPrompt.pipe(llm).pipe(message => {
  return message.content.split('\n')
})
```

Once we've generated our queries, we fetch relevant documents for each query and pass them into a function to *rerank* (that is, *reorder* according to relevancy) the final list of relevant documents.

The function `reciprocal_rank_fusion` takes a list of the search results of each query, so a list of lists of documents, where each inner list of documents is sorted by their relevance to that query. The RRF algorithm then calculates a new score for each document based on its ranks (or positions) in the different lists and sorts them to create a final reranked list.

After calculating the fused scores, the function sorts the documents in descending order of these scores to get the final reranked list, which is then returned:

Python

```
def reciprocal_rank_fusion(results: list[list], k=60):
    """reciprocal rank fusion on multiple lists of ranked documents
       and an optional parameter k used in the RRF formula
    """

    # Initialize a dictionary to hold fused scores for each document
    # Documents will be keyed by their contents to ensure uniqueness
    fused_scores = {}
    documents = {}

    # Iterate through each list of ranked documents
    for docs in results:
        # Iterate through each document in the list,
        # with its rank (position in the list)
        for rank, doc in enumerate(docs):
            # Use the document contents as the key for uniqueness
            doc_str = doc.page_content
            # If the document hasn't been seen yet,
            # - initialize score to 0
            # - save it for later
            if doc_str not in fused_scores:
                fused_scores[doc_str] = 0
                documents[doc_str] = doc
            # Update the score of the document using the RRF formula:
            # 1 / (rank + k)
```

```
            fused_scores[doc_str] += 1 / (rank + k)

    # Sort the documents based on their fused scores in descending order
    # to get the final reranked results
    reranked_doc_strs = sorted(
        fused_scores, key=lambda d: fused_scores[d], reverse=True
    )
    # retrieve the corresponding doc for each doc_str
    return [
        documents[doc_str]
        for doc_str in reranked_doc_strs
    ]


retrieval_chain = generate_queries | retriever.batch | reciprocal_rank_fusion
```

JavaScript

```
function reciprocalRankFusion(results, k = 60) {
  // Initialize a dictionary to hold fused scores for each document
  // Documents will be keyed by their contents to ensure uniqueness
  const fusedScores = {}
  const documents = {}

  results.forEach(docs => {
    docs.forEach((doc, rank) => {
      // Use the document contents as the key for uniqueness
      const key = doc.pageContent
      // If the document hasn't been seen yet,
      // - initialize score to 0
      // - save it for later
      if (!(key in fusedScores)) {
        fusedScores[key] = 0
        documents[key] = 0
      }
      // Update the score of the document using the RRF formula:
      // 1 / (rank + k)
      fusedScores[key] += 1 / (rank + k)
    })
  })

  // Sort the documents based on their fused scores in descending order
  // to get the final reranked results
  const sorted = Object.entries(fusedScores).sort((a, b) => b[1] - a[1])
  // retrieve the corresponding doc for each key
  return sorted.map(([key]) => documents[key])
}

const retrievalChain = queryGen
  .pipe(retriever.batch.bind(retriever))
  .pipe(reciprocalRankFusion)
```

Notice that the function also takes a k parameter, which determines how much influence documents in each query's result sets have over the final list of documents. A higher value indicates that lower-ranked documents have more influence.

Finally, we combine our new retrieval chain (now using RRF) with the full chain we've seen before:

Python

```python
prompt = ChatPromptTemplate.from_template("""Answer the following question based
    on this context:

{context}

Question: {question}
""")

llm = ChatOpenAI(temperature=0)

@chain
def multi_query_qa(input):
    # fetch relevant documents
    docs = retrieval_chain.invoke(input)
    # format prompt
    formatted = prompt.invoke({"context": docs, "question": input})
    # generate answer
    answer = llm.invoke(formatted)
    return answer

multi_query_qa.invoke("""Who are some key figures in the ancient greek history
    of philosophy?""")
```

JavaScript

```javascript
const rewritePrompt = ChatPromptTemplate.fromTemplate(`Answer the following
    question based on this context:

{context}

Question: {question}
`)

const llm = new ChatOpenAI({temperature: 0})

const multiQueryQa = RunnableLambda.from(async input => {
    // fetch relevant documents
    const docs = await retrievalChain.invoke(input)
    // format prompt
    const formatted = await prompt.invoke({context: docs, question: input})
    // generate answer
    const answer = await llm.invoke(formatted)
    return answer
})
```

```
await multiQueryQa.invoke(`Who are some key figures in the ancient greek
    history of philosophy?`)
```

RAG-Fusion's strength lies in its ability to capture the user's intended expression, navigate complex queries, and broaden the scope of retrieved documents, enabling serendipitous discovery.

Hypothetical Document Embeddings

Hypothetical Document Embeddings (HyDE) is a strategy that involves creating a hypothetical document based on the user's query, embedding the document, and retrieving relevant documents based on vector similarity.[4] The intuition behind HyDE is that an LLM-generated hypothetical document will be more similar to the most relevant documents than the original query, as shown in Figure 3-7.

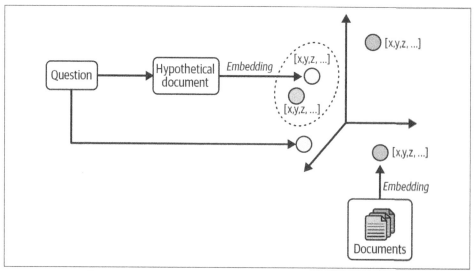

Figure 3-7. An illustration of HyDE closer in the vector space to the document embeddings than the plain query embeddings

First, define a prompt to generate a hypothetical document:

Python

```python
from langchain.prompts import ChatPromptTemplate
from langchain_core.output_parsers import StrOutputParser
from langchain_openai import ChatOpenAI
```

---

4 Luyu Gao et al., "Precise Zero-Shot Dense Retrieval Without Relevance Labels" (*https://oreil.ly/7aTnS*), arXiv, December 20, 2022.

```python
prompt_hyde = ChatPromptTemplate.from_template("""Please write a passage to
    answer the question.\n Question: {question} \n Passage:""")

generate_doc = (
    prompt_hyde | ChatOpenAI(temperature=0) | StrOutputParser()
)
```

JavaScript

```javascript
import {ChatOpenAI} from '@langchain/openai'
import {ChatPromptTemplate} from '@langchain/core/prompts'
import {RunnableLambda} from '@langchain/core/runnables';

const prompt = ChatPromptTemplate.fromTemplate(`Please write a passage to
    answer the question
Question: {question}
Passage:`)

const llm = new ChatOpenAI({temperature: 0})

const generateDoc = prompt.pipe(llm).pipe(msg => msg.content)
```

Next, we take the hypothetical document and use it as input to the `retriever`, which will generate its embedding and search for similar documents in the vector store:

Python

```python
retrieval_chain = generate_doc | retriever
```

JavaScript

```javascript
const retrievalChain = generateDoc.pipe(retriever)
```

Finally, we take the retrieved documents, pass them as context to the final prompt, and instruct the model to generate an output:

Python

```python
prompt = ChatPromptTemplate.from_template("""Answer the following question based
    on this context:

{context}

Question: {question}
""")

llm = ChatOpenAI(temperature=0)

@chain
def qa(input):
    # fetch relevant documents from the hyde retrieval chain defined earlier
    docs = retrieval_chain.invoke(input)
    # format prompt
    formatted = prompt.invoke({"context": docs, "question": input})
    # generate answer
```

```
answer = llm.invoke(formatted)
return answer

qa.invoke("""Who are some key figures in the ancient greek history of
    philosophy?""")
```

JavaScript

```
const prompt = ChatPromptTemplate.fromTemplate(`Answer the following
  question based on this context:

{context}

Question: {question}
`)

const llm = new ChatOpenAI({temperature: 0})

const qa = RunnableLambda.from(async input => {
  // fetch relevant documents from the hyde retrieval chain defined earlier
  const docs = await retrievalChain.invoke(input)
  // format prompt
  const formatted = await prompt.invoke({context: docs, question: input})
  // generate answer
  const answer = await llm.invoke(formatted)
  return answer
})

await qa.invoke(`Who are some key figures in the ancient greek history of
    philosophy?`)
```

To recap what we covered in this section, query transformation consists of taking the user's original query and doing the following:

- Rewriting into one or more queries
- Combining the results of those queries into a single set of the most relevant results

Rewriting the query can take many forms, but it's usually done in a similar fashion: take the user's original query—a prompt you wrote—and ask an LLM to write a new query or queries. Some examples of typical changes made are:

- Removing irrelevant/unrelated text from the query.
- Grounding the query with past conversation history. For instance, to make sense of a query such as *and what about in LA,* we need to combine it with a hypothetical past question about the weather in SF, to arrive at a useful query such as *weather in LA.*
- Casting a wider net for relevant documents by also fetching documents for related queries.

- Decomposing a complex question into multiple, simpler questions and then including results for all of them in the final prompt to generate an answer.

The right rewriting strategy to use will depend on your use case.

Now that we've covered the main query transformation strategies, let's discuss the second major question to answer in order to build a robust RAG system: How do we route queries to retrieve relevant data from multiple data sources?

Query Routing

Although using a single vector store is useful, the required data may live in a variety of data sources, including relational databases or other vector stores.

For example, you may have two vector stores: one for LangChain Python documentation and another for LangChain JS documentation. Given a user's question, we would like to *route* the query to the appropriate inferred data source to retrieve relevant docs. *Query routing* is a strategy used to forward a user's query to the relevant data source.

Logical Routing

In *logical routing*, we give the LLM knowledge of the various data sources at our disposal and then let the LLM reason which data source to apply based on the user's query, as shown in Figure 3-8.

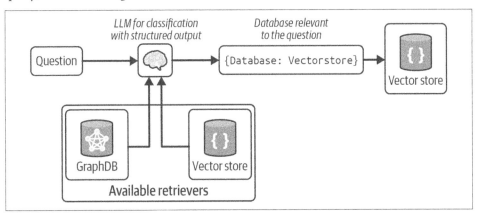

Figure 3-8. Query routing to relevant data sources

In order to achieve this, we make use of function-calling models like GPT-3.5 Turbo to help classify each query into one of the available routes. A *function call* involves defining a schema that the model can use to generate arguments of a function based on the query. This enables us to generate structured outputs that can be used to run other functions. The following Python code defines the schema for our router based on three docs for different languages:

Python

```python
from typing import Literal

from langchain_core.prompts import ChatPromptTemplate
from langchain_core.pydantic_v1 import BaseModel, Field
from langchain_openai import ChatOpenAI

# Data model
class RouteQuery(BaseModel):
    """Route a user query to the most relevant datasource."""

    datasource: Literal["python_docs", "js_docs"] = Field(
        ...,
        description="""Given a user question, choose which datasource would be
            most relevant for answering their question""",
    )

# LLM with function call
llm = ChatOpenAI(model="gpt-3.5-turbo", temperature=0)
structured_llm = llm.with_structured_output(RouteQuery)

# Prompt
system = """You are an expert at routing a user question to the appropriate data
    source.

Based on the programming language the question is referring to, route it to the
    relevant data source."""

prompt = ChatPromptTemplate.from_messages(
    [
        ("system", system),
        ("human", "{question}"),
    ]
)

# Define router
router = prompt | structured_llm
```

JavaScript

```javascript
import { ChatOpenAI } from "@langchain/openai";
import { z } from "zod";

const routeQuery = z.object({
  datasource: z.enum(["python_docs", "js_docs"]).describe(`Given a user
    question, choose which datasource would be most relevant for answering
    their question`),
}).describe("Route a user query to the most relevant datasource.")
```

```
const llm = new ChatOpenAI({model: "gpt-3.5-turbo", temperature: 0})
const structuredLlm = llm.withStructuredOutput(routeQuery, {name: "RouteQuery"})

const prompt = ChatPromptTemplate.fromMessages([
  ['system', `You are an expert at routing a user question to the appropriate
    data source.

Based on the programming language the question is referring to, route it to
  the relevant data source.`],
  ['human', '{question}']
])

const router = prompt.pipe(structuredLlm)
```

Now we invoke the LLM to extract the data source based on the predefined schema:

Python

```
question = """Why doesn't the following code work:

from langchain_core.prompts import ChatPromptTemplate

prompt = ChatPromptTemplate.from_messages(["human", "speak in {language}"])
prompt.invoke("french")
"""

result = router.invoke({"question": question})

result.datasource
# "python_docs"
```

JavaScript

```
const question = `Why doesn't the following code work:

from langchain_core.prompts import ChatPromptTemplate

prompt = ChatPromptTemplate.from_messages(["human", "speak in {language}"])
prompt.invoke("french")
`

await router.invoke({ question })
```

The output:

```
{
    datasource: "python_docs"
}
```

Notice how the LLM produced JSON output, conforming to the schema we defined earlier. This will be useful in many other tasks.

Once we've extracted the relevant data source, we can pass the value into another function to execute additional logic as required:

Python

```python
def choose_route(result):
    if "python_docs" in result.datasource.lower():
        ### Logic here
        return "chain for python_docs"
    else:
        ### Logic here
        return "chain for js_docs"

full_chain = router | RunnableLambda(choose_route)
```

JavaScript

```javascript
function chooseRoute(result) {
  if (result.datasource.toLowerCase().includes('python_docs')) {
    return 'chain for python_docs';
  } else {
    return 'chain for js_docs';
  }
}

const fullChain = router.pipe(chooseRoute)
```

Notice how we don't do an exact string comparison but instead first turn the generated output to lowercase, and then do a substring match. This makes our chain more resilient to the LLM going off script and producing output that doesn't quite conform to the schema we asked for.

 Resilience to the random nature of LLM outputs is an important theme to keep in mind when building your LLM applications.

Logical routing is most suitable when you have a defined list of data sources from which relevant data can be retrieved and utilized by the LLM to generate an accurate output. These can range from vector stores to databases and even APIs.

Semantic Routing

Unlike logical routing, *semantic routing* involves embedding various prompts that represent various data sources alongside the user's query and then performing vector similarity search to retrieve the most similar prompt. Figure 3-9 illustrates.

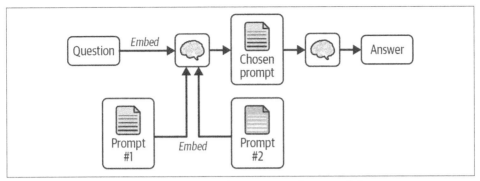

Figure 3-9. Semantic routing to improve the accuracy of retrieved documents

The following is an example of semantic routing:

Python

```python
from langchain.utils.math import cosine_similarity
from langchain_core.output_parsers import StrOutputParser
from langchain_core.prompts import PromptTemplate
from langchain_core.runnables import chain
from langchain_openai import ChatOpenAI, OpenAIEmbeddings

# Two prompts
physics_template = """You are a very smart physics professor. You are great at
    answering questions about physics in a concise and easy-to-understand manner.
    When you don't know the answer to a question, you admit that you don't know.

Here is a question:
{query}"""

math_template = """You are a very good mathematician. You are great at answering
    math questions. You are so good because you are able to break down hard
    problems into their component parts, answer the component parts, and then
    put them together to answer the broader question.

Here is a question:
{query}"""

# Embed prompts
embeddings = OpenAIEmbeddings()
prompt_templates = [physics_template, math_template]
prompt_embeddings = embeddings.embed_documents(prompt_templates)

# Route question to prompt
@chain
def prompt_router(query):
    # Embed question
    query_embedding = embeddings.embed_query(query)
    # Compute similarity
```

```
similarity = cosine_similarity([query_embedding], prompt_embeddings)[0]
# Pick the prompt most similar to the input question
most_similar = prompt_templates[similarity.argmax()]
return PromptTemplate.from_template(most_similar)

semantic_router = (
    prompt_router
    | ChatOpenAI()
    | StrOutputParser()
)

print(semantic_router.invoke("What's a black hole"))
```

JavaScript

```javascript
import {cosineSimilarity} from '@langchain/core/utils/math'
import {ChatOpenAI, OpenAIEmbeddings} from '@langchain/openai'
import {PromptTemplate} from '@langchain/core/prompts'
import {RunnableLambda} from '@langchain/core/runnables';

const physicsTemplate = `You are a very smart physics professor. You are great
  at answering questions about physics in a concise and easy-to-understand
  manner. When you don't know the answer to a question, you admit that you
  don't know.

Here is a question:
{query}`

const mathTemplate = `You are a very good mathematician. You are great at
  answering math questions. You are so good because you are able to break down
  hard problems into their component parts, answer the component parts, and
  then put them together to answer the broader question.

Here is a question:
{query}`

const embeddings = new OpenAIEmbeddings()

const promptTemplates = [physicsTemplate, mathTemplate]
const promptEmbeddings = await embeddings.embedDocuments(promptTemplates)

const promptRouter = RunnableLambda.from(query => {
  // Embed question
  const queryEmbedding = await embeddings.embedQuery(query)
  // Compute similarity
  const similarities = cosineSimilarity([queryEmbedding], promptEmbeddings)[0]
  // Pick the prompt most similar to the input question
  const mostSimilar = similarities[0] > similarities[1]
    ? promptTemplates[0]
    : promptTemplates[1]
  return PromptTemplate.fromTemplate(mostSimilar)
})
```

```
const semanticRouter = promptRouter.pipe(new ChatOpenAI())

await semanticRouter.invoke("What's a black hole")
```

Now that you've seen how to route a user's query to the relevant data source, let's discuss the third major question when building a robust RAG system: "How do we transform natural language to the query language of the target data source?"

Query Construction

As discussed earlier, RAG is an effective strategy to embed and retrieve relevant unstructured data from a vector store based on a query. But most data available for use in production apps is structured and typically stored in relational databases. In addition, unstructured data embedded in a vector store also contains structured metadata that possesses important information.

Query construction is the process of transforming a natural language query into the query language of the database or data source you are interacting with. See Figure 3-10.

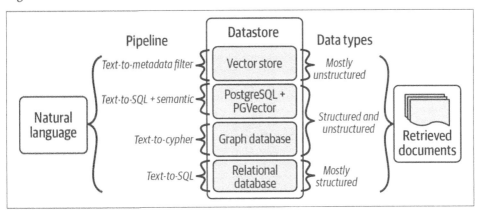

Figure 3-10. Illustration of query languages for various data sources

For example, consider the query: *What are movies about aliens in the year 1980?* This question contains an unstructured topic that can be retrieved via embeddings (*aliens*), but it also contains potential structured components (*year == 1980*).

The following sections dive deeper into the various forms of query construction.

Text-to-Metadata Filter

Most vector stores provide the ability to limit your vector search based on metadata. During the embedding process, we can attach metadata key-value pairs to vectors in an index and then later specify filter expressions when you query the index.

LangChain provides a `SelfQueryRetriever` that abstracts this logic and makes it easier to translate natural language queries into structured queries for various data sources. The self-querying utilizes an LLM to extract and execute the relevant metadata filters based on a user's query and predefined metadata schema:

Python

```python
from langchain.chains.query_constructor.base import AttributeInfo
from langchain.retrievers.self_query.base import SelfQueryRetriever
from langchain_openai import ChatOpenAI

fields = [
    AttributeInfo(
        name="genre",
        description="The genre of the movie",
        type="string or list[string]",
    ),
    AttributeInfo(
        name="year",
        description="The year the movie was released",
        type="integer",
    ),
    AttributeInfo(
        name="director",
        description="The name of the movie director",
        type="string",
    ),
    AttributeInfo(
        name="rating", description="A 1-10 rating for the movie", type="float"
    ),
]
description = "Brief summary of a movie"

llm = ChatOpenAI(temperature=0)

retriever = SelfQueryRetriever.from_llm(
    llm, db, description, fields,
)

print(retriever.invoke(
    "What's a highly rated (above 8.5) science fiction film?"))
```

JavaScript

```javascript
import { ChatOpenAI } from "@langchain/openai";
import { SelfQueryRetriever } from "langchain/retrievers/self_query";
import { FunctionalTranslator } from "@langchain/core/structured_query";

/**
 * First, we define the attributes we want to be able to query on.
 * in this case, we want to be able to query on the genre, year, director,
 * rating, and length of the movie.
 * We also provide a description of each attribute and the type of the attribute.
```

```
 * This is used to generate the query prompts.
 */
const fields = [
  {
    name: "genre",
    description: "The genre of the movie",
    type: "string or array of strings",
  },
  {
    name: "year",
    description: "The year the movie was released",
    type: "number",
  },
  {
    name: "director",
    description: "The director of the movie",
    type: "string",
  },
  {
    name: "rating",
    description: "The rating of the movie (1-10)",
    type: "number",
  },
  {
    name: "length",
    description: "The length of the movie in minutes",
    type: "number",
  },
];
const description = "Brief summary of a movie";

const llm = new ChatOpenAI();
const attributeInfos = fields.map((field) => new AttributeInfo(field.name,
  field.description, field.type));

const selfQueryRetriever = SelfQueryRetriever.fromLLM({
  llm,
  db,
  description,
  attributeInfo: attributeInfos,
  /**
   * We need to use a translator that translates the queries into a
   * filter format that the vector store can understand. LangChain provides one
   * here.
   */
  structuredQueryTranslator: new FunctionalTranslator(),
});

await selfQueryRetriever.invoke(
  "What's a highly rated (above 8.5) science fiction film?"
);
```

This results in a retriever that will take a user query, and split it into:

- A filter to apply on the metadata of each document first
- A query to use for semantic search on the documents

To do this, we have to describe which fields the metadata of our documents contain; that description will be included in the prompt. The retriever will then do the following:

1. Send the query generation prompt to the LLM.
2. Parse metadata filter and rewritten search query from the LLM output.
3. Convert the metadata filter generated by the LLM to the format appropriate for our vector store.
4. Issue a similarity search against the vector store, filtered to only match documents whose metadata passes the generated filter.

Text-to-SQL

SQL and relational databases are important sources of structured data, but they don't interact directly with natural language. Although we can simply use the LLM to translate a user's query to SQL queries, there is little margin for error.

Here are some useful strategies for effective text to SQL translations:

Database description
> To ground SQL queries, an LLM must be provided with an accurate description of the database. One common text-to-SQL prompt employs an idea reported in this paper and others: provide the LLM with a CREATE TABLE description for each table, including column names and types.[5] We can also provide a few (for instance, three) example rows from the table.

Few-shot examples
> Feeding the prompt with few-shot examples of question-query matches can improve the query generation accuracy. This can be achieved by simply appending standard static examples in the prompt to guide the agent on how it should build queries based on questions.

See Figure 3-11 for a visual of the process.

---

5 Nitarshan Rajkumar et al., "Evaluating the Text-to-SQL Capabilities of Large Language Models" (*https://oreil.ly/WOrzt*), arXiv, March 15, 2022.

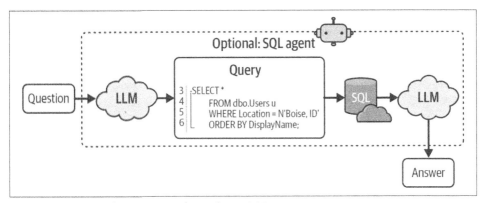

Figure 3-11. A user's query transformed to a SQL query

Here's a full code example:

Python

```python
from langchain_community.tools import QuerySQLDatabaseTool
from langchain_community.utilities import SQLDatabase
from langchain.chains import create_sql_query_chain
from langchain_openai import ChatOpenAI

# replace this with the connection details of your db
db = SQLDatabase.from_uri("sqlite:///Chinook.db")
llm = ChatOpenAI(model="gpt-4", temperature=0)

# convert question to sql query
write_query = create_sql_query_chain(llm, db)

# Execute SQL query
execute_query = QuerySQLDatabaseTool(db=db)

# combined
chain = write_query | execute_query

# invoke the chain
chain.invoke('How many employees are there?');
```

JavaScript

```javascript
import { ChatOpenAI } from "@langchain/openai";
import { createSqlQueryChain } from "langchain/chains/sql_db";
import { SqlDatabase } from "langchain/sql_db";
import { DataSource } from "typeorm";
import { QuerySqlTool } from "langchain/tools/sql";

const datasource = new DataSource({
  type: "sqlite",
  database: "./Chinook.db", // here should be the details of your database
});
```

```
const db = await SqlDatabase.fromDataSourceParams({
  appDataSource: datasource,
});
const llm = new ChatOpenAI({ model: "gpt-4", temperature: 0 });

// convert question to sql query
const writeQuery = await createSqlQueryChain({ llm, db, dialect: "sqlite" });

// execute query
const executeQuery = new QuerySqlTool(db);

// combined
const chain = writeQuery.pipe(executeQuery);

// invoke the chain
await chain.invoke('How many employees are there?');
```

We first convert the user's query to a SQL query appropriate to the dialect of our database. Then we execute that query on our database. Note that executing arbitrary SQL queries on your database generated by an LLM from user input is dangerous in a production application. To use these ideas in production, you need to consider a number of security measures to reduce the risk of unintended queries being run in your database. Here are some examples:

- Run the queries on your database with a user with read-only permissions.
- The database user running the queries should have access only to the tables you wish to make available for querying.
- Add a time-out to the queries run by this application; this would ensure that even if an expensive query is generated, it is canceled before taking up too many of your database resources.

This is not an exhaustive list of security considerations. Security of LLM applications is an area currently in development, with more security measures being added to the recommendations as new vulnerabilities are discovered.

Summary

This chapter discussed various state-of-the-art strategies to efficiently retrieve the most relevant documents based on a user's query and synthesize them with your prompt to aid the LLM to generate an accurate, up-to-date output.

As discussed, a robust, production-ready RAG system requires a wide range of effective strategies that can execute query transformation, query construction, routing, and indexing optimization.

Query transformation enables your AI app to transform an ambiguous or malformed user query into a representative query that's optimal for retrieval. Query construction enables your AI app to convert the user's query into the syntax of the query language of the database or data source where structured data lives. Routing enables your AI app to dynamically route the user's query to retrieve relevant information from the relevant data source.

In Chapter 4, we'll build on this knowledge to add memory to your AI chatbot so that it can remember and learn from each interaction. This will enable users to "chat" with the application in multiturn conversations like ChatGPT.

Using LangGraph to Add Memory to Your Chatbot

In Chapter 3, you learned how to provide your AI chatbot application with up-to-date and relevant context. This enables your chatbot to generate accurate responses based on the user's input. But that's not enough to build a production-ready application. How can you enable your application to actually "chat" back and forth with the user, while remembering prior conversations and relevant context?

Large language models are *stateless*, which means that each time the model is prompted to generate a new response it has no memory of the prior prompt or model response. In order to provide this historical information to the model, we need a robust memory system that will keep track of previous conversations and context. This historical information can then be included in the final prompt sent to the LLM, thus giving it "memory." Figure 4-1 illustrates this.

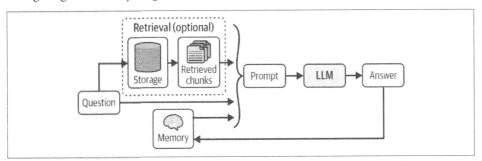

Figure 4-1. Memory and retrieval used to generate context-aware answers from an LLM

In this chapter, you'll learn how to build this essential memory system using Lang-Chain's built-in modules to make this development process easier.

Building a Chatbot Memory System

There are two core design decisions behind any robust memory system:

- How state is stored
- How state is queried

A simple way to build a chatbot memory system that incorporates effective solutions to these design decisions is to store and reuse the history of all chat interactions between the user and the model. The state of this memory system can be:

- Stored as a list of messages (refer to Chapter 1 to learn more about messages)
- Updated by appending recent messages after each turn
- Appended into the prompt by inserting the messages into the prompt

Figure 4-2 illustrates this simple memory system.

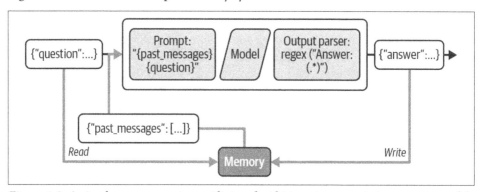

Figure 4-2. A simple memory system utilizing chat history in prompts to generate model answers

Here's a code example that illustrates a simple version of this memory system using LangChain:

Python

```python
from langchain_core.prompts import ChatPromptTemplate
from langchain_openai import ChatOpenAI

prompt = ChatPromptTemplate.from_messages([
    ("system", """You are a helpful assistant. Answer all questions to the best
        of your ability."""),
    ("placeholder", "{messages}"),
])

model = ChatOpenAI()
```

```
chain = prompt | model

chain.invoke({
    "messages": [
        ("human","""Translate this sentence from English to French: I love
            programming."""),
        ("ai", "J'adore programmer."),
        ("human", "What did you just say?"),
    ],
})
```

JavaScript

```javascript
import {ChatPromptTemplate} from '@langchain/core/prompts'
import {ChatOpenAI} from '@langchain/openai'

const prompt = ChatPromptTemplate.fromMessages([
  ["system", `You are a helpful assistant. Answer all questions to the best
    of your ability.`],
  ["placeholder", "{messages}"],
])

const model = new ChatOpenAI()

const chain = prompt.pipe(model)

await chain.invoke({
  "messages": [
    ["human",`Translate this sentence from English to French: I love
      programming.`],
    ["ai", "J'adore programmer."],
    ["human", "What did you just say?"],
  ],
})
```

The output:

```
I said, "J'adore programmer," which means "I love programming" in French.
```

Note how the incorporation of the previous conversation in the chain enabled the model to answer the follow-up question in a context-aware manner.

While this is simple and it works, when taking your application to production, you'll face some more challenges related to managing memory at scale, such as:

- You'll need to update the memory after every interaction, atomically (i.e., don't record only the question or only the answer in the case of failure).
- You'll want to store these memories in durable storage, such as a relational database.

- You'll want to control how many and which messages are stored for later, and how many of these are used for new interactions.

- You'll want to inspect and modify this state (for now, just a list of messages) outside a call to an LLM.

We'll now introduce some better tooling, which will help with this and all later chapters.

Introducing LangGraph

For the remainder of this chapter and the following chapters, we'll start to make use of LangGraph (*https://oreil.ly/TKCb6*), an open source library authored by LangChain. LangGraph was designed to enable developers to implement multiactor, multistep, stateful cognitive architectures, called *graphs*. That's a lot of words packed into a short sentence; let's take them one at a time. Figure 4-3 illustrates the multiactor aspect.

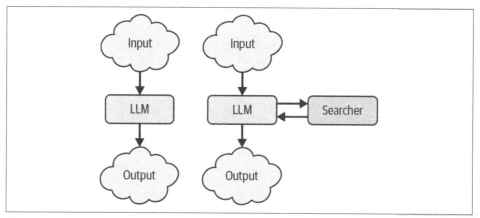

Figure 4-3. From single-actor applications to multiactor applications

A team of specialists can build something together that none of them could build alone. The same is true of LLM applications: an LLM prompt (great for answer generation and task planning and many more things) is much more powerful when paired up with a search engine (best at finding current facts), or even when paired with different LLM prompts. We have seen developers build some amazing applications, like Perplexity (*https://oreil.ly/bVlu7*) or Arc Search (*https://oreil.ly/NPOlF*), when they combine those two building blocks (and others) in novel ways.

And just as a human team needs more coordination than one person working by themselves, an application with multiple actors needs a coordination layer to do these things:

- Define the actors involved (the nodes in a graph) and how they hand off work to each other (the edges in that graph).

- Schedule execution of each actor at the appropriate time—in parallel if needed— with deterministic results.

Figure 4-4 illustrates the multistep dimension.

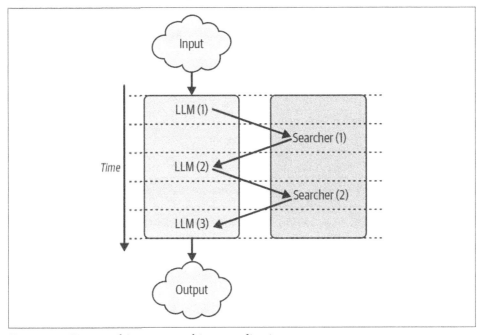

Figure 4-4. From multiactor to multistep applications

As each actor hands off work to another (for example, an LLM prompt asking a search tool for the results of a given search query), we need to make sense of the back-and-forth between multiple actors. We need to know what order it happens in, how many times each actor is called, and so on. To do this, we can model the interaction between the actors as happening across multiple discrete steps in time. When one actor hands off work to another actor, it results in the scheduling of the next step of the computation, and so on, until no more actors hand off work to others, and the final result is reached.

Figure 4-5 illustrates the stateful aspect.

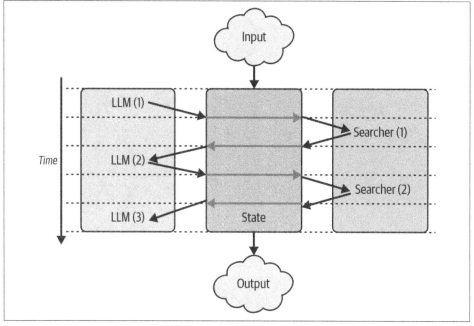

Figure 4-5. From multistep to stateful applications

Communication across steps requires tracking some state—otherwise, when you call the LLM actor the second time, you'd get the same result as the first time. It is very helpful to pull this state out of each of the actors and have all actors collaborate on updating a single central state. With a single central state, we can:

- Snapshot and store the central state during or after each computation.
- Pause and resume execution, which makes it easy to recover from errors.
- Implement human-in-the-loop controls (more on this in Chapter 8).

Each *graph* is then made up of the following:

State
> The data received from outside the application, modified and produced by the application while it's running.

Nodes
> Each step to be taken. Nodes are simply Python/JS functions, which receive the current state as input and can return an update to that state (that is, they can add to it and modify or remove existing data).

Edges

> The connections between nodes. Edges determine the path taken from the first node to the last, and they can be fixed (that is, after Node B, always visit node D) or conditional (evaluate a function to decide the next node to visit after node C).

LangGraph offers utilities to visualize these graphs and numerous features to debug their workings while in development. These graphs can then easily be deployed to serve production workloads at high scale.

If you followed the instructions in Chapter 1, you'll already have LangGraph installed. If not, you can install it by running one of the following commands in your terminal:

Python

```
pip install langgraph
```

JavaScript

```
npm i @langchain/langgraph
```

To help get you familiar with using LangGraph, we'll create a simple chatbot using LangGraph, which is a great example of the LLM call architecture with a single use of an LLM. This chatbot will respond directly to user messages. Though simple, it does illustrate the core concepts of building with LangGraph.

Creating a StateGraph

Start by creating a StateGraph. We'll add a node to represent the LLM call:

Python

```python
from typing import Annotated, TypedDict

from langgraph.graph import StateGraph, START, END
from langgraph.graph.message import add_messages


class State(TypedDict):
    # Messages have the type "list". The `add_messages`
    # function in the annotation defines how this state should
    # be updated (in this case, it appends new messages to the
    # list, rather than replacing the previous messages)
        messages: Annotated[list, add_messages]

builder = StateGraph(State)
```

JavaScript

```javascript
import {
  StateGraph,
  StateType,
  Annotation,
  messagesStateReducer,
  START, END
} from '@langchain/langgraph'

const State = {
  /**
   * The State defines three things:
   * 1. The structure of the graph's state (which "channels" are available to
   * read/write)
   * 2. The default values for the state's channels
   * 3. The reducers for the state's channels. Reducers are functions that
   * determine how to apply updates to the state. Below, new messages are
   * appended to the messages array.
   */
  messages: Annotation({
    reducer: messagesStateReducer,
    default: () => []
  }),
}

const builder = new StateGraph(State)
```

 The first thing you do when you define a graph is define the state of the graph. The *state* consists of the shape, or schema, of the graph state, as well as reducer functions that specify how to apply updates to the state. In this example, the state is a dictionary with a single key: messages. The messages key is annotated with the add_messages reducer function, which tells LangGraph to append new messages to the existing list, rather than overwrite it. State keys without an annotation will be overwritten by each update, storing the most recent value. You can write your own reducer functions, which are simply functions that receive as arguments— argument 1 is the current state, and argument 2 is the next value being written to the state—and should return the next state, that is, the result of merging the current state with the new value. The simplest example is a function that appends the next value to a list and returns that list.

So now our graph knows two things:

- Every node we define will receive the current State as input and return a value that updates that state.
- messages will be *appended* to the current list, rather than directly overwritten. This is communicated via the prebuilt add_messages (*https://oreil.ly/sK-Ry*) function in the Annotated syntax in the Python example or the reducer function for the JavaScript example.

Next, add the chatbot node. Nodes represent units of work. They are typically just functions:

Python

```python
from langchain_openai import ChatOpenAI

model = ChatOpenAI()

def chatbot(state: State):
    answer = model.invoke(state["messages"])
    return {"messages": [answer]}

# The first argument is the unique node name
# The second argument is the function or Runnable to run
builder.add_node("chatbot", chatbot)
```

JavaScript

```javascript
import {ChatOpenAI} from '@langchain/openai'
import {
  AIMessage,
  SystemMessage,
  HumanMessage
} from "@langchain/core/messages";

const model = new ChatOpenAI()

async function chatbot(state) {
  const answer = await model.invoke(state.messages)
  return {"messages": answer}
}

builder = builder.addNode('chatbot', chatbot)
```

This node receives the current state, does one LLM call, and then returns an update to the state containing the new message produced by the LLM. The add_messages reducer appends this message to the messages already in the state.

And finally let's add the edges:

Python

```python
builder.add_edge(START, 'chatbot')
builder.add_edge('chatbot', END)

graph = builder.compile()
```

JavaScript

```javascript
builder = builder
  .addEdge(START, 'chatbot')
  .addEdge('chatbot', END)

let graph = builder.compile()
```

This does a few things:

- It tells the graph where to start its work each time you run it.
- This instructs the graph where it should exit (this is optional, as LangGraph will stop execution once there's no more nodes to run).
- It compiles the graph into a runnable object, with the familiar `invoke` and `stream` methods.

We can also draw a visual representation of the graph:

Python

```python
graph.get_graph().draw_mermaid_png()
```

JavaScript

```javascript
await graph.getGraph().drawMermaidPng()
```

The graph we just made looks like Figure 4-6.

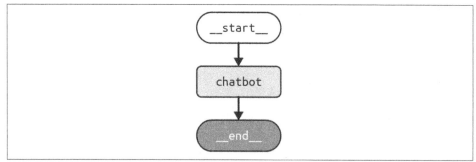

Figure 4-6. A simple chatbot

You can run it with the familiar `stream()` method you've seen in earlier chapters:

Python

```python
input = {"messages": [HumanMessage('hi!')]}
for chunk in graph.stream(input):
    print(chunk)
```

JavaScript

```javascript
const input = {messages: [new HumanMessage('hi!')]}
for await (const chunk of await graph.stream(input)) {
  console.log(chunk)
}
```

The output:

```
{ "chatbot": { "messages": [AIMessage("How can I help you?")] } }
```

Notice how the input to the graph was in the same shape as the `State` object we defined earlier; that is, we sent in a list of messages in the `messages` key of a dictionary. In addition, the `stream` function streams the full value of the state after each step of the graph.

Adding Memory to StateGraph

LangGraph has built-in persistence, which is used in the same way for the simplest graph to the most complex. Let's see what it looks like to apply it to this first architecture. We'll recompile our graph, now attaching a *checkpointer*, which is a storage adapter for LangGraph. LangGraph ships with a base class that any user can subclass to create an adapter for their favorite database; at the time of writing, LangGraph ships with several adapters maintained by LangChain:

- An in-memory adapter, which we'll use for our examples here
- A SQLite adapter, using the popular in-process database, appropriate for local apps and testing
- A Postgres adapter, optimized for the popular relational database and appropriate for large-scale applications.

Many developers have written adapters for other database systems, such as Redis or MySQL:

Python

```python
from langgraph.checkpoint.memory import MemorySaver

graph = builder.compile(checkpointer=MemorySaver())
```

JavaScript

```javascript
import {MemorySaver} from '@langchain/langgraph'

const graph = builder.compile({ checkpointer: new MemorySaver() })
```

This returns a runnable object with the same methods as the one used in the previous code block. But now, it stores the state at the end of each step, so every invocation after the first doesn't start from a blank slate. Any time the graph is called, it starts by using the checkpointer to fetch the most recent saved state, if any, and combines the new input with the previous state. And only then does it execute the first nodes.

Let's see the difference in action:

Python

```python
thread1 = {"configurable": {"thread_id": "1"}}
result_1 = graph.invoke(
    { "messages": [HumanMessage("hi, my name is Jack!")] },
    thread1
)
// { "chatbot": { "messages": [AIMessage("How can I help you, Jack?")] } }

result_2 = graph.invoke(
    { "messages": [HumanMessage("what is my name?")] },
    thread1
)
// { "chatbot": { "messages": [AIMessage("Your name is Jack")] } }
```

JavaScript

```javascript
const thread1 = {configurable: {thread_id: '1'}}
const result_1 = await graph.invoke(
  { "messages": [new HumanMessage("hi, my name is Jack!")] },
  thread1
)
// { "chatbot": { "messages": [AIMessage("How can I help you, Jack?")] } }

const result_2 = await graph.invoke(
  { "messages": [new HumanMessage("what is my name?")] },
  thread1
)
// { "chatbot": { "messages": [AIMessage("Your name is Jack")] } }
```

Notice the object thread1, which identifies the current interaction as belonging to a particular history of interactions—which are called *threads* in LangGraph. Threads are created automatically when first used. Any string is a valid identifier for a thread (usually, Universally Unique Identifiers [UUIDs] are used). The existence of threads helps you achieve an important milestone in your LLM application; it can now be used by multiple users with independent conversations that are never mixed up.

As before, the `chatbot` node is first called with a single message (the one we just passed in) and returns another message, both of which are then saved in the state.

The second time we execute the graph on the same thread, the `chatbot` node is called with three messages, the two saved from the first execution, and the next question from the user. This is the essence of memory: the previous state is still there, which makes it possible, for instance, to answer questions about something said before (and do many more interesting things, of which we will see more later).

You can also inspect and update the state directly; let's see how:

Python

```
graph.get_state(thread1)
```

JavaScript

```
await graph.getState(thread1)
```

This returns the current state of this thread.

And you can update the state like this:

Python

```
graph.update_state(thread1, [HumanMessage('I like LLMs!')])
```

JavaScript

```
await graph.updateState(thread1, [new HumanMessage('I like LLMs!')])
```

This would add one more message to the list of messages in the state, to be used the next time you invoke the graph on this thread.

Modifying Chat History

In many cases, the chat history messages aren't in the best state or format to generate an accurate response from the model. To overcome this problem, we can modify the chat history in three main ways: trimming, filtering, and merging messages.

Trimming Messages

LLMs have limited *context windows*; in other words, there is a maximum number of tokens that LLMs can receive as a prompt. As such, the final prompt sent to the model shouldn't exceed that limit (particular to each mode), as models will either refuse an overly long prompt or truncate it. In addition, excessive prompt information can distract the model and lead to hallucination.

An effective solution to this problem is to limit the number of messages that are retrieved from chat history and appended to the prompt. In practice, we need only to load and store the most recent messages. Let's use an example chat history with some preloaded messages.

Fortunately, LangChain provides the built-in `trim_messages` helper that incorporates various strategies to meet these requirements. For example, the trimmer helper enables specifying how many tokens we want to keep or remove from chat history.

Here's an example that retrieves the last `max_tokens` in the list of messages by setting a strategy parameter to `"last"`:

Python

```python
from langchain_core.messages import SystemMessage, trim_messages
from langchain_openai import ChatOpenAI

trimmer = trim_messages(
    max_tokens=65,
    strategy="last",
    token_counter=ChatOpenAI(model="gpt-4o"),
    include_system=True,
    allow_partial=False,
    start_on="human",
)

messages = [
    SystemMessage(content="you're a good assistant"),
    HumanMessage(content="hi! I'm bob"),
    AIMessage(content="hi!"),
    HumanMessage(content="I like vanilla ice cream"),
    AIMessage(content="nice"),
    HumanMessage(content="what's 2 + 2"),
    AIMessage(content="4"),
    HumanMessage(content="thanks"),
    AIMessage(content="no problem!"),
    HumanMessage(content="having fun?"),
    AIMessage(content="yes!"),
]

trimmer.invoke(messages)
```

JavaScript

```javascript
import {
  AIMessage,
  HumanMessage,
  SystemMessage,
  trimMessages,
} from "@langchain/core/messages";
import { ChatOpenAI } from "@langchain/openai";
```

```
const trimmer = trimMessages({
  maxTokens: 65,
  strategy: "last",
  tokenCounter: new ChatOpenAI({ modelName: "gpt-4o" }),
  includeSystem: true,
  allowPartial: false,
  startOn: "human",
});

const messages = [
  new SystemMessage("you're a good assistant"),
  new HumanMessage("hi! I'm bob"),
  new AIMessage("hi!"),
  new HumanMessage("I like vanilla ice cream"),
  new AIMessage("nice"),
  new HumanMessage("what's 2 + 2"),
  new AIMessage("4"),
  new HumanMessage("thanks"),
  new AIMessage("no problem!"),
  new HumanMessage("having fun?"),
  new AIMessage("yes!"),
]

const trimmed = await trimmer.invoke(messages);
```

The output:

```
[SystemMessage(content="you're a good assistant"),
 HumanMessage(content='what's 2 + 2'),
 AIMessage(content='4'),
 HumanMessage(content='thanks'),
 AIMessage(content='no problem!'),
 HumanMessage(content='having fun?'),
 AIMessage(content='yes!')]
```

Note the following:

- The parameter `strategy` controls whether to start from the beginning or the end of the list. Usually, you'll want to prioritize the most recent messages and cut older messages if they don't fit. That is, start from the end of the list. For this behavior, choose the value `last`. The other available option is `first`, which would prioritize the oldest messages and cut more recent messages if they don't fit.

- The `token_counter` is an LLM or chat model, which will be used to count tokens using the tokenizer appropriate to that model.

- We can add the parameter `include_system=True` to ensure that the trimmer keeps the system message.

- The parameter `allow_partial` determines whether to cut the last message's content to fit within the limit. In our example, we set this to `false`, which completely removes the message that would send the total over the limit.

- The parameter start_on="human" ensures that we never remove an AIMessage (that is, a response from the model) without also removing a corresponding HumanMessage (the question for that response).

Filtering Messages

As the list of chat history messages grows, a wider variety of types, subchains, and models may be utilized. LangChain's filter_messages helper makes it easier to filter the chat history messages by type, ID, or name.

Here's an example where we filter for human messages:

Python

```python
from langchain_core.messages import (
    AIMessage,
    HumanMessage,
    SystemMessage,
    filter_messages,
)

messages = [
    SystemMessage("you are a good assistant", id="1"),
    HumanMessage("example input", id="2", name="example_user"),
    AIMessage("example output", id="3", name="example_assistant"),
    HumanMessage("real input", id="4", name="bob"),
    AIMessage("real output", id="5", name="alice"),
]

filter_messages(messages, include_types="human")
```

JavaScript

```javascript
import {
  HumanMessage,
  SystemMessage,
  AIMessage,
  filterMessages,
} from "@langchain/core/messages";

const messages = [
  new SystemMessage({content: "you are a good assistant", id: "1"}),
  new HumanMessage({content: "example input", id: "2", name: "example_user"}),
  new AIMessage({content: "example output", id: "3", name: "example_assistant"}),
  new HumanMessage({content: "real input", id: "4", name: "bob"}),
  new AIMessage({content: "real output", id: "5", name: "alice"}),
];

filterMessages(messages, { includeTypes: ["human"] });
```

The output:

```
[HumanMessage(content='example input', name='example_user', id='2'),
 HumanMessage(content='real input', name='bob', id='4')]
```

Let's try another example where we filter to exclude users and IDs, and include message types:

Python

```
filter_messages(messages, exclude_names=["example_user", "example_assistant"])

"""
[SystemMessage(content='you are a good assistant', id='1'),
HumanMessage(content='real input', name='bob', id='4'),
AIMessage(content='real output', name='alice', id='5')]
"""

filter_messages(
    messages,
    include_types=[HumanMessage, AIMessage],
    exclude_ids=["3"]
)

"""
[HumanMessage(content='example input', name='example_user', id='2'),
 HumanMessage(content='real input', name='bob', id='4'),
 AIMessage(content='real output', name='alice', id='5')]
"""
```

JavaScript

```
filterMessages(
  messages,
  { excludeNames: ["example_user",
  "example_assistant"] }
);

/*
[SystemMessage(content='you are a good assistant', id='1'),
HumanMessage(content='real input', name='bob', id='4'),
AIMessage(content='real output', name='alice', id='5')]
*/

filterMessages(messages, { includeTypes: ["human", "ai"], excludeIds: ["3"] });

/*
[HumanMessage(content='example input', name='example_user', id='2'),
 HumanMessage(content='real input', name='bob', id='4'),
 AIMessage(content='real output', name='alice', id='5')]
*/
```

The `filter_messages` helper can also be used imperatively or declaratively, making it easy to compose with other components in a chain:

Python

```
model = ChatOpenAI()

filter_ = filter_messages(exclude_names=["example_user", "example_assistant"])

chain = filter_ | model
```

JavaScript

```
const model = new ChatOpenAI()

const filter = filterMessages({
  excludeNames: ["example_user", "example_assistant"]
})

const chain = filter.pipe(model)
```

Merging Consecutive Messages

Certain models don't support inputs, including consecutive messages of the same type (for instance, Anthropic chat models). LangChain's `merge_message_runs` utility makes it easy to merge consecutive messages of the same type:

Python

```
from langchain_core.messages import (
    AIMessage,
    HumanMessage,
    SystemMessage,
    merge_message_runs,
)

messages = [
    SystemMessage("you're a good assistant."),
    SystemMessage("you always respond with a joke."),
    HumanMessage(
        [{"type": "text", "text": "i wonder why it's called langchain"}]
    ),
    HumanMessage("and who is harrison chasing anyway"),
    AIMessage(
        '''Well, I guess they thought "WordRope" and "SentenceString" just
        didn\'t have the same ring to it!'''
    ),
    AIMessage("""Why, he's probably chasing after the last cup of coffee in the
        office!"""),
]

merge_message_runs(messages)
```

JavaScript

```javascript
import {
  HumanMessage,
  SystemMessage,
  AIMessage,
  mergeMessageRuns,
} from "@langchain/core/messages";

const messages = [
  new SystemMessage("you're a good assistant."),
  new SystemMessage("you always respond with a joke."),
  new HumanMessage({
    content: [{ type: "text", text: "i wonder why it's called langchain" }],
  }),
  new HumanMessage("and who is harrison chasing anyway"),
  new AIMessage(
    `Well, I guess they thought "WordRope" and "SentenceString" just didn\'t
      have the same ring to it!`
  ),
  new AIMessage(
    "Why, he's probably chasing after the last cup of coffee in the office!"
  ),
];

mergeMessageRuns(messages);
```

The output:

```
[SystemMessage(content="you're a good assistant.\nyou always respond with a
    joke."),
 HumanMessage(content=[{'type': 'text', 'text': "i wonder why it's called
    langchain"}, 'and who is harrison chasing anyway']),
 AIMessage(content='Well, I guess they thought "WordRope" and "SentenceString"
    just didn\'t have the same ring to it!\nWhy, he\'s probably chasing after
    the last cup of coffee in the office!')]
```

Notice that if the contents of one of the messages to merge is a list of content blocks, then the merged message will have a list of content blocks. And if both messages to merge have string contents, then those are concatenated with a newline character.

The `merge_message_runs` helper can be used imperatively or declaratively, making it easy to compose with other components in a chain:

Python

```python
model = ChatOpenAI()
merger = merge_message_runs()
chain = merger | model
```

JavaScript

```javascript
const model = new ChatOpenAI()
const merger = mergeMessageRuns()
const chain = merger.pipe(model)
```

Summary

This chapter covered the fundamentals of building a simple memory system that enables your AI chatbot to remember its conversations with a user. We discussed how to automate the storage and updating of chat history using LangGraph to make this easier. We also discussed the importance of modifying chat history and explored various strategies to trim, filter, and summarize chat messages.

In Chapter 5, you'll learn how to enable your AI chatbot to do more than just chat back: for instance, your new model will be able to make decisions, pick actions, and reflect on its past outputs.

Cognitive Architectures with LangGraph

So far, we've looked at the most common features of LLM applications:

- Prompting techniques in the Preface and Chapter 1
- RAG in Chapters 2 and 3
- Memory in Chapter 4

The next question should be: How do we assemble these pieces into a coherent application that achieves the goal we set out to solve? To draw a parallel with the world of bricks and mortar, a swimming pool and a one-story house are built of the same materials, but obviously serve very different purposes. What makes them uniquely suited to their different purposes is the plan for how those materials are combined—that is, their architecture. The same is true when building LLM applications. The most important decisions you have to make are how to assemble the different components you have at your disposal (such as RAG, prompting techniques, memory) into something that achieves your purpose.

Before we look at specific architectures, let's walk through an example. Any LLM application you might build will start from a purpose: what the app is designed to do. Let's say you want to build an email assistant—an LLM application that reads your emails before you do and aims to reduce the amount of emails you need to look at. The application might do this by archiving a few uninteresting ones, directly replying to some, and marking others as deserving of your attention later.

You probably also would want the app to be bound by some constraints in its action. Listing those constraints helps tremendously, as they will help inform the search for the right architecture. Chapter 8 covers these constraints in more detail and how to work with them. For this hypothetical email assistant, let's say we'd like it to do the following:

- Minimize the number of times it interrupts you (after all, the whole point is to save time).

- Avoid having your email correspondents receive a reply that you'd never have sent yourself.

This hints at the key trade-off often faced when building LLM apps: the trade-off between *agency* (or the capacity to act autonomously) and *reliability* (or the degree to which you can trust its outputs). Intuitively, the email assistant will be more useful if it takes more actions without your involvement, but if you take it too far, it will inevitably send emails you wish it hadn't.

One way to describe the degree of autonomy of an LLM application is to evaluate how much of the behavior of the application is determined by an LLM (versus code):

- Have an LLM decide the output of a step (for instance, write a draft reply to an email).

- Have an LLM decide the next step to take (for instance, for a new email, decide between the three actions it can take on an email: archive, reply, or mark for review).

- Have an LLM decide what steps are available to take (for instance, have the LLM write code that executes a dynamic action you didn't preprogram into the application).

We can classify a number of popular *recipes* for building LLM applications based on where they fall in this spectrum of autonomy, that is, which of the three tasks just mentioned are handled by an LLM and which remain in the hands of the developer or user. These recipes can be called *cognitive architectures*. In the artificial intelligence field, the term *cognitive architecture* has long been used to denote models of human reasoning (and their implementations in computers). An LLM cognitive architecture (the term was first applied to LLMs, to our knowledge, in a paper[1]) can be defined as a recipe for the steps to be taken by an LLM application (see Figure 5-1). A *step* is, for instance, retrieval of relevant documents (RAG), or calling an LLM with a chain-of-thought prompt.

---

1 Theodore R. Sumers et al., "Cognitive Architectures for Language Agents" (*https://oreil.ly/cuQnT*), arXiv, September 5, 2023, updated March 15, 2024.

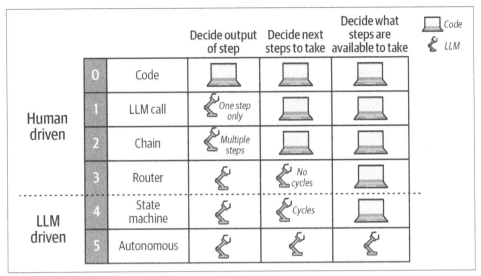

		Decide output of step	Decide next steps to take	Decide what steps are available to take
Human driven	0 Code	💻	💻	💻
	1 LLM call	🦾 One step only	💻	💻
	2 Chain	🦾 Multiple steps	💻	💻
	3 Router	🦾	🦾 No cycles	💻
LLM driven	4 State machine	🦾	🦾 Cycles	💻
	5 Autonomous	🦾	🦾	🦾

💻 Code   🦾 LLM

Figure 5-1. Cognitive architectures for LLM applications

Now let's look at each of the major architectures, or recipes, that you can use when building your application (as shown in Figure 5-1):

0: Code

> This is not an LLM cognitive architecture (hence we numbered it **0**), as it doesn't use LLMs at all. You can think of this as regular software you're used to writing. The first interesting architecture (for this book, at any rate) is actually the next one.

1: LLM call

> This is the majority of the examples we've seen in the book so far, with one LLM call only. This is useful mostly when it's part of a larger application that makes use of an LLM for achieving a specific task, such as translating or summarizing a piece of text.

2: Chain

> The next level up, so to speak, comes with the use of multiple LLM calls in a predefined sequence. For instance, a text-to-SQL application (which receives as input from the user a natural language description of some calculation to make over a database) could make use of two LLM calls in sequence:

> One LLM call to generate a SQL query, from the natural language query, provided by the user, and a description of the database contents, provided by the developer.

And another LLM call to write an explanation of the query appropriate for a nontechnical user, given the query generated in the previous call. This one could then be used to enable the user to check if the generated query matches his request.

3: Router

This next step comes from using the LLM to define the sequence of steps to take. That is, whereas the chain architecture always executes a static sequence of steps (however many) determined by the developer, the router architecture is characterized by using an LLM to choose between certain predefined steps. An example would be a RAG application with multiple indexes of documents from different domains, with the following steps:

1. An LLM call to pick which of the available indexes to use, given the user-supplied query and the developer-supplied description of the indexes.

2. A retrieval step that queries the chosen index for the most relevant documents for the user query.

3. Another LLM call to generate an answer, given the user-supplied query and the list of relevant documents fetched from the index.

That's as far as we'll go in this chapter. We will talk about each of these architectures in turn. The next chapters discuss the agentic architectures, which make even more use of LLMs. But first let's talk about some better tooling to help us on this journey.

Architecture #1: LLM Call

As an example of the LLM call architecture, we'll return to the chatbot we created in Chapter 4. This chatbot will respond directly to user messages.

Start by creating a StateGraph, to which we'll add a node to represent the LLM call:

Python

```python
from typing import Annotated, TypedDict

from langgraph.graph import StateGraph, START, END
from langgraph.graph.message import add_messages
from langchain_openai import ChatOpenAI


model = ChatOpenAI()

class State(TypedDict):
    # Messages have the type "list". The `add_messages`
    # function in the annotation defines how this state should
    # be updated (in this case, it appends new messages to the
    # list, rather than replacing the previous messages)
    messages: Annotated[list, add_messages]
```

```python
def chatbot(state: State):
    answer = model.invoke(state["messages"])
    return {"messages": [answer]}

builder = StateGraph(State)
builder.add_node("chatbot", chatbot)
builder.add_edge(START, 'chatbot')
builder.add_edge('chatbot', END)

graph = builder.compile()
```

JavaScript

```javascript
import {
  StateGraph,
  Annotation,
  messagesStateReducer,
  START, END
} from '@langchain/langgraph'
import {ChatOpenAI} from '@langchain/openai'

const model = new ChatOpenAI()

const State = {
  /**
   * The State defines three things:
   * 1. The structure of the graph's state (which "channels" are available to
   * read/write)
   * 2. The default values for the state's channels
   * 3. The reducers for the state's channels. Reducers are functions that
   * determine how to apply updates to the state. Below, new messages are
   * appended to the messages array.
   */
  messages: Annotation({
    reducer: messagesStateReducer,
    default: () => []
  }),
}

async function chatbot(state) {
  const answer = await model.invoke(state.messages)
  return {"messages": answer}
}

const builder = new StateGraph(State)
  .addNode('chatbot', chatbot)
  .addEdge(START, 'chatbot')
  .addEdge('chatbot', END)

const graph = builder.compile()
```

We can also draw a visual representation of the graph:

Python

```
graph.get_graph().draw_mermaid_png()
```

JavaScript

```
await graph.getGraph().drawMermaidPng()
```

The graph we just made looks like Figure 5-2.

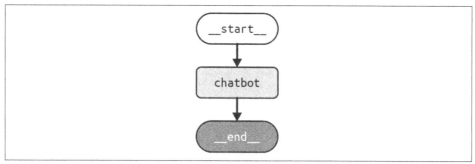

Figure 5-2. The LLM call architecture

You can run it with the familiar `stream()` method you've seen in earlier chapters:

Python

```
input = {"messages": [HumanMessage('hi!')]}
for chunk in graph.stream(input):
    print(chunk)
```

JavaScript

```
const input = {messages: [new HumanMessage('hi!')]}
for await (const chunk of await graph.stream(input)) {
  console.log(chunk)
}
```

The output:

```
{ "chatbot": { "messages": [AIMessage("How can I help you?")] } }
```

Notice how the input to the graph was in the same shape as the `State` object we defined earlier; that is, we sent in a list of messages in the `messages` key of a dictionary.

This is the simplest possible architecture for using an LLM, which is not to say that it should never be used. Here are some examples of where you might see it in action in popular products, among many others:

- AI-powered features such as summarize and translate (such as you can find in Notion, a popular writing software) can be powered by a single LLM call.

- Simple SQL query generation can be powered by a single LLM call, depending on the UX and target user the developer has in mind.

Architecture #2: Chain

This next architecture extends on all that by using multiple LLM calls, in a predefined sequence (that is, different invocations of the application do the same sequence of LLM calls, albeit with different inputs and results).

Let's take as an example a text-to-SQL application, which receives as input from the user a natural language description of some calculation to make over a database. We mentioned earlier that this could be achieved with a single LLM call, to generate a SQL query, but we can create a more sophisticated application by making use of multiple LLM calls in sequence. Some authors call this architecture *flow engineering*.[2]

First let's describe the flow in words:

1. One LLM call to generate a SQL query from the natural language query, provided by the user, and a description of the database contents, provided by the developer.

2. Another LLM call to write an explanation of the query appropriate for a nontechnical user, given the query generated in the previous call. This one could then be used to enable the user to check if the generated query matches his request.

You could also extend this even further (but we won't do that here) with additional steps to be taken after the preceding two:

3. Executes the query against the database, which returns a two-dimensional table.

4. Uses a third LLM call to summarize the query results into a textual answer to the original user question.

And now let's implement this with LangGraph:

Python

```
from typing import Annotated, TypedDict

from langchain_core.messages import HumanMessage, SystemMessage
from langchain_openai import ChatOpenAI
```

---

2 Tal Ridnik et al., "Code Generation with AlphaCodium: From Prompt Engineering to Flow Engineering" (*https://oreil.ly/0wHX4*), arXiv, January 16, 2024.

```python
from langgraph.graph import END, START, StateGraph
from langgraph.graph.message import add_messages

# useful to generate SQL query
model_low_temp = ChatOpenAI(temperature=0.1)
# useful to generate natural language outputs
model_high_temp = ChatOpenAI(temperature=0.7)

class State(TypedDict):
    # to track conversation history
    messages: Annotated[list, add_messages]
    # input
    user_query: str
    # output
    sql_query: str
    sql_explanation: str

class Input(TypedDict):
    user_query: str

class Output(TypedDict):
    sql_query: str
    sql_explanation: str

generate_prompt = SystemMessage(
    """You are a helpful data analyst who generates SQL queries for users based
    on their questions."""
)

def generate_sql(state: State) -> State:
    user_message = HumanMessage(state["user_query"])
    messages = [generate_prompt, *state["messages"], user_message]
    res = model_low_temp.invoke(messages)
    return {
        "sql_query": res.content,
        # update conversation history
        "messages": [user_message, res],
    }

explain_prompt = SystemMessage(
    "You are a helpful data analyst who explains SQL queries to users."
)

def explain_sql(state: State) -> State:
    messages = [
        explain_prompt,
        # contains user's query and SQL query from prev step
        *state["messages"],
    ]
    res = model_high_temp.invoke(messages)
    return {
```

```python
            "sql_explanation": res.content,
            # update conversation history
            "messages": res,
        }

builder = StateGraph(State, input=Input, output=Output)
builder.add_node("generate_sql", generate_sql)
builder.add_node("explain_sql", explain_sql)
builder.add_edge(START, "generate_sql")
builder.add_edge("generate_sql", "explain_sql")
builder.add_edge("explain_sql", END)

graph = builder.compile()
```

JavaScript

```javascript
import {
  HumanMessage,
  SystemMessage
} from "@langchain/core/messages";
import { ChatOpenAI } from "@langchain/openai";
import {
  StateGraph,
  Annotation,
  messagesStateReducer,
  START,
  END,
} from "@langchain/langgraph";

// useful to generate SQL query
const modelLowTemp = new ChatOpenAI({ temperature: 0.1 });
// useful to generate natural language outputs
const modelHighTemp = new ChatOpenAI({ temperature: 0.7 });

const annotation = Annotation.Root({
  messages: Annotation({ reducer: messagesStateReducer, default: () => [] }),
  user_query: Annotation(),
  sql_query: Annotation(),
  sql_explanation: Annotation(),
});

const generatePrompt = new SystemMessage(
  `You are a helpful data analyst who generates SQL queries for users based on
    their questions.`
);

async function generateSql(state) {
  const userMessage = new HumanMessage(state.user_query);
  const messages = [generatePrompt, ...state.messages, userMessage];
  const res = await modelLowTemp.invoke(messages);
  return {
    sql_query: res.content as string,
    // update conversation history
```

```
    messages: [userMessage, res],
  };
}

const explainPrompt = new SystemMessage(
  "You are a helpful data analyst who explains SQL queries to users."
);

async function explainSql(state) {
  const messages = [explainPrompt, ...state.messages];
  const res = await modelHighTemp.invoke(messages);
  return {
    sql_explanation: res.content as string,
    // update conversation history
    messages: res,
  };
}

const builder = new StateGraph(annotation)
  .addNode("generate_sql", generateSql)
  .addNode("explain_sql", explainSql)
  .addEdge(START, "generate_sql")
  .addEdge("generate_sql", "explain_sql")
  .addEdge("explain_sql", END);

const graph = builder.compile();
```

The visual representation of the graph is shown in Figure 5-3.

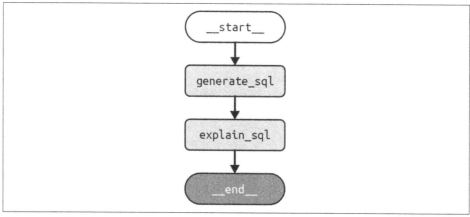

Figure 5-3. The chain architecture

Here's an example of inputs and outputs:

Python

```python
graph.invoke({
  "user_query": "What is the total sales for each product?"
})
```

JavaScript

```javascript
await graph.invoke({
  user_query: "What is the total sales for each product?"
})
```

The output:

```json
{
  "sql_query": "SELECT product_name, SUM(sales_amount) AS total_sales\nFROM
      sales\nGROUP BY product_name;",
  "sql_explanation": "This query will retrieve the total sales for each product
      by summing up the sales_amount column for each product and grouping the
      results by product_name.",
}
```

First, the `generate_sql` node is executed, which populates the `sql_query` key in the state (which will be part of the final output) and updates the `messages` key with the new messages. Then the `explain_sql` node runs, taking the SQL query generated in the previous step and populating the `sql_explanation` key in the state. At this point, the graph finishes running, and the output is returned to the caller.

Note also the use of separate input and output schemas when creating the `State Graph`. This lets you customize which parts of the state are accepted as input from the user and which are returned as the final output. The remaining state keys are used by the graph nodes internally to keep intermediate state and are made available to the user as part of the streaming output produced by `stream()`.

Architecture #3: Router

This next architecture moves up the autonomy ladder by assigning to LLMs the next of the responsibilities we outlined before: deciding the next step to take. That is, whereas the chain architecture always executes a static sequence of steps (however many), the router architecture is characterized by using an LLM to choose between certain predefined steps.

Let's use the example of a RAG application with access to multiple indexes of documents from different domains (refer to Chapter 2 for more on indexing). Usually you can extract better performance from LLMs by avoiding the inclusion of irrelevant information in the prompt. Therefore, in building this application, we should try to pick the right index to use for each query and use only that one. The key development in this architecture is to use an LLM to make this decision, effectively using an LLM to evaluate each incoming query and decide which index it should use for that *particular* query.

 Before the advent of LLMs, the usual way of solving this problem would be to build a classifier model using ML techniques and a dataset mapping example user queries to the right index. This could prove quite challenging, as it requires the following:

- Assembling that dataset by hand
- Generating enough *features* (quantitative attributes) from each user query to enable training a classifier for the task

LLMs, given their encoding of human language, can effectively serve as this classifier with zero, or very few, examples or additional training.

First, let's describe the flow in words:

1. An LLM call to pick which of the available indexes to use, given the user-supplied query, and the developer-supplied description of the indexes
2. A retrieval step that queries the chosen index for the most relevant documents for the user query
3. Another LLM call to generate an answer, given the user-supplied query and the list of relevant documents fetched from the index

And now let's implement it with LangGraph:

Python

```python
from typing import Annotated, Literal, TypedDict

from langchain_core.documents import Document
from langchain_core.messages import HumanMessage, SystemMessage
from langchain_core.vectorstores.in_memory import InMemoryVectorStore
from langchain_openai import ChatOpenAI, OpenAIEmbeddings

from langgraph.graph import END, START, StateGraph
from langgraph.graph.message import add_messages

embeddings = OpenAIEmbeddings()
# useful to generate SQL query
model_low_temp = ChatOpenAI(temperature=0.1)
# useful to generate natural language outputs
model_high_temp = ChatOpenAI(temperature=0.7)

class State(TypedDict):
```

```python
    # to track conversation history
    messages: Annotated[list, add_messages]
    # input
    user_query: str
    # output
    domain: Literal["records", "insurance"]
    documents: list[Document]
    answer: str

class Input(TypedDict):
    user_query: str

class Output(TypedDict):
    documents: list[Document]
    answer: str

# refer to Chapter 2 on how to fill a vector store with documents
medical_records_store = InMemoryVectorStore.from_documents([], embeddings)
medical_records_retriever = medical_records_store.as_retriever()

insurance_faqs_store = InMemoryVectorStore.from_documents([], embeddings)
insurance_faqs_retriever = insurance_faqs_store.as_retriever()

router_prompt = SystemMessage(
    """You need to decide which domain to route the user query to. You have two
        domains to choose from:
          - records: contains medical records of the patient, such as
          diagnosis, treatment, and prescriptions.
          - insurance: contains frequently asked questions about insurance
          policies, claims, and coverage.

Output only the domain name."""
)

def router_node(state: State) -> State:
    user_message = HumanMessage(state["user_query"])
    messages = [router_prompt, *state["messages"], user_message]
    res = model_low_temp.invoke(messages)
    return {
        "domain": res.content,
        # update conversation history
        "messages": [user_message, res],
    }

def pick_retriever(
    state: State,
) -> Literal["retrieve_medical_records", "retrieve_insurance_faqs"]:
    if state["domain"] == "records":
        return "retrieve_medical_records"
    else:
        return "retrieve_insurance_faqs"
```

```python
def retrieve_medical_records(state: State) -> State:
    documents = medical_records_retriever.invoke(state["user_query"])
    return {
        "documents": documents,
    }

def retrieve_insurance_faqs(state: State) -> State:
    documents = insurance_faqs_retriever.invoke(state["user_query"])
    return {
        "documents": documents,
    }

medical_records_prompt = SystemMessage(
    """You are a helpful medical chatbot who answers questions based on the
        patient's medical records, such as diagnosis, treatment, and
        prescriptions."""
)

insurance_faqs_prompt = SystemMessage(
    """You are a helpful medical insurance chatbot who answers frequently asked
        questions about insurance policies, claims, and coverage."""
)

def generate_answer(state: State) -> State:
    if state["domain"] == "records":
        prompt = medical_records_prompt
    else:
        prompt = insurance_faqs_prompt
    messages = [
        prompt,
        *state["messages"],
        HumanMessage(f"Documents: {state["documents"]}"),
    ]
    res = model_high_temp.invoke(messages)
    return {
        "answer": res.content,
        # update conversation history
        "messages": res,
    }

builder = StateGraph(State, input=Input, output=Output)
builder.add_node("router", router_node)
builder.add_node("retrieve_medical_records", retrieve_medical_records)
builder.add_node("retrieve_insurance_faqs", retrieve_insurance_faqs)
builder.add_node("generate_answer", generate_answer)
builder.add_edge(START, "router")
builder.add_conditional_edges("router", pick_retriever)
builder.add_edge("retrieve_medical_records", "generate_answer")
builder.add_edge("retrieve_insurance_faqs", "generate_answer")
builder.add_edge("generate_answer", END)

graph = builder.compile()
```

JavaScript

```javascript
import {
  HumanMessage,
  SystemMessage
} from "@langchain/core/messages";
import {
  ChatOpenAI,
  OpenAIEmbeddings
} from "@langchain/openai";
import {
  MemoryVectorStore
} from "langchain/vectorstores/memory";
import {
  DocumentInterface
} from "@langchain/core/documents";
import {
  StateGraph,
  Annotation,
  messagesStateReducer,
  START,
  END,
} from "@langchain/langgraph";

const embeddings = new OpenAIEmbeddings();
// useful to generate SQL query
const modelLowTemp = new ChatOpenAI({ temperature: 0.1 });
// useful to generate natural language outputs
const modelHighTemp = new ChatOpenAI({ temperature: 0.7 });

const annotation = Annotation.Root({
  messages: Annotation({ reducer: messagesStateReducer, default: () => [] }),
  user_query: Annotation(),
  domain: Annotation(),
  documents: Annotation(),
  answer: Annotation(),
});

// refer to Chapter 2 on how to fill a vector store with documents
const medicalRecordsStore = await MemoryVectorStore.fromDocuments(
  [],
  embeddings
);
const medicalRecordsRetriever = medicalRecordsStore.asRetriever();

const insuranceFaqsStore = await MemoryVectorStore.fromDocuments(
  [],
  embeddings
);
const insuranceFaqsRetriever = insuranceFaqsStore.asRetriever();

const routerPrompt = new SystemMessage(
  `You need to decide which domain to route the user query to. You have two
```

```
    domains to choose from:
        - records: contains medical records of the patient, such as diagnosis,
        treatment, and prescriptions.
        - insurance: contains frequently asked questions about insurance
        policies, claims, and coverage.

Output only the domain name.`
);

async function routerNode(state) {
  const userMessage = new HumanMessage(state.user_query);
  const messages = [routerPrompt, ...state.messages, userMessage];
  const res = await modelLowTemp.invoke(messages);
  return {
    domain: res.content as "records" | "insurance",
    // update conversation history
    messages: [userMessage, res],
  };
}

function pickRetriever(state) {
  if (state.domain === "records") {
    return "retrieve_medical_records";
  } else {
    return "retrieve_insurance_faqs";
  }
}

async function retrieveMedicalRecords(state) {
  const documents = await medicalRecordsRetriever.invoke(state.user_query);
  return {
    documents,
  };
}

async function retrieveInsuranceFaqs(state) {
  const documents = await insuranceFaqsRetriever.invoke(state.user_query);
  return {
    documents,
  };
}

const medicalRecordsPrompt = new SystemMessage(
  `You are a helpful medical chatbot who answers questions based on the
    patient's medical records, such as diagnosis, treatment, and
    prescriptions.`
);

const insuranceFaqsPrompt = new SystemMessage(
  `You are a helpful medical insurance chatbot who answers frequently asked
    questions about insurance policies, claims, and coverage.`
);
```

```
async function generateAnswer(state) {
  const prompt =
    state.domain === "records" ? medicalRecordsPrompt : insuranceFaqsPrompt;
  const messages = [
    prompt,
    ...state.messages,
    new HumanMessage(`Documents: ${state.documents}`),
  ];
  const res = await modelHighTemp.invoke(messages);
  return {
    answer: res.content as string,
    // update conversation history
    messages: res,
  };
}

const builder = new StateGraph(annotation)
  .addNode("router", routerNode)
  .addNode("retrieve_medical_records", retrieveMedicalRecords)
  .addNode("retrieve_insurance_faqs", retrieveInsuranceFaqs)
  .addNode("generate_answer", generateAnswer)
  .addEdge(START, "router")
  .addConditionalEdges("router", pickRetriever)
  .addEdge("retrieve_medical_records", "generate_answer")
  .addEdge("retrieve_insurance_faqs", "generate_answer")
  .addEdge("generate_answer", END);

const graph = builder.compile();
```

The visual representation is shown in Figure 5-4.

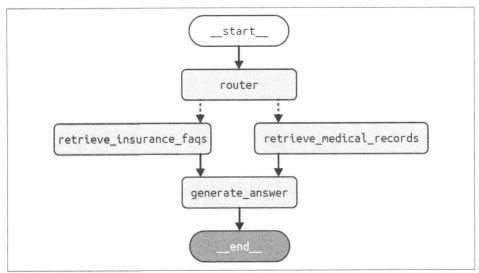

Figure 5-4. The router architecture

Notice how this is now starting to become more useful, as it shows the two possible paths through the graph, through `retrieve_medical_records` or through `retrieve_insurance_faqs`, and that for both of those, we first visit the `router` node and finish by visiting the `generate_answer` node. These two possible paths were implemented through the use of a conditional edge, implemented in the function `pick_retriever`, which maps the `domain` picked by the LLM to one of the two nodes mentioned earlier. The conditional edge is shown in Figure 5-4 as dotted lines from the source node to the destination nodes.

And now for example inputs and outputs, this time with streaming output:

Python

```python
input = {
    "user_query": "Am I covered for COVID-19 treatment?"
}
for c in graph.stream(input):
    print(c)
```

JavaScript

```javascript
const input = {
  user_query: "Am I covered for COVID-19 treatment?"
}
for await (const chunk of await graph.stream(input)) {
console.log(chunk)
}
```

The output (the actual answer is not shown, since it would depend on your documents):

```
{
    "router": {
        "messages": [
            HumanMessage(content="Am I covered for COVID-19 treatment?"),
            AIMessage(content="insurance"),
        ],
        "domain": "insurance",
    }
}
{
    "retrieve_insurance_faqs": {
        "documents": [...]
    }
}
{
    "generate_answer": {
        "messages": AIMessage(
            content="...",
        ),
        "answer": "...",
```

```
        }
    }
```

This output stream contains the values returned by each node that ran during this execution of the graph. Let's take it one at a time. The top-level key in each dictionary is the name of the node, and the value for that key is what that node returned:

1. The router node returned an update to messages (this would allow us to easily continue this conversation using the memory technique described earlier), and the domain the LLM picked for this user's query, in this case insurance.

2. Then the pick_retriever function ran and returned the name of the next node to run, based on the domain identified by the LLM call in the previous step.

3. Then the retrieve_insurance_faqs node ran, returning a set of relevant documents from that index. This means that on the drawing of the graph seen earlier, we took the left path, as decided by the LLM.

4. Finally, the generate_answer node ran, which took those documents and the original user query and produced an answer to the question, which was written to the state (along with a final update to the messages key).

Summary

This chapter talked about the key trade-off when building LLM applications: agency versus oversight. The more autonomous an LLM application is, the more it can do—but that raises the need for more mechanisms of control over its actions. We moved on to different cognitive architectures that strike different balances between agency and oversight.

Chapter 6 talks about the most powerful of the cognitive architectures we've seen so far: the agent architecture.

Agent Architecture

Building on the architectures described in Chapter 5, this chapter will cover what is perhaps the most important of all current LLM architectures, the agent architecture. First, we introduce what makes LLM agents unique, then we show how to build them and how to extend them for common use cases.

In the artificial intelligence field, there is a long history of creating (intelligent) agents, which can be most simply defined as "something that acts," in the words of Stuart Russell and Peter Norvig in their *Artificial Intelligence* (Pearson, 2020) textbook. The word *acts* actually carries a little more meaning than meets the eye:

- Acting requires some capacity for deciding what to do.
- Deciding what to do implies having access to more than one possible course of action. After all, a decision without options is no decision at all.
- In order to decide, the agent also needs access to information about the external environment (anything outside of the agent itself).

So an *agentic* LLM application must be one that uses an LLM to pick from one or more possible courses of action, given some context about the current state of the world or some desired next state. These attributes are usually implemented by mixing two prompting techniques we first met in the Preface:

Tool calling
> Include a list of external functions that the LLM can make use of in your prompt (that is, the actions it can decide to take) and provide instructions on how to format its choice in the output it generates. You'll see in a moment what this looks like in the prompt.

Chain-of-thought

Researchers have found that LLMs "make better decisions" when given instructions to reason about complex problems by breaking them down into granular steps to be taken in sequence. This is usually done either by adding instructions along the lines of "think step by step" or including examples of questions and their decomposition into several steps/actions.

Here's an example prompt using both tool calling and chain-of-thought:

```
Tools:
search: this tool accepts a web search query and returns the top results.
calculator: this tool accepts math expressions and returns their result.

If you want to use tools to arrive at the answer, output the list of tools and
inputs in CSV format, with the header row: tool,input.

Think step by step; if you need to make multiple tool calls to arrive at the
answer, return only the first one.

How old was the 30th president of the United States when he died?

tool,input
```

And the output, when run against `gpt-3.5-turbo` at temperature 0 (to ensure the LLM follows the desired output format, CSV) and newline as the stop sequence (which instructs the LLM to stop producing output when it reaches this character). This makes the LLM produce a single action (as expected, given the prompt asked for this):

```
search,30th president of the United States
```

The most recent LLMs and chat models have been fine-tuned to improve their performance for tool-calling and chain-of-thought applications, removing the need for adding specific instructions to the prompt:

```
add example prompt and output for tool-calling model
```

The Plan-Do Loop

What makes the agent architecture different from the architectures discussed in Chapter 5 is a concept we haven't covered yet: the LLM-driven loop.

Every programmer has encountered loops in their code before. By *loop*, we mean running the same code multiple times until a stop condition is hit. The key to the agent architecture is to have an LLM control the stop condition—that is, decide when to stop looping.

What we'll run in this loop will be some variation of the following:

- Planning an action or actions
- Executing said action(s)

Picking up on the example in the previous section, we'll next run the `search` tool with the input `30th president of the United States`, which produces this output:

```
Calvin Coolidge (born John Calvin Coolidge Jr.; /'kuːlɪdʒ/; July 4, 1872 - January
5, 1933) was an American attorney and politician who served as the 30th president
of the United States from 1923 to 1929. John Calvin Coolidge Jr.
```

And then we'll rerun the prompt, with a small addition:

```
Tools:
search: this tool accepts a web search query and returns the top results.
calculator: this tool accepts math expressions and returns their result.
output: this tool ends the interaction. Use it when you have the final answer.

If you want to use tools to arrive at the answer, output the list of tools and
inputs in CSV format, with this header row: tool,input

Think step by step; if you need to make multiple tool calls to arrive at
the answer, return only the first one.

How old was the 30th president of the United States when he died?

tool,input

search,30th president of the United States

search: Calvin Coolidge (born John Calvin Coolidge Jr.; /'kuːlɪdʒ/; July 4, 1872 -
January 5, 1933) was an American attorney and politician who served as the 30th
president of the United States from 1923 to 1929. John Calvin Coolidge Jr.

tool,input
```

And the output:

```
calculator,1933 - 1872
```

Notice we added two things:

- An "output" tool—which the LLM should use when it has found the final answer, and which we'd use as the signal to stop the loop.
- The result of the tool call from the preceding iteration, simply with the name of the tool and its (text) output. This is included in order to allow the LLM to move on to the next step in the interaction. In other words, we're telling the LLM, "Hey, we got the results you asked for, what do you want to do next?"

Let's continue with a third iteration:

```
Tools:
search: this tool accepts a web search query and returns the top results.
calculator: this tool accepts math expressions and returns their result.

If you want to use tools to arrive at the answer, output the list of tools and
inputs in CSV format, with this header row: tool,input.
output: this tool ends the interaction. Use it when you have the final answer.

Think step by step; if you need to make multiple tool calls to arrive at
the answer, return only the first one.

How old was the 30th president of the United States when he died?

tool,input

search,30th president of the United States

search: Calvin Coolidge (born John Calvin Coolidge Jr.; /ˈkuːlɪdʒ/; July 4, 1872 -
January 5, 1933) was an American attorney and politician who served as the 30th
president of the United States from 1923 to 1929. John Calvin Coolidge Jr.
tool,input

calculator,1933-1872

calculator: 61

tool, input
```

And the output:

```
output, 61
```

With the result from the calculator tool, the LLM now has enough information to provide the final answer, so it picked the output tool and chose "61" as the final answer.

This is what makes the agent architecture so useful—the LLM is given the agency to decide. The next step is to arrive at an answer and decide how many steps to take—that is, when to stop.

This architecture, called ReAct (*https://oreil.ly/M7hF-*), was first proposed by Shunyu Yao et al. The rest of this chapter explores how to improve the performance of the agent architecture, motivated by the email assistant example from Chapter 5.

But first, let's see what it looks like to implement the basic agent architecture using a chat model and LangGraph.

Building a LangGraph Agent

For this example, we need to install additional dependencies for the search tool we chose to use, DuckDuckGo. To install it for Python:

Python

```
pip install duckduckgo-search
```

And for JS, we also need to install a dependency for the calculator tool:

JavaScript

```
npm i duck-duck-scrape expr-eval
```

With that complete, let's get into the actual code to implement the agent architecture:

Python

```python
import ast
from typing import Annotated, TypedDict

from langchain_community.tools import DuckDuckGoSearchRun
from langchain_core.tools import tool
from langchain_openai import ChatOpenAI

from langgraph.graph import START, StateGraph
from langgraph.graph.message import add_messages
from langgraph.prebuilt import ToolNode, tools_condition

@tool
def calculator(query: str) -> str:
    """A simple calculator tool. Input should be a mathematical expression."""
    return ast.literal_eval(query)

search = DuckDuckGoSearchRun()
tools = [search, calculator]
model = ChatOpenAI(temperature=0.1).bind_tools(tools)

class State(TypedDict):
    messages: Annotated[list, add_messages]

def model_node(state: State) -> State:
    res = model.invoke(state["messages"])
    return {"messages": res}

builder = StateGraph(State)
builder.add_node("model", model_node)
builder.add_node("tools", ToolNode(tools))
builder.add_edge(START, "model")
builder.add_conditional_edges("model", tools_condition)
builder.add_edge("tools", "model")

graph = builder.compile()
```

JavaScript

```javascript
import {
  DuckDuckGoSearch
} from "@langchain/community/tools/duckduckgo_search";
import {
  Calculator
} from "@langchain/community/tools/calculator";
import {
  StateGraph,
  Annotation,
  messagesStateReducer,
  START,
} from "@langchain/langgraph";
import {
  ToolNode,
  toolsCondition
} from "@langchain/langgraph/prebuilt";

const search = new DuckDuckGoSearch();
const calculator = new Calculator();
const tools = [search, calculator];
const model = new ChatOpenAI({
  temperature: 0.1
}).bindTools(tools);

const annotation = Annotation.Root({
  messages: Annotation({
    reducer: messagesStateReducer,
    default: () => []
  }),
});

async function modelNode(state) {
  const res = await model.invoke(state.messages);
  return { messages: res };
}

const builder = new StateGraph(annotation)
  .addNode("model", modelNode)
  .addNode("tools", new ToolNode(tools))
  .addEdge(START, "model")
  .addConditionalEdges("model", toolsCondition)
  .addEdge("tools", "model");

const graph = builder.compile();
```

The visual representation is shown in Figure 6-1.

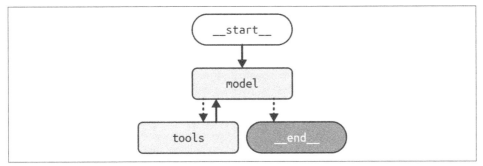

Figure 6-1. The agent architecture

A few things to notice here:

- We're using two tools in this example: a search tool and a calculator tool, but you could easily add more or replace the ones we used. In the Python example, you also see an example of creating a custom tool.

- We've used two convenience functions that ship with LangGraph. `ToolNode` serves as a node in our graph; it executes the tool calls requested in the latest AI message found in the state and returns a `ToolMessage` with the results of each. `ToolNode` also handles exceptions raised by tools—using the error message to build a `ToolMessage` that is then passed to the LLM—which may decide what to do with the error.

- `tools_condition` serves as a conditional edge function that looks at the latest AI message in the state and routes to the `tools` node if there are any tools to execute. Otherwise, it ends the graph.

- Finally, notice that this graph loops between the model and tools nodes. That is, the model itself is in charge of deciding when to end the computation, which is a key attribute of the agent architecture. Whenever we code a loop in LangGraph, we'll likely want to use a conditional edge, as that allows you to define the *stop condition* when the graph should exit the loop and stop executing.

Now let's see how it does in the previous example:

Python

```python
input = {
    "messages": [
        HumanMessage("""How old was the 30th president of the United States
            when he died?""")
    ]
}
for c in graph.stream(input):
    print(c)
```

JavaScript

```javascript
const input = {
  messages: [
    HumanMessage(`How old was the 30th president of the United States when he
      died?`)
  ]
}
for await (const c of await graph.stream(input)) {
  console.log(c)
}
```

The output:

```
{
    "model": {
        "messages": AIMessage(
            content="",
            tool_calls=[
                {
                    "name": "duckduckgo_search",
                    "args": {
                        "query": "30th president of the United States age at
                            death"
                    },
                    "id": "call_ZWRbPmjvo0fYkwyo4HCYUsar",
                    "type": "tool_call",
                }
            ],
        )
    }
}
{
    "tools": {
        "messages": [
            ToolMessage(
                content="Calvin Coolidge (born July 4, 1872, Plymouth, Vermont,
                    U.S.—died January 5, 1933, Northampton, Massachusetts) was
                    the 30th president of the United States (1923-29). Coolidge
                    acceded to the presidency after the death in office of
                    Warren G. Harding, just as the Harding scandals were coming
                    to light....",
                name="duckduckgo_search",
                tool_call_id="call_ZWRbPmjvo0fYkwyo4HCYUsar",
            )
        ]
    }
}
{
    "model": {
        "messages": AIMessage(
            content="Calvin Coolidge, the 30th president of the United States,
                died on January 5, 1933, at the age of 60.",
```

```
            )
        }
    }
```

Walking through this output:

1. First the model node executed and decided to call the duckduckgo_search tool, which led the conditional edge to route us to the tools node after.

2. The ToolNode executed the search tool and got the search results printed above, which actually contain the answer "Age and Year of Death . January 5, 1933 (aged 60)".

3. The model tool was called again, this time with the search results as the latest message, and produced the final answer (with no more tool calls); therefore, the conditional edge ended the graph.

Next, let's look at a few useful extensions to this basic agent architecture, customizing both planning and tool calling.

Always Calling a Tool First

In the standard agent architecture, the LLM is always called upon to decide what tool to call next. This arrangement has a clear advantage: it gives the LLM ultimate flexibility to adapt the behavior of the application to each user query that comes in. But this flexibility comes at a cost: unpredictability. If, for instance, you, the developer of the application, know that the search tool should always be called first, that can actually be beneficial to your application:

1. It will reduce overall latency, as it will skip the first LLM call that would generate that request to call the search tool.

2. It will prevent the LLM from erroneously deciding it doesn't need to call the search tool for some user queries.

On the other hand, if your application doesn't have a clear rule of the kind "you should always call this tool first," introducing such a constraint would actually make your application worse.

Let's see what it looks like to do this:

Python

```
import ast
from typing import Annotated, TypedDict
from uuid import uuid4

from langchain_community.tools import DuckDuckGoSearchRun
from langchain_core.messages import AIMessage, HumanMessage, ToolCall
```

```python
from langchain_core.tools import tool
from langchain_openai import ChatOpenAI

from langgraph.graph import START, StateGraph
from langgraph.graph.message import add_messages
from langgraph.prebuilt import ToolNode, tools_condition

@tool
def calculator(query: str) -> str:
    """A simple calculator tool. Input should be a mathematical expression."""
    return ast.literal_eval(query)

search = DuckDuckGoSearchRun()
tools = [search, calculator]
model = ChatOpenAI(temperature=0.1).bind_tools(tools)

class State(TypedDict):
    messages: Annotated[list, add_messages]

def model_node(state: State) -> State:
    res = model.invoke(state["messages"])
    return {"messages": res}

def first_model(state: State) -> State:
    query = state["messages"][-1].content
    search_tool_call = ToolCall(
        name="duckduckgo_search", args={"query": query}, id=uuid4().hex
    )
    return {"messages": AIMessage(content="", tool_calls=[search_tool_call])}

builder = StateGraph(State)
builder.add_node("first_model", first_model)
builder.add_node("model", model_node)
builder.add_node("tools", ToolNode(tools))
builder.add_edge(START, "first_model")
builder.add_edge("first_model", "tools")
builder.add_conditional_edges("model", tools_condition)
builder.add_edge("tools", "model")

graph = builder.compile()
```

JavaScript

```javascript
import {
  DuckDuckGoSearch
} from "@langchain/community/tools/duckduckgo_search";
import {
  Calculator
} from "@langchain/community/tools/calculator";
import {
  AIMessage,
} from "@langchain/core/messages";
import {
```

```
  StateGraph,
  Annotation,
  messagesStateReducer,
  START,
} from "@langchain/langgraph";
import {
  ToolNode,
  toolsCondition
} from "@langchain/langgraph/prebuilt";

const search = new DuckDuckGoSearch();
const calculator = new Calculator();
const tools = [search, calculator];
const model = new ChatOpenAI({ temperature: 0.1 }).bindTools(tools);

const annotation = Annotation.Root({
  messages: Annotation({ reducer: messagesStateReducer, default: () => [] }),
});

async function firstModelNode(state) {
  const query = state.messages[state.messages.length - 1].content;
  const searchToolCall = {
    name: "duckduckgo_search",
    args: { query },
    id: Math.random().toString(),
  };
  return {
    messages: [new AIMessage({ content: "", tool_calls: [searchToolCall] })],
  };
}

async function modelNode(state) {
  const res = await model.invoke(state.messages);
  return { messages: res };
}

const builder = new StateGraph(annotation)
  .addNode("first_model", firstModelNode)
  .addNode("model", modelNode)
  .addNode("tools", new ToolNode(tools))
  .addEdge(START, "first_model")
  .addEdge("first_model", "tools")
  .addEdge("tools", "model")
  .addConditionalEdges("model", toolsCondition);

const graph = builder.compile();
```

The visual representation is shown in Figure 6-2.

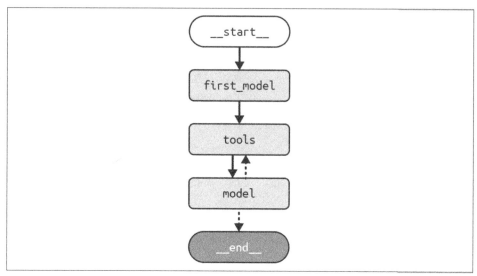

Figure 6-2. Modifying the agent architecture to always call a specific tool first

Notice the differences compared to the previous section:

- Now, we start all invocations by calling `first_model`, which doesn't call an LLM at all. It just creates a tool call for the search tool, using the user's message verbatim as the search query. The previous architecture would have the LLM generate this tool call (or some other response it deemed better).

- After that, we proceed to `tools`, which is identical to the previous example, and from there we proceed to the `agent` node as before.

Now let's see some example output, for the same query as before:

Python

```python
input = {
    "messages": [
        HumanMessage("""How old was the 30th president of the United States
            when he died?""")
    ]
}
for c in graph.stream(input):
print(c)
```

JavaScript

```javascript
const input = {
  messages: [
    HumanMessage(`How old was the 30th president of the United States when he
        died?`)
  ]
```

```
  }
  for await (const c of await graph.stream(input)) {
    console.log(c)
  }
```

The output:

```
{
    "first_model": {
        "messages": AIMessage(
            content="",
            tool_calls=[
                {
                    "name": "duckduckgo_search",
                    "args": {
                        "query": "How old was the 30th president of the United
                            States when he died?"
                    },
                    "id": "9ed4328dcdea4904b1b54487e343a373",
                    "type": "tool_call",
                }
            ],
        )
    }
}
{
    "tools": {
        "messages": [
            ToolMessage(
                content="Calvin Coolidge (born July 4, 1872, Plymouth, Vermont,
                    U.S.—died January 5, 1933, Northampton, Massachusetts) was
                    the 30th president of the United States (1923-29). Coolidge
                    acceded to the presidency after the death in office of
                    Warren G. Harding, just as the Harding scandals were coming
                    to light....",
                name="duckduckgo_search",
                tool_call_id="9ed4328dcdea4904b1b54487e343a373",
            )
        ]
    }
}
{
    "model": {
        "messages": AIMessage(
            content="Calvin Coolidge, the 30th president of the United States,
                was born on July 4, 1872, and died on January 5, 1933. To
                calculate his age at the time of his death, we can subtract his
                birth year from his death year. \n\nAge at death = Death year -
                Birth year\nAge at death = 1933 - 1872\nAge at death = 61
                years\n\nCalvin Coolidge was 61 years old when he died.",
        )
    }
}
```

This time, we skipped the initial LLM call. We first went to `first_model` node, which directly returned a tool call for the search tool. From there we went to the previous flow—that is, we executed the search tool and finally went back to the `model` node to generate the final answer.

Next let's go over what you can do when you have many tools you want to make available to the LLM.

Dealing with Many Tools

LLMs are far from perfect, and they currently struggle more when given multiple choices or excessive information in a prompt. These limitations also extend to the planning of the next action to take. When given many tools (say, more than 10) the planning performance (that is, the LLM's ability to choose the right tool) starts to suffer. The solution to this problem is to reduce the number of tools the LLM can choose from. But what if you do have many tools you want to see used for different user queries?

One elegant solution is to use a RAG step to preselect the most relevant tools for the current query and then feed the LLM only that subset of tools instead of the entire arsenal. This can also help to reduce the cost of calling the LLM (commercial LLMs usually charge based on the length of the prompt and outputs). On the other hand, this RAG step introduces additional latency to your application, so should only be taken when you see performance decreasing after adding more tools.

Let's see how to do this:

Python

```python
import ast
from typing import Annotated, TypedDict

from langchain_community.tools import DuckDuckGoSearchRun
from langchain_core.documents import Document
from langchain_core.messages import HumanMessage
from langchain_core.tools import tool
from langchain_core.vectorstores.in_memory import InMemoryVectorStore
from langchain_openai import ChatOpenAI, OpenAIEmbeddings

from langgraph.graph import START, StateGraph
from langgraph.graph.message import add_messages
from langgraph.prebuilt import ToolNode, tools_condition

@tool
def calculator(query: str) -> str:
    """A simple calculator tool. Input should be a mathematical expression."""
    return ast.literal_eval(query)

search = DuckDuckGoSearchRun()
```

```python
tools = [search, calculator]

embeddings = OpenAIEmbeddings()
model = ChatOpenAI(temperature=0.1)

tools_retriever = InMemoryVectorStore.from_documents(
    [Document(tool.description, metadata={"name": tool.name}) for tool in tools],
    embeddings,
).as_retriever()

class State(TypedDict):
    messages: Annotated[list, add_messages]
    selected_tools: list[str]

def model_node(state: State) -> State:
    selected_tools = [
        tool for tool in tools if tool.name in state["selected_tools"]
    ]
    res = model.bind_tools(selected_tools).invoke(state["messages"])
    return {"messages": res}

def select_tools(state: State) -> State:
    query = state["messages"][-1].content
    tool_docs = tools_retriever.invoke(query)
    return {"selected_tools": [doc.metadata["name"] for doc in tool_docs]}

builder = StateGraph(State)
builder.add_node("select_tools", select_tools)
builder.add_node("model", model_node)
builder.add_node("tools", ToolNode(tools))
builder.add_edge(START, "select_tools")
builder.add_edge("select_tools", "model")
builder.add_conditional_edges("model", tools_condition)
builder.add_edge("tools", "model")

graph = builder.compile()
```

JavaScript

```javascript
import { DuckDuckGoSearch } from "@langchain/community/tools/duckduckgo_search";
import { Calculator } from "@langchain/community/tools/calculator";
import { ChatOpenAI } from "@langchain/openai";
import { OpenAIEmbeddings } from "@langchain/openai";
import { Document } from "@langchain/core/documents";
import { MemoryVectorStore } from "langchain/vectorstores/memory";
import {
  StateGraph,
  Annotation,
  messagesStateReducer,
  START,
} from "@langchain/langgraph";
import { ToolNode, toolsCondition } from "@langchain/langgraph/prebuilt";
import { HumanMessage } from "@langchain/core/messages";
```

```
const search = new DuckDuckGoSearch();
const calculator = new Calculator();
const tools = [search, calculator];

const embeddings = new OpenAIEmbeddings();
const model = new ChatOpenAI({ temperature: 0.1 });

const toolsStore = await MemoryVectorStore.fromDocuments(
  tools.map(
    (tool) =>
      new Document({
        pageContent: tool.description,
        metadata: { name: tool.constructor.name },
      })
  ),
  embeddings
);
const toolsRetriever = toolsStore.asRetriever();

const annotation = Annotation.Root({
  messages: Annotation({ reducer: messagesStateReducer, default: () => [] }),
  selected_tools: Annotation(),
});

async function modelNode(state) {
  const selectedTools = tools.filter((tool) =>
    state.selected_tools.includes(tool.constructor.name)
  );
  const res = await model.bindTools(selectedTools).invoke(state.messages);
  return { messages: res };
}

async function selectTools(state) {
  const query = state.messages[state.messages.length - 1].content;
  const toolDocs = await toolsRetriever.invoke(query as string);
  return {
    selected_tools: toolDocs.map((doc) => doc.metadata.name),
  };
}

const builder = new StateGraph(annotation)
  .addNode("select_tools", selectTools)
  .addNode("model", modelNode)
  .addNode("tools", new ToolNode(tools))
  .addEdge(START, "select_tools")
  .addEdge("select_tools", "model")
  .addConditionalEdges("model", toolsCondition)
  .addEdge("tools", "model");
```

You can see the visual representation in Figure 6-3.

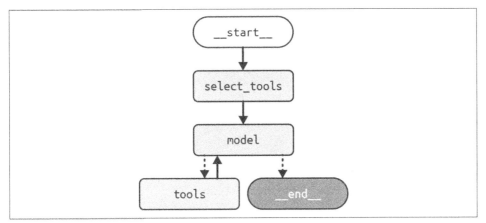

Figure 6-3. Modifying the agent architecture to deal with many tools

 This is very similar to the regular agent architecture. The only difference is that we stop by the `select_tools` node before entering the actual agent loop. After that, it works just as the regular agent architecture we've seen before.

Now let's see some example output for the same query as before:

Python

```python
input = {
  "messages": [
    HumanMessage("""How old was the 30th president of the United States when
        he died?""")
  ]
}
for c in graph.stream(input):
print(c)
```

JavaScript

```javascript
const input = {
  messages: [
    HumanMessage(`How old was the 30th president of the United States when he
        died?`)
  ]
}
for await (const c of await graph.stream(input)) {
  console.log(c)
}
```

The output:

```
{
    "select_tools": {
        "selected_tools': ['duckduckgo_search', 'calculator']
    }
}
{
    "model": {
        "messages": AIMessage(
            content="",
            tool_calls=[
                {
                    "name": "duckduckgo_search",
                    "args": {
                        "query": "30th president of the United States"
                    },
                    "id": "9ed4328dcdea4904b1b54487e343a373",
                    "type": "tool_call",
                }
            ],
        )
    }
}
{
    "tools": {
        "messages": [
            ToolMessage(
                content="Calvin Coolidge (born July 4, 1872, Plymouth, Vermont,
                    U.S.—died January 5, 1933, Northampton, Massachusetts) was
                    the 30th president of the United States (1923-29). Coolidge
                    acceded to the presidency after the death in office of
                    Warren G. Harding, just as the Harding scandals were coming
                    to light....",
                name="duckduckgo_search",
                tool_call_id="9ed4328dcdea4904b1b54487e343a373",
            )
        ]
    }
}
{
    "model": {
        "messages": AIMessage(
            content="Calvin Coolidge, the 30th president of the United States,
                was born on July 4, 1872, and died on January 5, 1933. To
                calculate his age at the time of his death, we can subtract his
                birth year from his death year. \n\nAge at death = Death year -
                Birth year\nAge at death = 1933 - 1872\nAge at death = 61
                years\n\nCalvin Coolidge was 61 years old when he died.",
        )
    }
}
```

Notice how the first thing we did was query the retriever to get the most relevant tools for the current user query. Then, we proceeded to the regular agent architecture.

Summary

This chapter introduced the concept of *agency* and discussed what it takes to make an LLM application *agentic*: giving the LLM the ability to decide between multiple options by using external information.

We walked through the standard agent architecture built with LangGraph and looked at two useful extensions: how to always call a specific tool first and how to deal with many tools.

Chapter 7 looks at additional extensions to the agent architecture.

Agents II

Chapter 6 introduced the *agent* architecture, the most powerful of the LLM architectures we have seen up until now. It is hard to overstate the potential of this combination of chain-of-thought prompting, tool use, and looping.

This chapter discusses two extensions to the agent architecture that improve performance for some use cases:

Reflection
Taking another page out of the repertoire of human thought patterns, this is about giving your LLM app the opportunity to analyze its past output and choices, together with the ability to remember reflections from past iterations.

Multi-agent
Much the same way as a team can accomplish more than a single person, there are problems that can be best tackled by teams of LLM agents.

Let's start with reflection.

Reflection

One prompting technique we haven't covered yet is *reflection* (also known as *self-critique*). *Reflection* is the creation of a loop between a creator prompt and a reviser prompt. This mirrors the creation process for many human-created artifacts, such as this chapter you're reading now, which is the result of a back and forth between the authors, reviewers, and editor until all are happy with the final product.

As with many of the prompting techniques we have seen so far, reflection can be combined with other techniques, such as chain-of-thought and tool calling. In this section, we'll look at reflection in isolation.

A parallel can be drawn to the modes of human thinking known as *System 1* (reactive or instinctive) and *System 2* (methodical and reflective), first introduced by Daniel Kahneman in the book *Thinking, Fast and Slow* (Farrar, Straus and Giroux, 2011). When applied correctly, self-critique can help LLM applications get closer to something that resembles System 2 behavior (Figure 7-1).

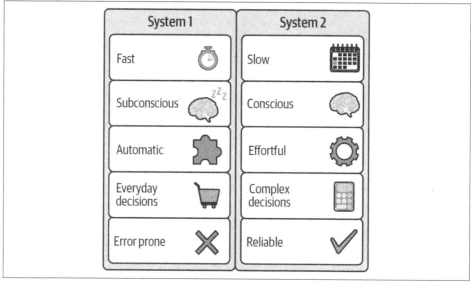

Figure 7-1. System 1 and System 2 thinking

We'll implement reflection as a graph with two nodes: generate and reflect. This graph will be tasked with writing three-paragraph essays, with the generate node writing or revising drafts of the essay, and reflect writing a critique to inform the next revision. We'll run the loop a fixed number of times, but a variation on this technique would be to have the reflect node decide when to finish. Let's see what it looks like:

Python

```python
from typing import Annotated, TypedDict

from langchain_core.messages import (
    AIMessage,
    BaseMessage,
    HumanMessage,
    SystemMessage,
)
from langchain_openai import ChatOpenAI

from langgraph.graph import END, START, StateGraph
from langgraph.graph.message import add_messages

model = ChatOpenAI()
```

```python
class State(TypedDict):
    messages: Annotated[list[BaseMessage], add_messages]

generate_prompt = SystemMessage(
    """You are an essay assistant tasked with writing excellent 3-paragraph
        essays."""
    "Generate the best essay possible for the user's request."
    """If the user provides critique, respond with a revised version of your
        previous attempts."""
)

def generate(state: State) -> State:
    answer = model.invoke([generate_prompt] + state["messages"])
    return {"messages": [answer]}

reflection_prompt = SystemMessage(
    """You are a teacher grading an essay submission. Generate critique and
        recommendations for the user's submission."""
    """Provide detailed recommendations, including requests for length, depth,
        style, etc."""
)

def reflect(state: State) -> State:
    # Invert the messages to get the LLM to reflect on its own output
    cls_map = {AIMessage: HumanMessage, HumanMessage: AIMessage}
    # First message is the original user request.
    # We hold it the same for all nodes
    translated = [reflection_prompt, state["messages"][0]] + [
        cls_map[msg.__class__](content=msg.content)
            for msg in state["messages"][1:]
    ]
    answer = model.invoke(translated)
    # We treat the output of this as human feedback for the generator
    return {"messages": [HumanMessage(content=answer.content)]}

def should_continue(state: State):
    if len(state["messages"]) > 6:
        # End after 3 iterations, each with 2 messages
        return END
    else:
        return "reflect"

builder = StateGraph(State)
builder.add_node("generate", generate)
builder.add_node("reflect", reflect)
builder.add_edge(START, "generate")
builder.add_conditional_edges("generate", should_continue)
builder.add_edge("reflect", "generate")

graph = builder.compile()
```

JavaScript

```javascript
import {
  AIMessage,
  BaseMessage,
  SystemMessage,
  HumanMessage,
} from "@langchain/core/messages";
import { ChatOpenAI } from "@langchain/openai";
import {
  StateGraph,
  Annotation,
  messagesStateReducer,
  START,
  END,
} from "@langchain/langgraph";

const model = new ChatOpenAI();

const annotation = Annotation.Root({
  messages: Annotation({ reducer: messagesStateReducer, default: () => [] }),
});

// fix multiline string
const generatePrompt = new SystemMessage(
  `You are an essay assistant tasked with writing excellent 3-paragraph essays.
  Generate the best essay possible for the user's request.
  If the user provides critique, respond with a revised version of your
    previous attempts.`
);

async function generate(state) {
  const answer = await model.invoke([generatePrompt, ...state.messages]);
  return { messages: [answer] };
}

const reflectionPrompt = new SystemMessage(
  `You are a teacher grading an essay submission. Generate critique and
    recommendations for the user's submission.
  Provide detailed recommendations, including requests for length, depth,
    style, etc.`
);

async function reflect(state) {
  // Invert the messages to get the LLM to reflect on its own output
  const clsMap: { [key: string]: new (content: string) => BaseMessage } = {
    ai: HumanMessage,
    human: AIMessage,
  };
  // First message is the original user request.
  // We hold it the same for all nodes
  const translated = [
    reflectionPrompt,
```

```
      state.messages[0],
      ...state.messages
        .slice(1)
        .map((msg) => new clsMap[msg._getType()](msg.content as string)),
  ];
  const answer = await model.invoke(translated);
  // We treat the output of this as human feedback for the generator
  return { messages: [new HumanMessage({ content: answer.content })] };
}

function shouldContinue(state) {
  if (state.messages.length > 6) {
    // End after 3 iterations, each with 2 messages
    return END;
  } else {
    return "reflect";
  }
}

const builder = new StateGraph(annotation)
  .addNode("generate", generate)
  .addNode("reflect", reflect)
  .addEdge(START, "generate")
  .addConditionalEdges("generate", shouldContinue)
  .addEdge("reflect", "generate");

const graph = builder.compile();
```

The visual representation of the graph is shown in Figure 7-2.

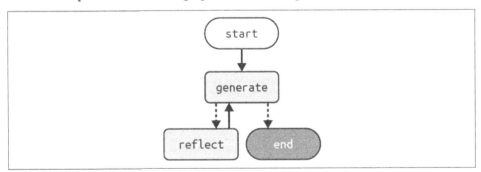

Figure 7-2. The reflection architecture

Notice how the `reflect` node tricks the LLM into thinking it is critiquing essays written by the user. And in tandem, the `generate` node is made to think that the critique comes from the user. This subterfuge is required because dialogue-tuned LLMs are trained on pairs of human-AI messages, so a sequence of many messages from the same participant would result in poor performance.

One more thing to note: you might, at first glance, expect the end to come after a revise step, but in this architecture we have a fixed number of iterations of the generate-reflect loop; therefore we terminate after generate (so that the last set of revisions requested are dealt with). A variation on this architecture would instead have the reflect step make the decision to end the process (once it had no more comments).

Let's see what one of the critiques looks like:

```
{
    'messages': [
        HumanMessage(content='Your essay on the topicality of "The Little Prince"
            and its message in modern life is well-written and insightful. You
            have effectively highlighted the enduring relevance of the book\'s
            themes and its importance in today\'s society. However, there are a
            few areas where you could enhance your essay:\n\n1. **Depth**:
            While you touch upon the themes of cherishing simple joys,
            nurturing connections, and understanding human relationships,
            consider delving deeper into each of these themes. Provide specific
            examples from the book to support your points and explore how these
            themes manifest in contemporary life.\n\n2. **Analysis**: Consider
            analyzing how the book\'s messages can be applied to current
            societal issues or personal experiences. For instance, you could
            discuss how the Little Prince\'s perspective on materialism relates
            to consumer culture or explore how his approach to relationships
            can inform interpersonal dynamics in the digital age.\n\n3.
            **Length**: Expand on your ideas by adding more examples,
            discussing counterarguments, or exploring the cultural impact of
            "The Little Prince" in different parts of the world. This will
            enrich the depth of your analysis and provide a more comprehensive
            understanding of the book\'s relevance.\n\n4. **Style**: Your essay
            is clear and well-structured. To enhance the engagement of your
            readers, consider incorporating quotes from the book to illustrate
            key points or including anecdotes to personalize your analysis.
            \n\n5. **Conclusion**: Conclude your essay by summarizing the
            enduring significance of "The Little Prince" and how its messages
            can inspire positive change in modern society. Reflect on the
            broader implications of the book\'s themes and leave the reader
            with a lasting impression.\n\nBy expanding on your analysis,
            incorporating more examples, and deepening your exploration of the
            book\'s messages, you can create a more comprehensive and
            compelling essay on the topicality of "The Little Prince" in modern
            life. Well done on your thoughtful analysis, and keep up the good
            work!', id='70c22b1d-ec96-4dc3-9fd0-d2c6463f9e2c'),
    ],
}
```

And the final output:

```
{
    'messages': [
        AIMessage(content='"The Little Prince" by Antoine de Saint-Exupéry
            stands as a timeless masterpiece that continues to offer profound
            insights into human relationships and values, resonating with
            readers across generations. The narrative of the Little Prince\'s
            travels and encounters with a myriad of characters serves as a rich
            tapestry of allegorical representations, ....', response_metadata=
            {'token_usage': {'completion_tokens': 420, 'prompt_tokens': 2501,
            'total_tokens': 2921}, 'model_name': 'gpt-3.5-turbo',
            'system_fingerprint': None, 'finish_reason': 'stop', 'logprobs':
            None}, id='run-2e8f9f13-f625-4820-9c8b-b64e1c23daa2-0',
            usage_metadata={'input_tokens': 2501, 'output_tokens': 420,
            'total_tokens': 2921}),
    ],
}
```

This simple type of reflection can sometimes improve performance by giving the LLM multiple attempts at refining its output and by letting the reflection node adopt a different persona while critiquing the output.

There are several possible variations of this architecture. For one, we could combine the reflection step with the agent architecture of Chapter 6, adding it as the last node right before sending output to the user. This would make the critique appear to come from the user, and give the application a chance to improve its final output without direct user intervention. Obviously this approach would come at the expense of higher latency.

In certain use cases, it could be helpful to ground the critique with external information. For instance, if you were writing a code-generation agent, you could have a step before `reflect` that would run the code through a linter or compiler and report any errors as input to `reflect`.

 Whenever this approach is possible, we strongly recommend giving it a try, as it's likely to increase the quality of the final output.

Subgraphs in LangGraph

Before we dive into multi-agent architectures, let's look at an important technical concept in LangGraph that enables it. *Subgraphs* are graphs that are used as part of another graph. Here are some use cases for subgraphs:

- Building multi-agent systems (discussed in the next section).
- When you want to reuse a set of nodes in multiple graphs, you can define them once in a subgraph and then use them in multiple parent graphs.
- When you want different teams to work on different parts of the graph independently, you can define each part as a subgraph, and as long as the subgraph interface (the input and output schemas) is respected, the parent graph can be built without knowing any details of the subgraph.

There are two ways to add subgraph nodes to a parent graph:

Add a node that calls the subgraph directly
This is useful when the parent graph and the subgraph share state keys, and you don't need to transform state on the way in or out.

Add a node with a function that invokes the subgraph
This is useful when the parent graph and the subgraph have different state schemas, and you need to transform state before or after calling the subgraph.

Let's look at each in turn.

Calling a Subgraph Directly

The simplest way to create subgraph nodes is to attach a subgraph directly as a node. When doing so, it is important that the parent graph and the subgraph share state keys, because those shared keys will be used to communicate. (If your graph and subgraph do not share any keys, see the next section.)

 If you pass extra keys to the subgraph node (that is, in addition to the shared keys), they will be ignored by the subgraph node. Similarly, if you return extra keys from the subgraph, they will be ignored by the parent graph.

Let's see what it looks like in action:

Python

```python
from langgraph.graph import START, StateGraph
from typing import TypedDict

class State(TypedDict):
    foo: str # this key is shared with the subgraph

class SubgraphState(TypedDict):
    foo: str # this key is shared with the parent graph
    bar: str
```

```python
# Define subgraph
def subgraph_node(state: SubgraphState):
    # note that this subgraph node can communicate with the parent graph
    # via the shared "foo" key
    return {"foo": state["foo"] + "bar"}

subgraph_builder = StateGraph(SubgraphState)
subgraph_builder.add_node(subgraph_node)
...
subgraph = subgraph_builder.compile()

# Define parent graph
builder = StateGraph(State)
builder.add_node("subgraph", subgraph)
...
graph = builder.compile()
```

JavaScript

```javascript
import { StateGraph, Annotation, START } from "@langchain/langgraph";

const StateAnnotation = Annotation.Root({
  foo: Annotation(),
});

const SubgraphStateAnnotation = Annotation.Root({
  // note that this key is shared with the parent graph state
  foo: Annotation(),
  bar: Annotation(),
});

// Define subgraph
const subgraphNode = async (state) => {
  // note that this subgraph node can communicate with
  // the parent graph via the shared "foo" key
  return { foo: state.foo + "bar" };
};

const subgraph = new StateGraph(SubgraphStateAnnotation)
  .addNode("subgraph", subgraphNode);
  ...
  .compile();

// Define parent graph
const parentGraph = new StateGraph(StateAnnotation)
  .addNode("subgraph", subgraph)
  .addEdge(START, "subgraph")
  // Additional parent graph setup would go here
  .compile();
```

Calling a Subgraph with a Function

You might want to define a subgraph with a completely different schema. In that case, you can create a node with a function that invokes the subgraph. This function will need to transform the input (parent) state to the subgraph state before invoking the subgraph and transform the results back to the parent state before returning the state update from the node.

Let's see what it looks like:

Python

```python
class State(TypedDict):
    foo: str

class SubgraphState(TypedDict):
    # none of these keys are shared with the parent graph state
    bar: str
    baz: str

# Define subgraph
def subgraph_node(state: SubgraphState):
    return {"bar": state["bar"] + "baz"}

subgraph_builder = StateGraph(SubgraphState)
subgraph_builder.add_node(subgraph_node)
...
subgraph = subgraph_builder.compile()

# Define parent graph
def node(state: State):
    # transform the state to the subgraph state
    response = subgraph.invoke({"bar": state["foo"]})
    # transform response back to the parent state
    return {"foo": response["bar"]}

builder = StateGraph(State)
# note that we are using `node` function instead of a compiled subgraph
builder.add_node(node)
...
graph = builder.compile()
```

JavaScript

```javascript
import { StateGraph, START, Annotation } from "@langchain/langgraph";

const StateAnnotation = Annotation.Root({
  foo: Annotation(),
});

const SubgraphStateAnnotation = Annotation.Root({
  // note that none of these keys are shared with the parent graph state
```

```
  bar: Annotation(),
  baz: Annotation(),
});

// Define subgraph
const subgraphNode = async (state) => {
  return { bar: state.bar + "baz" };
};

const subgraph = new StateGraph(SubgraphStateAnnotation)
  .addNode("subgraph", subgraphNode);
  ...
  .compile();

// Define parent graph
const subgraphWrapperNode = async (state) => {
  // transform the state to the subgraph state
  const response = await subgraph.invoke({
    bar: state.foo,
  });
  // transform response back to the parent state
  return {
    foo: response.bar,
  };
}

const parentGraph = new StateGraph(StateAnnotation)
  .addNode("subgraph", subgraphWrapperNode)
  .addEdge(START, "subgraph")
  // Additional parent graph setup would go here
  .compile();
```

Now that we know how to use subgraphs, let's take a look at one of the big use cases for them: multi-agent architectures.

Multi-Agent Architectures

As LLM agents grow in size, scope, or complexity, several issues can show up and impact their performance, such as the following:

- The agent is given too many tools to choose from and makes poor decisions about which tool to call next (Chapter 6 discussed some approaches to this problem).

- The context grows too complex for a single agent to keep track of; that is, the size of the prompts and the number of things they mention grows beyond the capability of the model you're using.

- You want to use a specialized subsystem for a particular area, for instance, planning, research, solving math problems, and so on.

To tackle these problems, you might consider breaking your application into multiple smaller, independent agents and composing them into a multi-agent system. These independent agents can be as simple as a prompt and an LLM call or as complex as a ReAct agent (introduced in Chapter 6). Figure 7-3 illustrates several ways to connect agents in a multi-agent system.

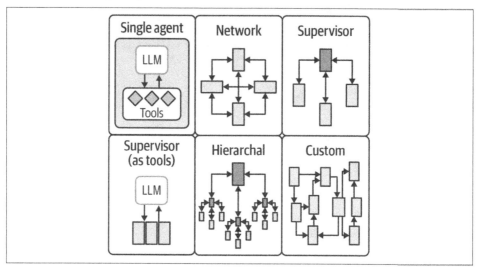

Figure 7-3. Multiple strategies for coordinating multiple agents

Let's look at Figure 7-3 in more detail:

Network
> Each agent can communicate with every other agent. Any agent can decide which other agent is to be executed next.

Supervisor
> Each agent communicates with a single agent, called the *supervisor*. The supervisor agent makes decisions on which agent (or agents) should be called next. A special case of this architecture implements the supervisor agent as an LLM call with tools, as covered in Chapter 6.

Hierarchical
> You can define a multi-agent system with a supervisor of supervisors. This is a generalization of the supervisor architecture and allows for more complex control flows.

Custom multi-agent workflow
> Each agent communicates with only a subset of agents. Parts of the flow are deterministic, and only select agents can decide which other agents to call next.

The next section dives deeper into the supervisor architecture, which we think has a good balance of capability and ease of use.

Supervisor Architecture

In this architecture, we add each agent to the graph as a node and also add a supervisor node, which decides which agents should be called next. We use conditional edges to route execution to the appropriate agent node based on the supervisor's decision. Refer back to Chapter 5 for an introduction to LangGraph, which goes over the concepts of nodes, edges, and more.

Let's first see what the supervisor node looks like:

Python

```python
from typing import Literal
from langchain_openai import ChatOpenAI
from pydantic import BaseModel

class SupervisorDecision(BaseModel):
    next: Literal["researcher", "coder", "FINISH"]

model = ChatOpenAI(model="gpt-4o", temperature=0)
model = model.with_structured_output(SupervisorDecision)

agents = ["researcher", "coder"]

system_prompt_part_1 = f"""You are a supervisor tasked with managing a
conversation between the following workers: {agents}. Given the following user
request, respond with the worker to act next. Each worker will perform a
task and respond with their results and status. When finished,
respond with FINISH."""

system_prompt_part_2 = f"""Given the conversation above, who should act next? Or
    should we FINISH? Select one of: {', '.join(agents)}, FINISH"""

def supervisor(state):
    messages = [
        ("system", system_prompt_part_1),
        *state["messages"],
        ("system",      system_prompt_part_2)
    ]
    return model.invoke(messages)
```

JavaScript

```javascript
import { ChatOpenAI } from 'langchain-openai';
import { z } from 'zod';

const SupervisorDecision = z.object({
  next: z.enum(['researcher', 'coder', 'FINISH']),
});
```

```
const model = new ChatOpenAI({ model: 'gpt-4o', temperature: 0 });
const modelWithStructuredOutput = model.withStructuredOutput(SupervisorDecision);

const agents = ['researcher', 'coder'];

const systemPromptPart1 = `You are a supervisor tasked with managing a
  conversation between the following workers: ${agents.join(', ')}. Given the
  following user request, respond with the worker to act next. Each worker
  will perform a task and respond with their results and status. When
  finished, respond with FINISH.`;

const systemPromptPart2 = `Given the conversation above, who should act next? Or
  should we FINISH? Select one of: ${agents.join(', ')}, FINISH`;

const supervisor = async (state) => {
  const messages = [
    { role: 'system', content: systemPromptPart1 },
    ...state.messages,
    { role: 'system', content: systemPromptPart2 }
  ];

  return await modelWithStructuredOutput.invoke({ messages });
};
```

 The code in the prompt requires the names of your subagents to be self-explanatory and distinct. For instance, if they were simply called agent_1 and agent_2, the LLM would have no information to decide which one is appropriate for each task. If needed, you could modify the prompt to add a description of each agent, which could help the LLM in picking an agent for each query.

Now let's see how to integrate this supervisor node into a larger graph that includes two other subagents, which we will call researcher and coder. Our overall goal with this graph is to handle queries that can be answered either by the researcher by itself or the coder by itself, or even both of them in succession. This example doesn't include implementations for either the researcher or coder—the key idea is they could be any other LangGraph graph or node:

Python

```
from typing import Literal
from langchain_openai import ChatOpenAI
from langgraph.graph import StateGraph, MessagesState, START

model = ChatOpenAI()

class AgentState(BaseModel):
    next: Literal["researcher", "coder", "FINISH"]
```

```python
def researcher(state: AgentState):
    response = model.invoke(...)
    return {"messages": [response]}

def coder(state: AgentState):
    response = model.invoke(...)
    return {"messages": [response]}

builder = StateGraph(AgentState)
builder.add_node(supervisor)
builder.add_node(researcher)
builder.add_node(coder)

builder.add_edge(START, "supervisor")
# route to one of the agents or exit based on the supervisor's decision
builder.add_conditional_edges("supervisor", lambda state: state["next"])
builder.add_edge("researcher", "supervisor")
builder.add_edge("coder", "supervisor")

supervisor = builder.compile()
```

JavaScript

```javascript
import {
  StateGraph,
  Annotation,
  MessagesAnnotation,
  START,
  END,
} from "@langchain/langgraph";
import { ChatOpenAI } from "@langchain/openai";

const model = new ChatOpenAI({
  model: "gpt-4o",
});

const StateAnnotation = Annotation.Root({
  ...MessagesAnnotation.spec,
  next: Annotation(),
});

const researcher = async (state) => {
  const response = await model.invoke(...);
  return { messages: [response] };
};

const coder = async (state) => {
  const response = await model.invoke(...);
  return { messages: [response] };
};

const graph = new StateGraph(StateAnnotation)
  .addNode("supervisor", supervisor)
```

```
.addNode("researcher", researcher)
.addNode("coder", coder)
.addEdge(START, "supervisor")
// route to one of the agents or exit based on the supervisor's decision
.addConditionalEdges("supervisor", async (state) =>
  state.next === 'FINISH' ? END : state.next)
.addEdge("researcher", "supervisor")
.addEdge("coder", "supervisor")
.compile();
```

A few things to notice: In this example, both subagents (researcher and coder) can see each other's work, as all progress is recorded in the messages list. This isn't the only way to organize this. Each of the subagents could be more complex. For instance, a subagent could be its own graph that maintains internal state and only outputs a summary of the work it did.

After each agent executes, we route back to the supervisor node, which decides if there is more work to be done and which agent to delegate that to if so. This routing isn't a hard requirement for this architecture; we could have each subagent make a decision as to whether its output should be returned directly to the user. To do that, we'd replace the hard edge between, say, researcher and supervisor, with a conditional edge (which would read some state key updated by researcher).

Summary

This chapter covered two important extensions to the agent architecture: reflection and multi-agent architectures. The chapter also looked at how to work with subgraphs in LangGraph, which are a key building block for multi-agent systems.

These extensions add more power to the LLM agent architecture, but they shouldn't be the first thing you reach for when creating a new agent. The best place to start is usually the straightforward architecture we discussed in Chapter 6.

Chapter 8 returns to the trade-off between reliability and agency, which is the key design decision when building LLM apps today. This is especially important when using the agent or multi-agent architectures, as their power comes at the expense of reliability if left unchecked. After diving deeper into why this trade-off exists, Chapter 8 will cover the most important techniques at your disposal to navigate that decision, and ultimately improve your LLM applications and agents.

Patterns to Make the Most of LLMs

LLMs today have some major limitations, but that doesn't mean your dream LLM app is impossible to build. The experience that you design for users of your application needs to work around, and ideally with, the limitations.

Chapter 5 touched on the key trade-off we face when building LLM apps: the trade-off between *agency* (the LLM's capacity to act autonomously) and *reliability* (the degree to which we can trust its outputs). Intuitively, any LLM application will be more useful to us if it takes more actions without our involvement, but if we let agency go too far, the application will inevitably do things we wish it hadn't.

Figure 8-1 illustrates this trade-off.

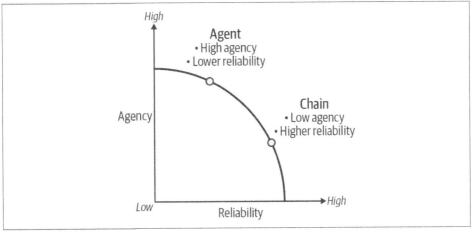

Figure 8-1. The agency-reliability trade-off

To borrow a concept from other fields,[1] we can visualize the trade-off as a *frontier*—all points on the frontier's curved line are optimal LLM architectures for some application, marking different choices between agency and reliability. (Refer to Chapter 5 for an overview of different LLM application architectures.) As an example, notice how the chain architecture has relatively low agency but higher reliability, whereas the Agent architecture has higher agency at the expense of lower reliability.

Let's briefly touch on a number of additional (but still important) objectives that you might want your LLM application to have. Each LLM app will be designed for a different mix of one or more of these objectives:

Latency
    Minimize time to get final answer

Autonomy
    Minimize interruptions for human input

Variance
    Minimize variation between invocations

This is not meant as an exhaustive list of all possible objectives, but rather as illustrative of the trade-offs you face when building your application. Each objective is somewhat at odds with all the others (for instance, the easiest path to higher reliability requires either higher latency or lower autonomy). Each objective would nullify the others if given full weight (for instance, the minimal latency app is the one that does nothing at all). Figure 8-2 illustrates this concept.

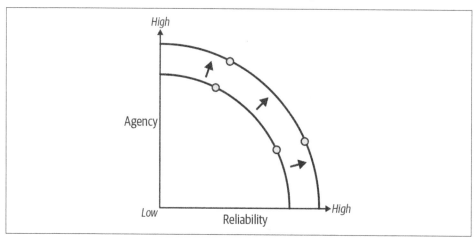

Figure 8-2. Shifting the frontier, or more agency, for the same reliability

---

What we really want as application developers is to shift the frontier outward. For the same level of reliability, we'd like to achieve higher agency; and for the same level of agency, we'd like to achieve higher reliability. This chapter covers a number of techniques you can use to achieve this:

Streaming/intermediate output
> Higher latency is easier to accept if there is some communication of progress/intermediate output throughout.

Structured output
> Requiring an LLM to produce output in a predefined format makes it more likely that it will conform to expectations.

Human in the loop
> Higher-agency architectures benefit from human intervention while they're running: interrupting, approving, forking, or undoing.

Double texting modes
> The longer an LLM app takes to answer, the more likely it is that the user might send it new input before the previous one has finished being processed.

Structured Output

It is often crucial to have LLMs return structured output, either because a downstream use of that output expects a things in a specific *schema* (a definition of the names and types of the various fields in a piece of structured output) or purely to reduce variance to what would otherwise be completely free-form text output.

There are a few different strategies you can use for this with different LLMs:

Prompting
> This is when you ask the LLM (very nicely) to return output in the desired format (for instance, JSON, XML, or CSV). Prompting's big advantage is that it works to some extent with any LLM; the downside is that it acts more as a suggestion to the LLM and not as a guarantee that the output will come out in this format.

Tool calling
> This is available for LLMs that have been fine-tuned to pick from a list of possible output schemas, and to produce something that conforms to the chosen one. This usually involves writing, for each of the possible output schemas: a name to identify it, a description to help the LLM decide when it is the appropriate choice, and a schema for the desired output format (usually in JSONSchema notation).

JSON mode
> This is a mode available in some LLMs (such as recent OpenAI models) that enforces the LLM to output a valid JSON document.

Different models may support different variants of these, with slightly different parameters. To make it easy to get LLMs to return structured output, LangChain models implement a common interface, a method called `.with_structured_output`. By invoking this method—and passing in a JSON schema or a Pydantic (in Python) or Zod (in JS) model—the model will add whatever model parameters and output parsers are necessary to produce and return the structured output. When a particular model implements more than one of the preceding strategies, you can configure which method to use.

Let's create a schema to use:

Python

```python
from pydantic import BaseModel, Field


class Joke(BaseModel):
    setup: str = Field(description="The setup of the joke")
    punchline: str = Field(description="The punchline to the joke")
```

JavaScript

```javascript
import { z } from "zod";

const joke = z.object({
  setup: z.string().describe("The setup of the joke"),
  punchline: z.string().describe("The punchline to the joke"),
});
```

Notice how we take care to add a description to each field. This is key because—together with the name of the field—this is the information the LLM will use to decide what part of the output should go in each field. We could also have defined a schema in raw JSONSchema notation, which would look like this:

```json
{'properties': {'setup': {'description': 'The setup of the joke',
    'title': 'Setup',
    'type': 'string'},
  'punchline': {'description': 'The punchline to the joke',
    'title': 'Punchline',
    'type': 'string'}},
 'required': ['setup', 'punchline'],
 'title': 'Joke',
 'type': 'object'}
```

And now let's get an LLM to generate output that conforms to this schema:

Python

```python
from langchain_openai import ChatOpenAI

model = ChatOpenAI(model="gpt-3.5-turbo", temperature=0)
model = model.with_structured_output(Joke)

model.invoke("Tell me a joke about cats")
```

JavaScript

```javascript
import { ChatOpenAI } from "@langchain/openai";

let model = new ChatOpenAI({
  model: "gpt-3.5-turbo",
  temperature: 0
});
model = model.withStructuredOutput(joke);

await structuredLlm.invoke("Tell me a joke about cats");
```

An example of output

```
{
    setup: "Why don't cats play poker in the wild?",
    punchline: "Too many cheetahs."
}
```

A couple of things to notice:

- We create the instance of the model as usual, specifying the model name to use and other parameters.
- Low temperature is usually a good fit for structured output, as it reduces the chance the LLM will produce invalid output that doesn't conform to the schema.
- Afterward, we attach the schema to the model, which returns a new object, which will produce output that matches the schema provided. When you pass in a Pydantic or Zod object for schema, this will be used for validation as well; that is, if the LLM produces output that doesn't conform, a validation error will be returned to you instead of the failed output.
- Finally, we invoke the model with our (free-form) input, and receive back output that matches the structure we desired.

This pattern of using structured output can be very useful both as a standalone tool and as a part of a larger application; for instance, refer back to Chapter 5, where we make use of this capability to implement the routing step of the router architecture.

Intermediate Output

The more complex your LLM architecture becomes, the more likely it will take longer to execute. If you think back to the architecture diagrams in Chapters 5 and 6, every time you see multiple steps (or nodes) connected in sequence or in a loop, that is an indication that the time it takes for a full invocation is increasing.

This increase in latency—if not addressed—can be a blocker to user adoption of LLM applications, with most users expecting computer applications to produce some output within seconds. There are several strategies to make the higher latency more palatable, but they all fall under the umbrella of *streaming output*, that is, receiving output from the application while it is still running.

For this section, we'll use the last architecture described in "Dealing with Many Tools" on page 148. Refer back to Chapter 6 for the full code snippet.

To generate intermediate output with LangGraph, all you have to do is to invoke the graph with the `stream` method, which will yield the output of each node as soon as each finishes. Let's see what that looks like:

Python

```python
input = {
    "messages": [
        HumanMessage("""How old was the 30th president of the United States
            when he died?""")
    ]
}
for c in graph.stream(input, stream_mode='updates'):
    print(c)
```

JavaScript

```javascript
const input = {
  messages: [
    new HumanMessage(`How old was the 30th president of the United States when
      he died?`)
  ]
}
const output = await graph.stream(input, streamMode: 'updates')
for await (const c of output) {
  console.log(c)
}
```

The output:

```
{
    "select_tools": {
        "selected_tools": ['duckduckgo_search', 'calculator']
    }
}
{
```

```
"model": {
    "messages": AIMessage(
        content="",
        tool_calls=[
            {
                "name": "duckduckgo_search",
                "args": {
                    "query": "30th president of the United States"
                },
                "id": "9ed4328dcdea4904b1b54487e343a373",
                "type": "tool_call",
            }
        ],
    )
}
}
{
    "tools": {
        "messages": [
            ToolMessage(
                content="Calvin Coolidge (born July 4, 1872, Plymouth, Vermont,
                    U.S.–died January 5, 1933, Northampton, Massachusetts) was
                    the 30th president of the United States (1923-29). Coolidge
                    acceded to the presidency after the death in office of
                    Warren G. Harding, just as the Harding scandals were coming
                    to light....",
                name="duckduckgo_search",
                tool_call_id="9ed4328dcdea4904b1b54487e343a373",
            )
        ]
    }
}
{
    "model": {
        "messages": AIMessage(
            content="Calvin Coolidge, the 30th president of the United States,
                was born on July 4, 1872, and died on January 5, 1933. To
                calculate his age at the time of his death, we can subtract his
                birth year from his death year. \n\nAge at death = Death year -
                Birth year\nAge at death = 1933 - 1872\nAge at death = 61
                years\n\nCalvin Coolidge was 61 years old when he died.",
        )
    }
}
```

Notice how each output entry is a dictionary with the name of the node that emitted as the key and the output of that node as the value. This gives you two key pieces of information:

- Where the application currently is; that is, if you think back to the architecture diagrams shown in previous chapters, where in that diagram are we currently?

- Each update to the shared state of the application, which together build up to the final output of the graph.

In addition, LangGraph supports more stream modes:

- `updates`. This is the default mode, described above.
- `values`. This mode yields the current state of the graph every time it changes, that is after each set of nodes finishes executing. This can be useful when the way you display output to your users closely tracks the shape of the graph state.
- `debug`. This mode yields detailed events every time something happens in your graph, including:
  - checkpoint events, whenever a new checkpoint of the current state is saved to the database
  - task events, emitted whenever a node is about to start running
  - task_result events, emitted whenever a node finishes running
- Finally, you can combine these modes; for instance, requesting both `updates` and `values` by passing a list.

You control the stream mode with the `stream_mode` argument to `stream()`.

Streaming LLM Output Token-by-Token

Sometimes you may also want to get streaming output from each LLM call inside your larger LLM application. This can be useful for various projects, such as when building an interactive chatbot, where you want each word to be displayed as soon as it is produced by the LLM.

You can achieve this with LangGraph as well:

Python

```python
input = {
    "messages": [
        HumanMessage("""How old was the 30th president of the United States
            when he died?""")
    ]
}
output = app.astream_events(input, version="v2")

async for event in output:
    if event["event"] == "on_chat_model_stream":
        content = event["data"]["chunk"].content
        if content:
            print(content)
```

JavaScript

```javascript
const input = {
  messages: [
    new HumanMessage(`How old was the 30th president of the United States when
      he died?`)
  ]
}

const output = await agent.streamEvents(input, {version: "v2"});

for await (const { event, data } of output) {
  if (event === "on_chat_model_stream") {
    const msg = data.chunk as AIMessageChunk;
    if (msg.content) {
      console.log(msg.content);
    }
  }
}
```

This will emit each word (technically each token) as soon as it is received from
the LLM. You can find more details on this pattern from LangChain (*https://oreil.ly/
ExYll*).

Human-in-the-Loop Modalities

As we walk the autonomy (or agency) ladder, we find ourselves increasingly giving
up control (or oversight) in exchange for capability (or autonomy). The shared state
pattern used in LangGraph (see Chapter 5 for an introduction) makes it easier to
observe, interrupt, and modify the application. This makes it possible to use many
different *human-in-the-loop* modes, or ways for the developer/end user of an application to influence what the LLM is up to.

For this section, we'll again use the last architecture described in "Dealing with
Many Tools" on page 148. Refer back to Chapter 6 for the full code snippet. For all
human-in-the-loop modes, we first need to attach a checkpointer to the graph; refer
to "Adding Memory to StateGraph" on page 105 for more details on this:

Python

```python
from langgraph.checkpoint.memory import MemorySaver

graph = builder.compile(checkpointer=MemorySaver())
```

JavaScript

```javascript
import {MemorySaver} from '@langchain/langgraph'

graph = builder.compile({ checkpointer: new MemorySaver() })
```

This returns an instance of the graph that stores the state at the end of each step, so every invocation after the first doesn't start from a blank slate. Any time the graph is called, it starts by using the checkpointer to fetch the most recent saved state—if any—and combines the new input with the previous state. And only then does it execute the first nodes. This is key to enabling human-in-the-loop modalities, which all rely on the graph remembering the previous state.

The first mode, interrupt, is the simplest form of control—the user is looking at streaming output of the application as it is produced, and manually interrupts it when he sees fit (see Figure 8-3). The state is saved as of the last complete step prior to the user hitting the interrupt button. From there the user can choose to:

- Resume from that point onward, and the computation will proceed as if it hadn't been interrupted (see "Resume" on page 183).
- Send new input into the application (e.g., a new message in a chatbot), which will cancel any future steps that were pending and start dealing with the new input (see "Restart" on page 184).
- Do nothing and nothing else will run.

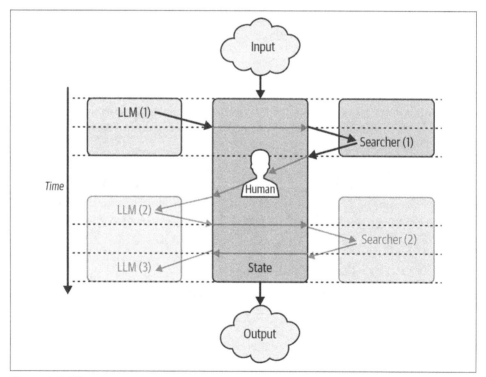

Figure 8-3. The interrupt pattern

Let's see how to do this in LangGraph:

Python

```python
import asyncio

event = asyncio.Event()

input = {
    "messages": [
        HumanMessage("""How old was the 30th president of the United States
            when he died?""")
    ]
}

config = {"configurable": {"thread_id": "1"}}

async with aclosing(graph.astream(input, config)) as stream:
    async for chunk in stream:
        if event.is_set():
            break
        else:
            ... # do something with the output

# Somewhere else in your application

event.set()
```

JavaScript

```javascript
const controller = new AbortController()

const input = {
  "messages": [
    new HumanMessage(`How old was the 30th president of the United States when
      he died?`)
  ]
}

const config = {"configurable": {"thread_id": "1"}}

try {
  const output = await graph.stream(input, {
    ...config,
    signal: controller.signal
  });
  for await (const chunk of output) {
    console.log(chunk); // do something with the output
  }
} catch (e) {
  console.log(e);
}
```

```
// Somewhere else in your application
controller.abort()
```

This makes use of an event or signal, so that you can control interruption from outside of the running application. Notice in the Python code block the use of `aclosing`; this ensures the stream is properly closed when interrupted. Notice in JS the use of the `try-catch` statement, as interrupting the run will result in an `abort` exception being raised. Finally notice that usage of the checkpointer requires passing in an identifier for this thread, to distinguish this interaction with the graph from all others.

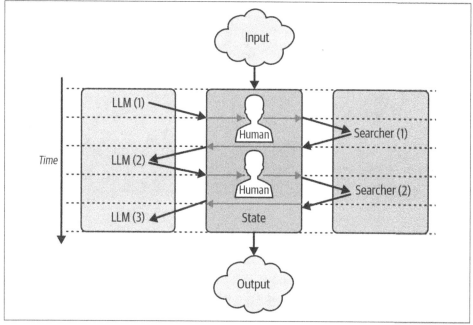

Figure 8-4. The authorize *pattern*

A second control mode is `authorize`, where the user defines ahead of time that they want the application to hand off control to them every time a particular node is about to be called (see Figure 8-4). This is usually implemented for tool confirmation—before any tool (or particular tools) is called, the application will pause and ask for confirmation, at which point the user can, again:

- Resume computation, accepting the tool call.
- Send a new message to guide the bot in a different direction, in which case the tool will not be called.
- Do nothing.

Here's the code:

Python

```python
input = {
    "messages": [
        HumanMessage("""How old was the 30th president of the United States
            when he died?""")
    ]
}

config = {"configurable": {"thread_id": "1"}}

output = graph.astream(input, config, interrupt_before=['tools'])

async for c in output:
    ... # do something with the output
```

JavaScript

```javascript
const input = {
  "messages": [
    new HumanMessage(`How old was the 30th president of the United States when
      he died?`)
  ]
}

const config = {"configurable": {"thread_id": "1"}}

const output = await graph.stream(input, {
  ...config,
  interruptBefore: ['tools']
});
for await (const chunk of output) {
  console.log(chunk); // do something with the output
}
```

This will run the graph up until it is about to enter the node called tools, thus giving you the chance to inspect the current state, and decide whether to proceed or not. Notice that interrupt_before is a list where order is not important; if you pass multiple node names, it will interrupt before entering each of them.

Resume

To proceed from an interrupted graph—such as when using one of the previous two patterns—you just need to re-invoke the graph with null input (or None in Python). This is taken as a signal to continue processing the previous non-null input:

Python

```python
config = {"configurable": {"thread_id": "1"}}

output = graph.astream(None, config, interrupt_before=['tools'])
```

```
async for c in output:
    ... # do something with the output
```

JavaScript

```
const config = {"configurable": {"thread_id": "1"}}

const output = await graph.stream(null, {
  ...config,
  interruptBefore: ['tools']
});
for await (const chunk of output) {
  console.log(chunk); // do something with the output
}
```

Restart

If instead you want an interrupted graph to start over from the first node, with additional new input, you just need to invoke it with new input:

Python

```
input = {
    "messages": [
        HumanMessage("""How old was the 30th president of the United States
            when he died?""")
    ]
}

config = {"configurable": {"thread_id": "1"}}

output = graph.astream(input, config)

async for c in output:
    ... # do something with the output
```

JavaScript

```
const input = {
  "messages": [
    new HumanMessage(`How old was the 30th president of the United States when
      he died?`)
  ]
}

const config = {"configurable": {"thread_id": "1"}}

const output = await graph.stream(input, config);

for await (const chunk of output) {
  console.log(chunk); // do something with the output
}
```

This will keep the current state of the graph, merge it with the new input, and start again from the first node.

If you want to lose the current state, just change the thread_id, which will start a new interaction from a blank slate. Any string value is a valid thread_id; we'd recommend using UUIDs (or other unique identifiers) as thread IDs.

Edit state

Sometimes you might want to update the state of the graph before resuming; this is possible with the update_state method. You'll usually want to first inspect the current state with get_state.

Here's what it looks like:

Python

```
config = {"configurable": {"thread_id": "1"}}

state = graph.get_state(config)

# something you want to add or replace
update = { }

graph.update_state(config, update)
```

JavaScript

```
const config = "configurable": {"thread_id": "1"}

const state = await graph.getState(config)

// something you want to add or replace
const update = { }

await graph.updateState(config, update)
```

This will create a new checkpoint containing your update. After this, you're ready to resume the graph from this new point. See "Resume" on page 183 to find out how.

Fork

You can also browse the history of all past states the graph has passed through, and any of them can be visited again, for instance, to get an alternative answer. This can be very useful in more creative applications, where each run through the graph is expected to produce different output.

Let's see what it looks like:

Python

```python
config = {"configurable": {"thread_id": "1"}}

history = [
    state for state in
    graph.get_state_history(config)
]

# replay a past state
graph.invoke(None, history[2].config)
```

JavaScript

```javascript
const config = "configurable": {"thread_id": "1"}

const history = await Array.fromAsync(graph.getStateHistory(config))

// replay a past state
await graph.invoke(null, history[2].config)
```

Notice how we collect the history into a list/array in both languages; `get_state_history` returns an iterator of states (to allow consuming lazily). The states returned from the history method are sorted with the most recent first and the oldest last.

The true power of the human-in-the-loop controls comes from mixing them in whatever way suits your application.

Multitasking LLMs

This section covers the problem of handling concurrent input for LLM applications. This is a particularly relevant problem given that LLMs are quite slow, much more so when producing long outputs or when chained in multistep architectures (like you can do with LangGraph). Even as LLMs become faster, dealing with concurrent inputs will continue to be a challenge, as latency improvements will also unlock the door for more and more complex use cases, in much the same way as even the most productive person still faces the need to prioritize competing demands on their time.

Let's walk through the options.

Refuse concurrent inputs

Any input received while processing a previous one is rejected. This is the simplest strategy, but unlikely to cover all needs, as it effectively means handing off concurrency management to the caller.

Handle independently

Another simple option is to treat any new input as an independent invocation, creating a new thread (a container for remembering state) and producing output in that context. This has the obvious downside of needing to be shown to the user as two separate and unreconcilable invocations, which isn't always possible or desirable. On the other hand, it has the upside of scaling to arbitrarily large sizes, and is something you'll use to some extent in your application almost certainly. For instance, this is how you would think about the problem of getting a chatbot to "chat" with two different users concurrently.

Queue concurrent inputs

Any input received while processing a previous one is queued up and handled when the current one is finished. This strategy has some pros:

- It supports receiving an arbitrary number of concurrent requests.
- Because we wait for current input to finish processing, it doesn't matter if the new input arrives almost immediately after we start handling the current input or immediately before we finish; the end result will be the same, as we will finish processing the current input before moving on to the next.

The strategy suffers from a few drawbacks as well:

- It may take a while to process all queued inputs; in fact, the queue may grow unbounded if inputs are produced at a rate faster than processed.
- The inputs may be stale by the time they get processed, given that they are queued before seeing the response to the previous one, and not altered afterwards. This strategy is not appropriate when new inputs depend on previous answers.

Interrupt

When a new input is received while another is being processed, abandon processing of the current one and restart the chain with the new input. This strategy can vary by what is kept of the interrupted run. Here are a few options:

- Keep nothing. The previous input is completely forgotten, as if it had never been sent or processed.
- Keep the last completed step. In a checkpointing app (which stores progress as it moves through the computation), keep the state produced by the last completed step, discard any pending state updates from the currently executing step, and start handling the new input in that context.

- Keep the last completed step, as well as the current in-progress step. Attempt to interrupt the current step while taking care to save any incomplete updates to state that were being produced at the time. This is likely to not generalize beyond the simplest architectures.

- Wait for the current node (but not any subsequent nodes) to finish, then save and interrupt.

This option has some pros compared to queuing concurrent inputs:

- New input is handled as soon as possible, reducing latency and the chance of producing stale outputs.

- For the "keep nothing" variant, the final output doesn't depend on when the new input was received.

But it also has drawbacks:

- Effectively, this strategy is still limited to processing one input at a time; any old input is abandoned when new input is received.

- Keeping partial state updates for the next run requires the state to be designed with that in mind; if not, then your application is likely to end up in an invalid state. For instance, OpenAI chat models require an AI message requesting tool calls to be immediately followed by tool messages with the tool outputs. If your run is interrupted in between, you either defensively clean up the intermediate state or risk being unable to progress further.

- The final outputs produced are very sensitive to when the new input is received; new input will be handled in the context of the (incomplete) progress previously made toward handling the previous input. This can result in brittle or unpredictable outcomes if you don't design accordingly.

Fork and merge

Another option is to handle new input in parallel, forking the state of the thread as it is when the new input is received and merging the final states as inputs finish being handled. This option requires designing your state to either be mergeable without conflicts (e.g., using conflict-free replicated data types [CRDTs] or other conflict resolution algorithms) or having the user manually resolve conflicts before you're able to make sense of the output or send new input in this thread. If either of those two requirements is met, this is likely to be the best option overall. This way, new input is handled in a timely manner, output is independent of time received, and it supports an arbitrary number of concurrent runs.

Some of these strategies are implemented in LangGraph Platform, which will be covered in Chapter 9.

Summary

In this chapter, we returned to the main trade-off you face when building LLM applications: agency versus reliability. We learned that there are strategies to partially beat the odds and get more reliability without sacrificing agency, and vice versa.

We started by covering structured outputs, which can improve the predictability of LLM-generated text. Next, we discussed emitting streaming/intermediate output from your application, which can make high latency (an inevitable side effect of agency currently) applications pleasant to use.

We also walked through a variety of human-in-the-loop controls—that is, techniques to give back some oversight to the end user of your LLM application—which can often make the difference in making high-agency architectures reliable. Finally, we talked about the problem of handling concurrent input to your application, a particularly salient problem for LLM apps given their high latency.

In the next chapter, you'll learn how to deploy your AI application into production.

## CHAPTER 9

Deployment: Launching Your AI Application into Production

So far, we've explored the key concepts, ideas, and tools to help you build the core functionality of your AI application. You've learned how to utilize LangChain and LangGraph to generate LLM outputs, index and retrieve data, and enable memory and agency.

But your application is limited to your local environment, so external users can't access its features yet.

In this chapter, you'll learn the best practices for deploying your AI application into production. We'll also explore various tools to debug, collaborate, test, and monitor your LLM applications.

Let's get started.

Prerequisites

In order to effectively deploy your AI application, you need to utilize various services to host your application, store and retrieve data, and monitor your application. In the deployment example in this chapter, we will incorporate the following services:

Vector store
  Supabase

Monitoring and debugging
  LangSmith

Backend API
  LangGraph Platform

We will dive deeper into each of these components and services and see how to adapt them for your use case. But first, let's install necessary dependencies and set up the environment variables.

If you'd like to follow the example, fork this LangChain template (*https://oreil.ly/ brqVm*) to your GitHub account. This repository contains the full logic of a retrieval agent-based AI application.

Install Dependencies

First, follow the instructions in the *README.md* file (*https://oreil.ly/N5eqe*) to install the project dependencies.

If you're not using the template, you can install the dependencies individually from the respective *pyproject.toml* or *package.json* files.

Second, create a *.env* file and store the following variables:

```
OPENAI_API_KEY=
SUPABASE_URL=
SUPABASE_SERVICE_ROLE_KEY=

# for tracing
LANGCHAIN_TRACING_V2=true
LANGCHAIN_ENDPOINT="https://api.smith.langchain.com"
LANGCHAIN_API_KEY=
```

Next, we'll walk through the process of retrieving the values for each of these variables.

Large Language Model

The LLM is responsible for generating the output based on a given query. LangChain provides access to popular LLM providers, including OpenAI, Anthropic, Google, and Cohere.

In this deployment example, we'll utilize OpenAI by retrieving the API keys (*https:// oreil.ly/MIpY5*), as shown in Figure 9-1. Once you've retrieved your API keys, input the value as OPENAI_API_KEY in your *.env* file.

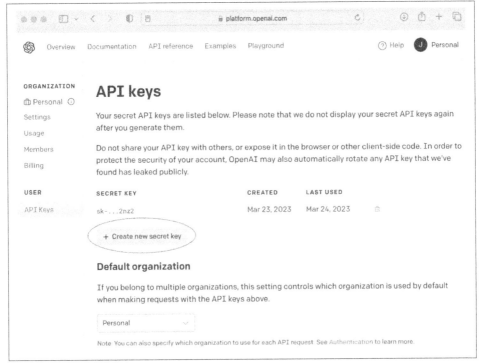

Figure 9-1. OpenAI API keys dashboard

Vector Store

As discussed in previous chapters, a vector store is a special database responsible for storing and managing vector representations of your data—in other words, embeddings. A vector store enables similarity search and context retrieval to help the LLM generate accurate answers based on the user's query.

For our deployment, we'll use Supabase—a PostgreSQL database—as the vector store. Supabase utilizes the `pgvector` extension to store embeddings and query vectors for similarity search.

If you haven't yet done it, create a Supabase account (*https://oreil.ly/CXDsx*). Once you've created an account, click "New project" on the dashboard page. Follow the steps and save the database password after creating it, as shown in Figure 9-2.

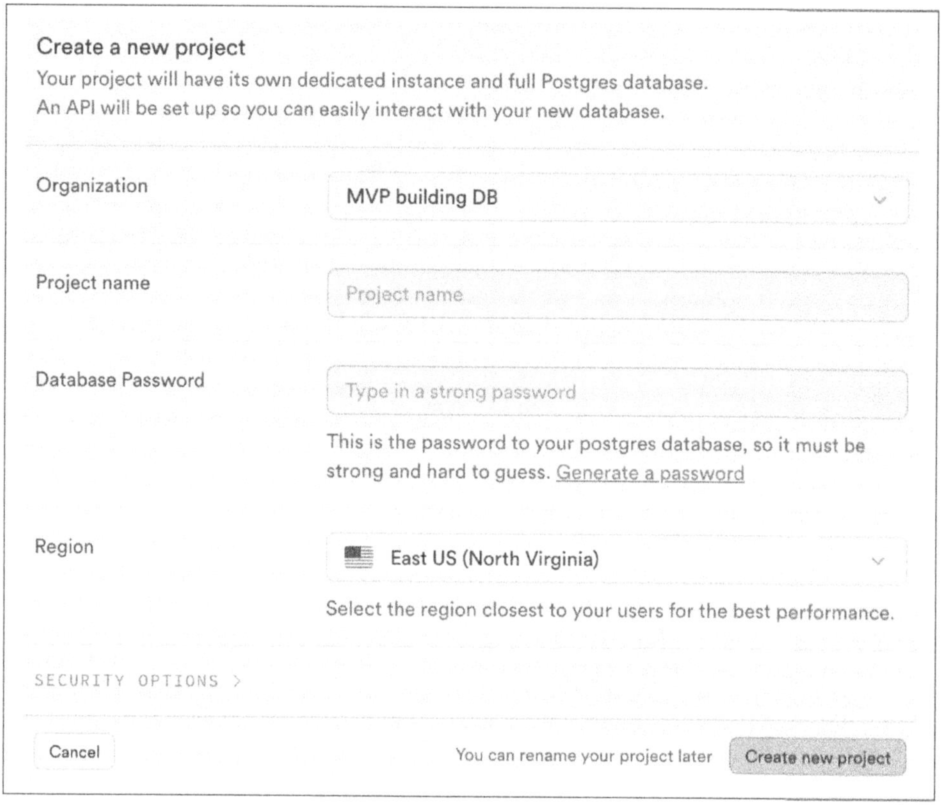

Create a new project

Your project will have its own dedicated instance and full Postgres database.
An API will be set up so you can easily interact with your new database.

Organization	MVP building DB ⌄
Project name	Project name
Database Password	Type in a strong password
	This is the password to your postgres database, so it must be strong and hard to guess. Generate a password
Region	🏴 East US (North Virginia) ⌄
	Select the region closest to your users for the best performance.

SECURITY OPTIONS >

Cancel   You can rename your project later   Create new project

Figure 9-2. Supabase project creation dashboard

Once your Supabase project is created, navigate to the Project Settings tab and select API under Configuration. Under this new tab, you will see Project URL and Project API keys.

In your *.env* file, copy and paste the Project URL as the value to SUPABASE_URL and the service_role secret API key as the value to SUPABASE_SERVICE_ROLE_KEY.

Navigate to the SQL editor in the Supabase menu and run the following SQL scripts. First, let's enable pgvector:

```
## Enable the pgvector extension to work with embedding vectors
create extension vector;
```

Now create a table called documents to store vectors of your data:

```
## Create a table to store your documents

create table documents (
  id bigserial primary key,
  content text, -- corresponds to Document.pageContent
  metadata jsonb, -- corresponds to Document.metadata
```

```
    embedding vector(1536) -- 1536 works for OpenAI embeddings, change if needed
);
```

You should now see the documents table in the Supabase database.

Now you can create a script to generate the embeddings of your data, store them, and query from the database. Open the Supabase SQL editor again and run the following script:

```
## Create a function to search for documents
create function match_documents (
    query_embedding vector(1536),
    match_count int DEFAULT null,
    filter jsonb DEFAULT '{}'
) returns table (
    id bigint,
    content text,
    metadata jsonb,
    embedding jsonb,
    similarity float
)
language plpgsql
as $$
#variable_conflict use_column
begin
    return query
    select
      id,
      content,
      metadata,
      (embedding::text)::jsonb as embedding,
      1 - (documents.embedding <=> query_embedding) as similarity
    from documents
    where metadata @> filter
    order by documents.embedding <=> query_embedding
    limit match_count;
end;
$$;
```

The match_documents database function takes a query_embedding vector and compares it to embeddings in the documents table using cosine similarity. It calculates a similarity score for each document (1 - (documents.embedding <=> query_embedding)), then returns the most similar matches. The results are:

1. Filtered first by the metadata criteria specified in the filter argument (using JSON containment @>).

2. Ordered by similarity score (highest first).

3. Limited to the number of matches specified in match_count.

Once the vector similarity function is generated, you can use Supabase as a vector store by importing the class and providing the necessary parameters. Here's an example of how it works:

Python

```
import os

from langchain_community.vectorstores import SupabaseVectorStore
from langchain_openai import OpenAIEmbeddings
from supabase.client import Client, create_client

supabase_url = os.environ.get("SUPABASE_URL")
supabase_key = os.environ.get("SUPABASE_SERVICE_ROLE_KEY")
supabase: Client = create_client(supabase_url, supabase_key)

embeddings = OpenAIEmbeddings()


## Assuming you've already generated embeddings of your data

vector_store = SupabaseVectorStore(
    embedding=embeddings,
    client=supabase,
    table_name="documents",
    query_name="match_documents",
)

## Test that similarity search is working

query = "What is this document about?"
matched_docs = vector_store.similarity_search(query)

print(matched_docs[0].page_content)
```

JavaScript

```
import {
  SupabaseVectorStore
} from "@langchain/community/vectorstores/supabase";
import { OpenAIEmbeddings } from "@langchain/openai";

import { createClient } from "@supabase/supabase-js";

const embeddings = new OpenAIEmbeddings();

const supabaseClient = createClient(
  process.env.SUPABASE_URL,
  process.env.SUPABASE_SERVICE_ROLE_KEY
);

const vectorStore = new SupabaseVectorStore(embeddings, {
  client: supabaseClient,
```

```
    tableName: "documents",
    queryName: "match_documents",
  });

  // Example documents structure of your data

  const document1: Document = {
    pageContent: "The powerhouse of the cell is the mitochondria",
    metadata: { source: "https://example.com" },
  };

  const document2: Document = {
    pageContent: "Buildings are made out of brick",
    metadata: { source: "https://example.com" },
  };

  const documents = [document1, document2]

  //Embed and store the data in the database

  await vectorStore.addDocuments(documents, { ids: ["1", "2"] });

  // Query the Vector Store

  const filter = { source: "https://example.com" };

  const similaritySearchResults = await vectorStore.similaritySearch(
    "biology",
    2,
    filter
  );

  for (const doc of similaritySearchResults) {
    console.log(`* ${doc.pageContent} [${JSON.stringify(doc.metadata, null)}]`);
  }
```

The output:

```
The powerhouse of the cell is the mitochondria [{"source":"https://example.com"}]
```

You can review the full logic of the Supabase vector store implementation in the Github LangChain template mentioned previously.

Backend API

As discussed in previous chapters, LangGraph is a low-level open source framework used to build complex agentic systems powered by LLMs. LangGraph enables fine-grained control over the flow and state of your application, built-in persistence, and advanced human-in-the-loop and memory features. Figure 9-3 illustrates LangGraph's control flow.

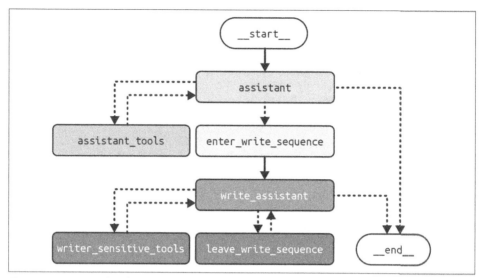

Figure 9-3. Example of LangGraph API control flow

To deploy an AI application that utilizes LangGraph, we will use LangGraph Platform. LangGraph Platform is a managed service for deploying and hosting Lang-Graph agents at scale.

As your agentic use case gains traction, uneven task distribution among agents can overload the system, leading to downtime. LangGraph Platform manages horizontally scaling task queues, servers, and a robust Postgres checkpointer to handle many concurrent users and efficiently store large states and threads. This ensures fault-tolerant scalability.

LangGraph Platform is designed to support real-world interaction patterns. In addition to streaming and human-in-the-loop features, LangGraph Platform enables the following:

- Double texting to handle new user inputs on ongoing graph threads
- Asynchronous background jobs for long-running tasks
- Cron jobs for running common tasks on a schedule

LangGraph Platform also provides an integrated solution for collaborating on, deploying, and monitoring agentic AI applications. It includes LangGraph Studio (*https://oreil.ly/2Now-*)—a visual playground for debugging, editing, and testing agents. LangGraph Studio also enables you to share your LangGraph agent with team members for collaborative feedback and rapid iteration, as Figure 9-4 shows.

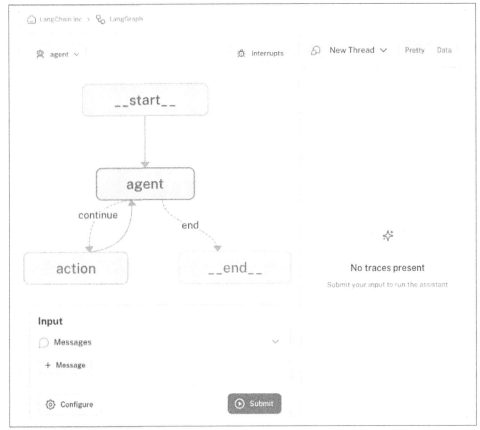

Figure 9-4. Snapshot of LangGraph Studio UI

Additionally, LangGraph Platform simplifies agentic deployment by enabling one-click submissions.

Create a LangSmith Account

LangSmith is an all-in-one developer platform that enables you to debug, collaborate, test, and monitor your LLM applications. LangGraph Platform is seamlessly integrated with LangSmith and is accessible from within the LangSmith UI.

To deploy your application on LangGraph Platform, you need to create a LangSmith account (*https://oreil.ly/2WVCn*). Once you're logged in to the dashboard, navigate to the Settings page, then scroll to the API Keys section and click Create API Key. You should see a UI similar to Figure 9-5.

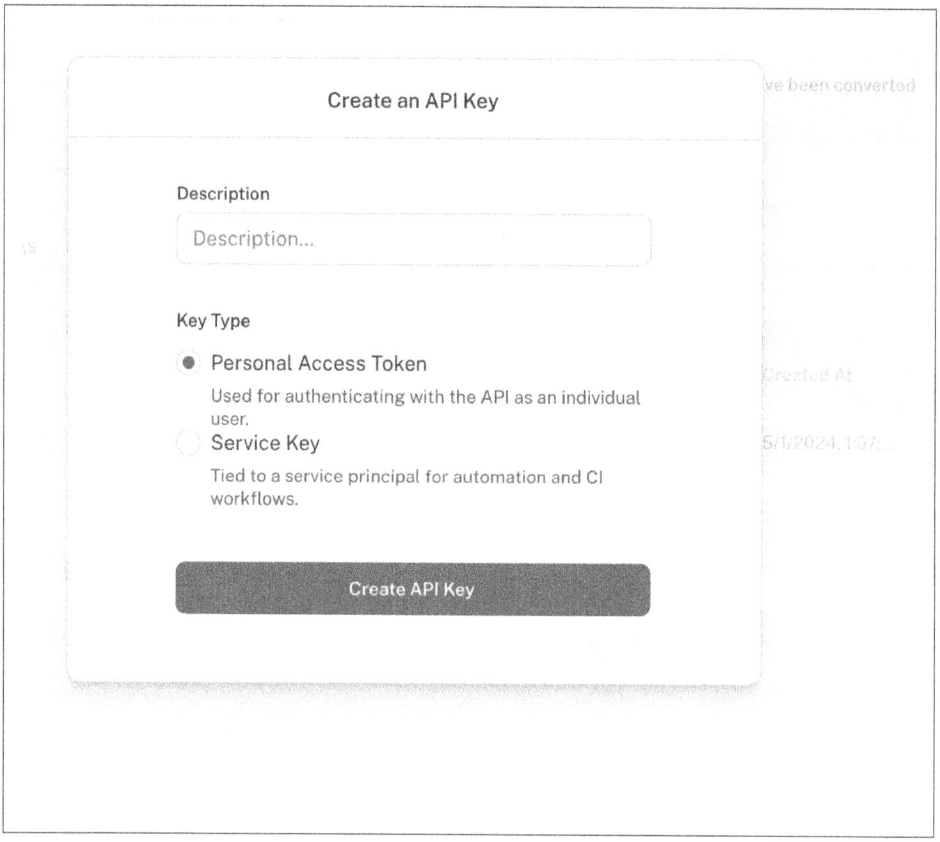

Figure 9-5. Create LangSmith API Key UI

Copy the API Key value as your LANGCHAIN_API_KEY in your *.env* file.

Navigate to "Usage and billing" and set up your billing details. Then click the "Plans and Billings" tab and the "Upgrade to Plus" button to get instructions on transitioning to a LangSmith Plus plan, which will enable LangGraph Platform usage. If you'd prefer to use a free self-hosted deployment, you can follow the instructions here (*https://oreil.ly/TBgSQ*). Please note that this option requires management of the infrastructure, including setting up and maintaining required databases and Redis instances.

Understanding the LangGraph Platform API

Before deploying your AI application on LangGraph Platform, it's important to understand how each component of the LangGraph API works. These components can generally be split into data models and features.

Data Models

The LangGraph Platform API consists of a few core data models:

- Assistants
- Threads
- Runs
- Cron jobs

Assistants

An *assistant* is a configured instance of a `CompiledGraph`. It abstracts the cognitive architecture of the graph and contains instance-specific configuration and metadata. Multiple assistants can reference the same graph but can contain different configuration and metadata—which may differentiate the behavior of the assistants. An assistant (that is, the graph) is invoked as part of a run.

The LangGraph Platform API provides several endpoints for creating and managing assistants.

Threads

A *thread* contains the accumulated state of a group of runs. If a run is executed on a thread, then the state of the underlying graph of the assistant will be persisted to the thread. A thread's current and historical state can be retrieved. To persist state, a thread must be created prior to executing a run. The state of a thread at a particular point in time is called a *checkpoint*.

The LangGraph Platform API provides several endpoints for creating and managing threads and thread state.

Runs

A *run* is an invocation of an assistant. Each run may have its own input, configuration, and metadata—which may affect the execution and output of the underlying graph. A run can optionally be executed on a thread.

The LangGraph Platform API provides several endpoints for creating and managing runs.

Cron jobs

LangGraph Platform supports *cron jobs*, which enable graphs to be run on a user-defined schedule. The user specifies a schedule, an assistant, and an input. Then LangGraph Platform creates a new thread with the specified assistant and sends the specified input to that thread.

Features

The LangGraph Platform API also offers several features to support complex agent architectures, including the following:

- Streaming
- Human-in-the-loop
- Double texting
- Stateless runs
- Webhooks

Streaming

Streaming is critical for ensuring that LLM applications feel responsive to end users. When creating a streaming run, the streaming mode determines what data is streamed back to the API client. The LangGraph Platform API supports five streaming modes:

Values
Stream the full state of the graph after each super-step is executed.

Messages
Stream complete messages (at the end of node execution) as well as tokens for any messages generated inside a node. This mode is primarily meant for powering chat applications. This is only an option if your graph contains a `messages` key.

Updates
Stream updates to the state of the graph after each node is executed.

Events
Stream all events (including the state of the graph) that occur during graph execution. This can be used to do token-by-token streaming for LLMs.

Debug
Stream debug events throughout graph execution.

Human-in-the-loop

If left to run autonomously, a complex agent can take unintended actions, leading to catastrophic application outcomes. To prevent this, human intervention is recommended, especially at checkpoints where application logic involves invoking certain tools or accessing specific documents. LangGraph Platform enables you to insert this human-in-the-loop behavior to ensure your graph doesn't have undesired outcomes.

Double texting

Graph execution may take longer than expected, and often users may send one message and then, before the graph has finished running, send a second message. This is known as *double texting*. For example, a user might notice a typo in their original request and edit the prompt and resend it. In such scenarios, it's important to prevent your graphs from behaving in unexpected ways and ensure a smooth user experience. LangGraph Platform provides four different solutions to handle double texting:

Reject
> This rejects any follow-up runs and does not allow double texting.

Enqueue
> This option continues the first run until it completes the whole run, then sends the new input as a separate run.

Interrupt
> This option interrupts the current execution but saves all the work done up until that point. It then inserts the user input and continues from there. If you enable this option, your graph should be able to handle weird edge cases that may arise.

Rollback
> This option rolls back all work done up until that point. It then sends the user input in—as if it just followed the original run input.

Stateless runs

All runs use the built-in checkpointer to store checkpoints for runs. However, it can often be useful to just kick off a run without worrying about explicitly creating a thread and keeping those checkpointers around. *Stateless* runs allow you to do this by exposing an endpoint that does these things:

- Takes in user input
- Creates a thread
- Runs the agent, but skips all checkpointing steps
- Cleans up the thread afterwards

Stateless runs are retried while keeping memory intact. However, in the case of stateless background runs, if the task worker dies halfway, the entire run will be retried from scratch.

Webhooks

LangGraph Platform also supports completion *webhooks*. A webhook URL is provided, which notifies your application whenever a run completes.

Deploying Your AI Application on LangGraph Platform

At this point, you have created accounts for the recommended services, filled in your *.env* file with values of all necessary environment variables, and completed the core logic for your AI application. Next, we will take the necessary steps to effectively deploy your application.

Create a LangGraph API Config

Prior to deployment, you need to configure your application with a LangGraph API configuration file called *langgraph.json* (*https://oreil.ly/aVDhd*). Here's an example of what the file looks like in a Python repository:

Python

```
{
    "dependencies": ["./my_agent"],
    "graphs": {
        "agent": "./my_agent/agent.py:graph"
    },
    "env": ".env"
}
```

And here's an example repository structure:

```
my-app/
├── my_agent # all project code lies within here
│   ├── utils # utilities for your graph
│   │   ├── __init__.py
│   │   ├── tools.py # tools for your graph
│   │   ├── nodes.py # node functions for you graph
│   │   └── state.py # state definition of your graph
│   ├── requirements.txt # package dependencies
│   ├── __init__.py
│   └── agent.py # code for constructing your graph
├── .env # environment variables
└── langgraph.json # configuration file for LangGraph
```

Note that the *langgraph.json* file is placed on the same level or higher than the files that contain compiled graphs and associated dependencies.

In addition, the dependencies are specified in a *requirements.txt* file. But they can also be specified in *pyproject.toml*, *setup.py*, or *package.json* files.

Here's what each of the properties mean:

Dependencies
Array of dependencies for LangGraph Platform API server

Graphs
Mapping from graph ID to path where the compiled graph or a function that makes a graph is defined

Env
Path to your *.env* file or a mapping from environment variable to its value (you can learn more about configurations for the `langgraph.json` file here (*https://oreil.ly/bPA0W*))

Test Your LangGraph App Locally

Testing your application locally ensures that there are no errors or dependency conflicts prior to deployment. To do this, we will utilize the LangGraph CLI, which includes commands to run a local development server with hot reloading and debugging capabilities.

For Python, install the Python `langgraph-cli` package (note: this requires Python 3.11 or higher):

```
pip install -U "langgraph-cli[inmem]"
```

Or for JavaScript, install the package as follows:

```
npm i @langchain/langgraph-cli
```

Once the CLI is installed, run the following command to start the API:

```
langgraph dev
```

This will start up the LangGraph API server locally. If this runs successfully, you should see something like this:

```
Ready!
API: http://localhost:2024
Docs: http://localhost:2024/docs
```

The LangGraph Platform API reference is available with each deployment at the */docs* URL path (*http://localhost:2024/docs*).

The easiest way to interact with your local API server is to use the auto-launched LangGraph Studio UI. Alternatively, you can interact with the local API server using cURL, as seen in this example:

```
curl --request POST \
    --url http://localhost:8123/runs/stream \
    --header 'Content-Type: application/json' \
    --data '{
    "assistant_id": "agent",
    "input": {
        "messages": [
            {
                "role": "user",
                "content": "How are you?"
            }
        ]
    },
    "metadata": {},
    "config": {
        "configurable": {}
    },
    "multitask_strategy": "reject",
    "stream_mode": [
        "values"
    ]
}'
```

If you receive a valid response, your application is functioning well. Next, we can interact with the server using the LangGraph SDK.

Here's an example both initializing the SDK client and invoking the graph:

Python

```
from langgraph_sdk import get_client

# only pass the url argument to get_client() if you changed the default port
# when calling langgraph up
client = get_client()
# Using the graph deployed with the name "agent"
assistant_id = "agent"
thread = await client.threads.create()


input = {"messages": [{"role": "user", "content": "what's the weather in sf"}]}
async for chunk in client.runs.stream(
    thread["thread_id"],
    assistant_id,
    input=input,
    stream_mode="updates",
):
    print(f"Receiving new event of type: {chunk.event}...")
```

```
      print(chunk.data)
      print("\n\n")
```

JavaScript

```javascript
import { Client } from "@langchain/langgraph-sdk";

// only set the apiUrl if you changed the default port when calling langgraph up
const client = new Client();
// Using the graph deployed with the name "agent"
const assistantId = "agent";
const thread = await client.threads.create();

const input = {
  messages: [{ "role": "user", "content": "what's the weather in sf"}]
}

const streamResponse = client.runs.stream(
  thread["thread_id"],
  assistantId,
  {
    input: input,
    streamMode: "updates",
  }
);
for await (const chunk of streamResponse) {
  console.log(`Receiving new event of type: ${chunk.event}...`);
  console.log(chunk.data);
  console.log("\n\n");
}
```

If your LangGraph application is working correctly, you should see your graph output displayed in the console.

Deploy from the LangSmith UI

At this point, you should have completed all prerequisite steps and your LangGraph API should be working locally. Your next step is to navigate to your LangSmith dashboard panel and click the Deployments tab. You should see a UI similar to Figure 9-6.

Figure 9-6. LangGraph Platform deployment UI page

Next, click the New Deployment button in the top right corner of the page.

If you don't see a page with the New Deployment button, it's likely that you haven't yet upgraded to a LangSmith Plus plan according to the instructions in the "Usage and billing" setting.

You should now see a page of three form fields to complete.

Deployment details

1. Select "Import with GitHub" and follow the GitHub OAuth workflow to install and authorize LangChain's hosted-langserve GitHub app to access the selected repositories. After installation is complete, return to the Create New Deployment panel and select the GitHub repository to deploy from the drop-down menu.

2. Specify a name for the deployment and the full path to the LangGraph API config file, including the filename. For example, if the file *langgraph.json* is in the root of the repository, simply specify *langgraph.json*.

3. Specify the desired `git` reference (branch name) of your repository to deploy.

Development type

Select Production from the dropdown. This will enable a production deployment that can serve up to 500 requests/second and is provisioned with highly available storage and automatic backups.

Environment variables

Provide the properties and values in your *.env* here. For sensitive values, like your OPENAI_API_KEY, make sure to tick the Secret box before inputting the value.

Once you've completed the fields, click the button to submit the deployment and wait for a few seconds for the build to complete. You should see a new revision associated with the deployment.

Since LangGraph Platform is integrated within LangSmith, you can gain deeper visibility into your app and track and monitor usage, errors, performance, and costs in production too. Figure 9-7 shows a visual Trace Count summary chart showing successful, pending, and error traces over a given time period. You can also view all monitoring info for your server by clicking the "All charts" button.

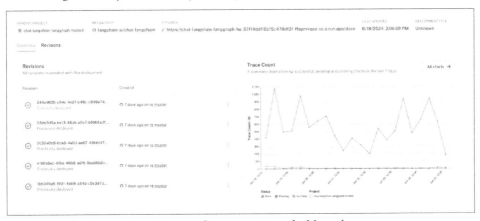

Figure 9-7. Deployment revisions and trace count on dashboard

To view the build and deployment logs, select the desired revision from the Revisions tab, then choose the Deploy tab to view the full deployment logs history. You can also adjust the date and time range.

To create a new deployment, click the New Revision button in the navigation bar. Fill out the necessary fields, including the LangGraph API config file path, git reference, and environment variables, as done previously.

Finally, you can access the API documentation by clicking the API docs link, which should display a similar page to the UI shown in Figure 9-8.

Figure 9-8. LangGraph API documentation

Launch LangGraph Studio

LangGraph Studio provides a specialized agent IDE for visualizing, interacting with, and debugging complex agentic applications. It enables developers to modify an agent result (or the logic underlying a specific node) halfway through the agent's trajectory. This creates an iterative process by letting you interact with and manipulate the state at that point in time.

Once you've deployed your AI application, click the LangGraph Studio button at the top righthand corner of the deployment dashboard, as you can see in Figure 9-9.

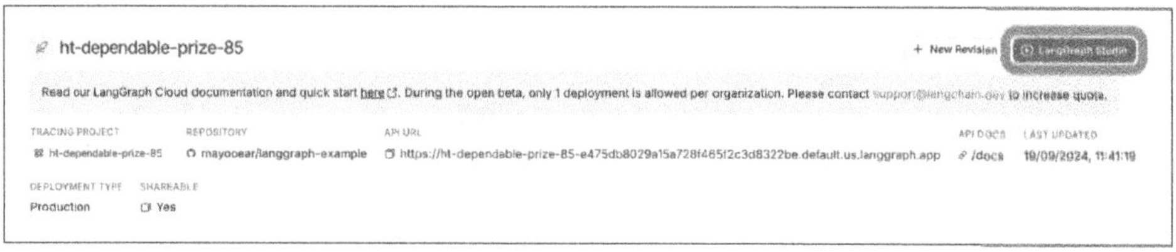

Figure 9-9. LangGraph deployment UI

After clicking the button, you should see the LangGraph Studio UI (for example, see Figure 9-10).

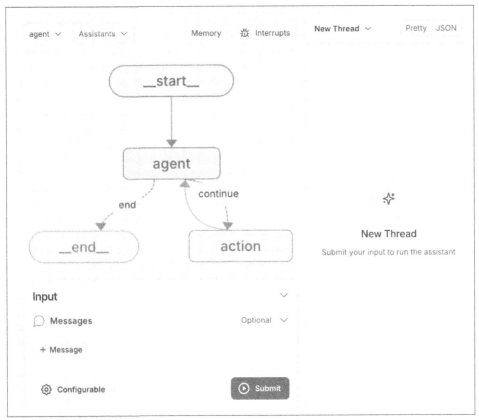

Figure 9-10. LangGraph Studio UI

To invoke a graph and start a new run, follow these steps:

1. Select a graph from the drop-down menu in the top left corner of the lefthand pane. The graph in Figure 9-10 is called *agent*.

2. In the Input section, click the "+ Message" icon and input a *human* message, but the input will vary depending on your application state definitions.

3. Click Submit to invoke the selected graph.

4. View the output of the invocation in the right-hand pane.

The output of your invoked graph should look like Figure 9-11.

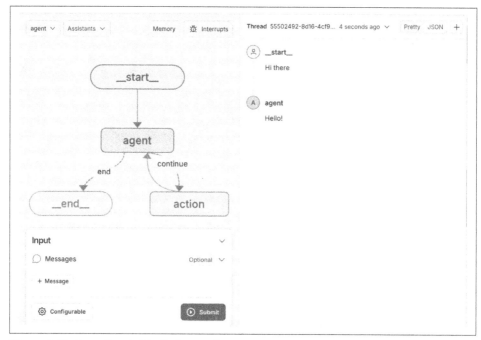

Figure 9-11. LangGraph Studio invocation output

In addition to invocation, LangGraph Studio enables you to change run configurations, create and edit threads, interrupt your graphs, edit graph code, and enable human-in-the-loop intervention. You can read the full guide (*https://oreil.ly/xUU37*) to learn more.

 LangGraph Studio is also available as a desktop application (for Apple silicon), which enables you to test your AI application locally.

If you've followed the installation guide in the GitHub template and successfully deployed your AI application, it's now live for production use. But before you share to external users or use the backend API in existing applications, it's important to be aware of key security considerations.

Security

Although AI applications are powerful, they are vulnerable to several security risks that may lead to data corruption or loss, unauthorized access to confidential information, and compromised performance. These risks may carry adverse legal, reputational, and financial consequences.

To mitigate these risks, it's recommended to follow general application security best practices, including the following:

Limit permissions

Scope permissions specific to the application's need. Granting broad or excessive permissions can introduce significant security vulnerabilities. To avoid such vulnerabilities, consider using read-only credentials, disallowing access to sensitive resources, and using sandboxing techniques (such as running inside a container).

Anticipate potential misuse

Always assume that any system access or credentials may be used in any way allowed by the permissions they are assigned. For example, if a pair of database credentials allows deleting data, it's safest to assume that any LLM able to use those credentials may in fact delete data.

Defense in depth

It's often best to combine multiple layered security approaches rather than rely on any single layer of defense to ensure security. For example, use both read-only permissions and sandboxing to ensure that LLMs are only able to access data that is explicitly meant for them to use.

Here are three example scenarios implementing these mitigation strategies:

File access

A user may ask an agent with access to the file system to delete files that should not be deleted or read the content of files that contain sensitive information. To mitigate this risk, limit the agent to only use a specific directory and only allow it to read or write files that are safe to read or write. Consider further sandboxing the agent by running it in a container.

API access

A user may ask an agent with write access to an external API to write malicious data to the API or delete data from that API. To mitigate, give the agent read-only API keys, or limit it to only use endpoints that are already resistant to such misuse.

Database access

> A user may ask an agent with access to a database to drop a table or mutate the schema. To mitigate, scope the credentials to only the tables that the agent needs to access and consider issuing read-only credentials.

In addition to the preceding security measures, you can take further steps to mitigate abuse of your AI application. Due to the dependency of external LLM API providers (such as OpenAI), there is a direct cost associated with running your application. To prevent abuse of your API and exponential costs, you can implement the following:

Account creation verification

> This typically includes a form of authentication login, such as email or phone number verification.

Rate limiting

> Implement a rate-limiting mechanism in the middleware of the application to prevent users from making too many requests in a short period of time. This should check the number of requests a user has made in the last X minutes and "timeout" or "ban" the user if the abuse is severe.

Implement prompt injection guardrails

> *Prompt injection* occurs when a malicious user injects a prompt in an attempt to trick the LLM to act in unintended ways. This usually includes extracting confidential data or generating unrelated outputs. To mitigate this, you should ensure the LLM has proper permission scoping and that the application's prompts are specific and strict to the desired outcomes.

Summary

Throughout this chapter, you've learned the best practices for deploying your AI application and enabling users to interact with it. We explored recommended services to handle various key components of the application in production, including the LLM, vector store, and backend API.

We also discussed using LangGraph Platform as a managed service for deploying and hosting LangGraph agents at scale—in conjunction with LangGraph Studio—to visualize, interact with, and debug your application.

Finally, we briefly explored various security best practices to mitigate data breach risks often associated with AI applications.

In Chapter 10, you'll learn how to effectively evaluate, monitor, benchmark, and improve the performance of your AI application.

Testing: Evaluation, Monitoring, and Continuous Improvement

In Chapter 9, you learned how to deploy your AI application into production and utilize LangGraph Platform to host and debug your app.

Although your app can respond to user inputs and execute complex tasks, its underlying LLM is nondeterministic and prone to hallucination. As discussed in previous chapters, LLMs can generate inaccurate and outdated outputs due to a variety of reasons including the prompt, format of user's input, and retrieved context. In addition, harmful or misleading LLM outputs can significantly damage a company's brand and customer loyalty.

To combat this tendency toward hallucination, you need to build an efficient system to test, evaluate, monitor, and continuously improve your LLM applications' performance. This robust testing process will enable you to quickly debug and fix AI-related issues before and after your app is in production.

In this chapter, you'll learn how to build an iterative testing system across the key stages of the LLM app development life-cycle and maintain high performance of your application.

Testing Techniques Across the LLM App Development Cycle

Before we construct the testing system, let's briefly review how testing can be applied across the three key stages of LLM app development:

Design

> In this stage, LLM tests are applied directly to your application. These tests can be assertions executed at runtime that feed failures back to the LLM for self-correction. The purpose of testing at this stage is error handling within your app before it affects users.

Preproduction

> In this stage, tests are run right before deployment into production. The purpose of testing at this stage is to catch and fix any regressions before the app is released to real users.

Production

> In this stage, tests are run while your application is in production to help monitor and catch errors affecting real users. The purpose is to identify issues and feed them back into the design or preproduction phases.

The combination of testing across these stages creates a continuous improvement cycle where these steps are repeated: design, test, deploy, monitor, fix, and redesign. See Figure 10-1.

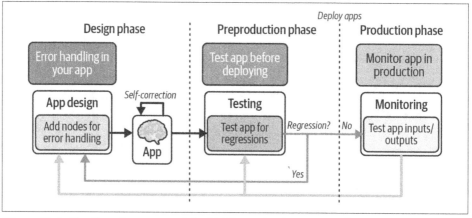

Figure 10-1. The three key stages of the LLM app development cycle

In essence, this cycle helps you to identify and fix production issues in an efficient and quick manner.

Let's dive deeper into testing techniques across each of these stages.

The Design Stage: Self-Corrective RAG

As discussed previously, your application can incorporate error handling at runtime that feeds errors to the LLM for self-correction. Let's explore a RAG use case using LangGraph as the framework to orchestrate error handling.

Basic RAG-driven AI applications are prone to hallucination due to inaccurate or incomplete retrieval of relevant context to generate outputs. But you can utilize an LLM to grade retrieval relevance and fix hallucination issues.

LangGraph enables you to effectively implement the control flow of this process, as shown in Figure 10-2.

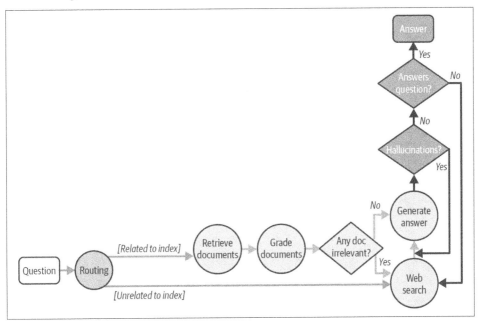

Figure 10-2. Self-corrective RAG control flow

The control flow steps are as follows:

1. In the routing step, each question is routed to the relevant retrieval method, that is, vector store and web search.

2. If, for example, the question is routed to a vector store for retrieval, the LLM in the control flow will retrieve and grade the documents for relevancy.

3. If the document is relevant, the LLM proceeds to generate an answer.

4. The LLM will check the answer for hallucinations and only proceed to display the answer to the user if the output is accurate and relevant.

5. As a fallback, if the retrieved document is irrelevant or the generated answer doesn't answer the user's question, the flow utilizes web search to retrieve relevant information as context.

This process enables your app to iteratively generate answers, self-correct errors and hallucinations, and improve the quality of outputs.

Let's run through an example code implementation of this control flow. First, download the required packages and initialize relevant API keys. For these examples, you'll need to set your OpenAI and LangSmith API keys as environment variables.

First, we'll create an index of three blog posts:

Python

```python
from langchain.text_splitter import RecursiveCharacterTextSplitter
from langchain_community.document_loaders import WebBaseLoader
from langchain_community.vectorstores import InMemoryVectorStore
from langchain_openai import OpenAIEmbeddings
from langchain_core.prompts import ChatPromptTemplate
from pydantic import BaseModel, Field
from langchain_openai import ChatOpenAI


# --- Create an index of documents ---

urls = [
    "https://blog.langchain.dev/top-5-langgraph-agents-in-production-2024/",
    "https://blog.langchain.dev/langchain-state-of-ai-2024/",
    "https://blog.langchain.dev/introducing-ambient-agents/",
]

docs = [WebBaseLoader(url).load() for url in urls]
docs_list = [item for sublist in docs for item in sublist]

text_splitter = RecursiveCharacterTextSplitter.from_tiktoken_encoder(
    chunk_size=250, chunk_overlap=0
)
doc_splits = text_splitter.split_documents(docs_list)

# Add to vectorDB
vectorstore = InMemoryVectorStore.from_documents(
    documents=doc_splits,
    embedding=OpenAIEmbeddings(),
)
retriever = vectorstore.as_retriever()

# Retrieve the relevant documents
results = retriever.invoke(
    "What are 2 LangGraph agents used in production in 2024?")

print("Results: \n", results)
```

```javascript
import { RecursiveCharacterTextSplitter } from '@langchain/textsplitters';
import {
  CheerioWebBaseLoader
} from "@langchain/community/document_loaders/web/cheerio";
import {
  InMemoryVectorStore
} from '@langchain/community/vectorstores/in_memory';
import { OpenAIEmbeddings } from '@langchain/openai';
import { ChatPromptTemplate } from '@langchain/core/prompts';
import { z } from 'zod';
import { ChatOpenAI } from '@langchain/openai';

const urls = [
  'https://blog.langchain.dev/top-5-langgraph-agents-in-production-2024/',
  'https://blog.langchain.dev/langchain-state-of-ai-2024/',
  'https://blog.langchain.dev/introducing-ambient-agents/',
];

// Load documents from URLs
const loadDocs = async (urls) => {
  const docs = [];
  for (const url of urls) {
    const loader = new CheerioWebBaseLoader(url);
    const loadedDocs = await loader.load();
    docs.push(...loadedDocs);
  }
  return docs;
};

const docsList = await loadDocs(urls);

// Initialize the text splitter
const textSplitter = new RecursiveCharacterTextSplitter({
  chunkSize: 250,
  chunkOverlap: 0,
});

// Split the documents into smaller chunks
const docSplits = textSplitter.splitDocuments(docsList);

// Add to vector database
const vectorstore = await InMemoryVectorStore.fromDocuments(
  docSplits,
  new OpenAIEmbeddings()
);

// The `retriever` object can now be used for querying
const retriever = vectorstore.asRetriever();

const question = 'What are 2 LangGraph agents used in production in 2024?';
```

```
const docs = retriever.invoke(question);

console.log('Retrieved documents: \n', docs[0].page_content);
```

As discussed previously, the LLM will grade the relevancy of the retrieved documents from the index. We can construct this instruction in a system prompt:

Python

```python
### Retrieval Grader

from langchain_core.prompts import ChatPromptTemplate
from langchain_core.pydantic_v1 import BaseModel, Field
from langchain_openai import ChatOpenAI


# Data model
class GradeDocuments(BaseModel):
    """Binary score for relevance check on retrieved documents."""

    binary_score: str = Field(
        description="Documents are relevant to the question, 'yes' or 'no'"
    )


# LLM with function call
llm = ChatOpenAI(model="gpt-3.5-turbo", temperature=0)
structured_llm_grader = llm.with_structured_output(GradeDocuments)

# Prompt
system = """You are a grader assessing relevance of a retrieved document to a
    user question.
    If the document contains keyword(s) or semantic meaning related to the
    question, grade it as relevant.
    Give a binary score 'yes' or 'no' to indicate whether the document is
    relevant to the question."""
grade_prompt = ChatPromptTemplate.from_messages(
    [
        ("system", system),
        ("human", """Retrieved document: \n\n {document} \n\n User question:
            {question}"""),
    ]
)

retrieval_grader = grade_prompt | structured_llm_grader
question = "agent memory"
docs = retriever.get_relevant_documents(question)
doc_txt = docs[0].page_content # as an example
retrieval_grader.invoke({"question": question, "document": doc_txt})
```

JavaScript

```javascript
import { ChatPromptTemplate } from "@langchain/core/prompts";
import { z } from "zod";
import { ChatOpenAI } from "@langchain/openai";

// Define the schema using Zod
const GradeDocumentsSchema = z.object({
  binary_score: z.string().describe(`Documents are relevant to the question,
      'yes' or 'no'`),
});

// Initialize LLM with structured output using Zod schema
const llm = new ChatOpenAI({ model: "gpt-3.5-turbo", temperature: 0 });
const structuredLLMGrader = llm.withStructuredOutput(GradeDocumentsSchema);

// System and prompt template
const systemMessage = `You are a grader assessing relevance of a retrieved
  document to a user question.
If the document contains keyword(s) or semantic meaning related to the
  question, grade it as relevant.
Give a binary score 'yes' or 'no' to indicate whether the document is relevant
  to the question.`;

const gradePrompt = ChatPromptTemplate.fromMessages([
  { role: "system", content: systemMessage },
  {
    role: "human",
    content: "Retrieved document: \n\n {document} \n\n
      User question: {question}",
  },
]);

// Combine prompt with the structured output
const retrievalGrader = gradePrompt.pipe(structuredLLMGrader);

const question = "agent memory";
const docs = await retriever.getRelevantDocuments(question);

await retrievalGrader.invoke({
  question,
  document: docs[1].pageContent,
});
```

The output:

```
binary_score='yes'
```

Notice the use of Pydantic/Zod to help model the binary decision output in a format that can be used to programmatically decide which node in the control flow to move toward.

In LangSmith, you can see a trace of the logic flow across the nodes discussed previously (see Figure 10-3).

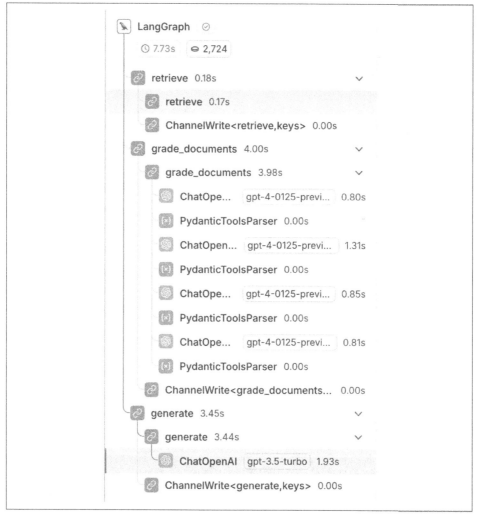

Figure 10-3. LangSmith trace results

Let's test to see what happens when the input question cannot be answered by the retrieved documents in the index.

First, utilize LangGraph to make it easier to construct, execute, and debug the full control flow. See the full graph definition in the book's GitHub repository (*https://oreil.ly/v63Vr*). Notice that we've added a transform_query node to help rewrite the input query in a format that web search can use to retrieve higher-quality results.

As a final step, we set up our web search tool and execute the graph using the out-of-context question. The LangSmith trace shows that the web search tool was used as a fallback to retrieve relevant information prior to the final LLM generated answer (see Figure 10-4).

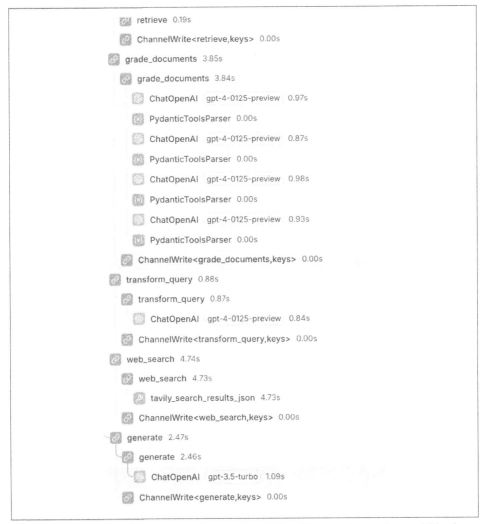

Figure 10-4. LangSmith trace of self-corrective RAG utilizing web search as a fallback

Let's move on to the next stage in LLM app testing: preproduction.

The Preproduction Stage

The purpose of the preproduction stage of testing is to measure and evaluate the performance of your application prior to production. This will enable you to efficiently assess the accuracy, latency, and cost of utilizing the LLM.

Creating Datasets

Prior to testing, you need to define a set of scenarios you'd like to test and evaluate. A *dataset* is a collection of examples that provide inputs and expected outputs used to evaluate your LLM app.

These are three common methods to build datasets for valuation:

Manually curated examples
> These are handwritten examples based on expected user inputs and ideal generated outputs. A small dataset consists of between 10 and 50 quality examples. Over time, more examples can be added to the dataset based on edge cases that emerge in production.

Application logs
> Once the application is in production, you can store real-time user inputs and later add them to the dataset. This will help ensure the dataset is realistic and covers the most common user questions.

Synthetic data
> These are artificially generated examples that simulate various scenarios and edge cases. This enables you to generate new inputs by sampling existing inputs, which is useful when you don't have enough real data to test on.

In LangSmith, you can create a new dataset by selecting Datasets and Testing in the sidebar and clicking the "+ New Dataset" button on the top right of the app, as shown in Figure 10-5.

In the opened window, enter the relevant dataset details, including a name, description, and dataset type. If you'd like to use your own dataset, click the "Upload a CSV dataset" button.

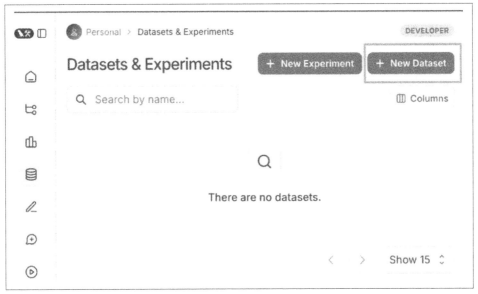

Figure 10-5. Creating a new dataset in the LangSmith UI

LangSmith offers three different dataset types:

kv *(key-value) dataset*
- *Inputs* and *outputs* are represented as arbitrary key-value pairs.
- The kv dataset is the most versatile, and it is the default type. The kv dataset is suitable for a wide range of evaluation scenarios.
- This dataset type is ideal for evaluating chains and agents that require multiple inputs or generate multiple outputs.

llm *(large language model) dataset*
- The llm dataset is designed for evaluating completion style language models.
- The inputs dictionary contains a single input key mapped to the prompt string.
- The outputs dictionary contains a single output key mapped to the corresponding response string.
- This dataset type simplifies evaluation for LLMs by providing a standardized format for inputs and outputs.

chat *dataset*

- The chat dataset is designed for evaluating LLM structured chat messages as inputs and outputs.
- The *inputs* dictionary contains a single *input* key mapped to a list of serialized chat messages.
- The *outputs* dictionary contains a single *output* key mapped to a list of serialized chat messages.
- This dataset type is useful for evaluating conversational AI systems or chatbots.

The most flexible option is the key-value data type (see Figure 10-6).

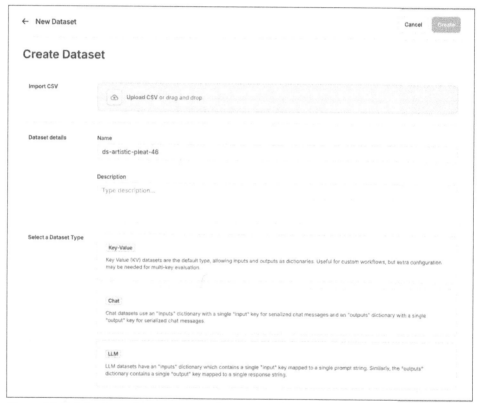

Figure 10-6. Selecting a dataset type in the LangSmith UI

Next, add examples to the dataset by clicking Add Example. Provide the input and output examples as JSON objects, as shown in Figure 10-7.

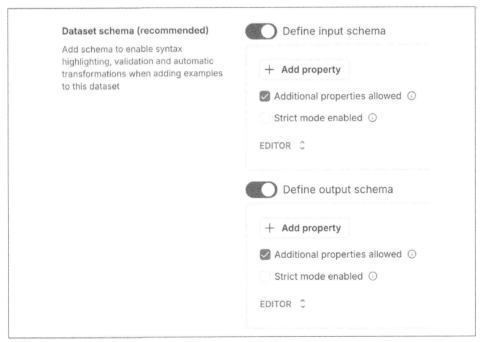

Figure 10-7. Add key-value dataset examples in the LangSmith UI

You can also define a schema for your dataset in the "Dataset schema" section, as shown in Figure 10-8.

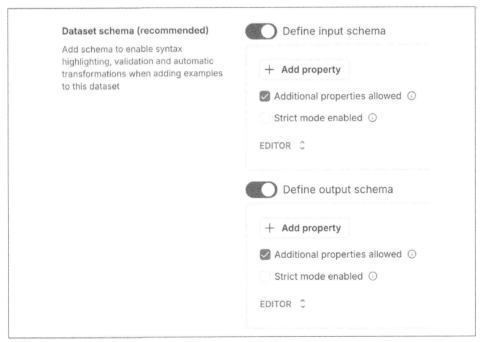

Figure 10-8. Adding a dataset schema in the LangSmith UI

Defining Your Evaluation Criteria

After creating your dataset, you need to define evaluation metrics to assess your application's outputs before deploying into production. This batch evaluation on a predetermined test suite is often referred to as *offline evaluation*.

For offline evaluation, you can optionally label expected outputs (that is, ground truth references) for the data points you are testing on. This enables you to compare your application's response with the ground truth references, as shown in Figure 10-9.

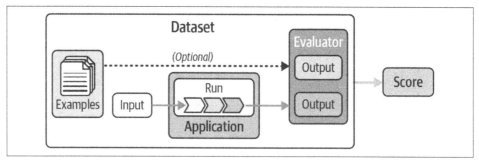

Figure 10-9. AI evaluation diagram

There are three main evaluators to score your LLM app performance:

Human evaluators
> If you can't express your testing requirements as code, you can use human feedback to express qualitative characteristics and label app responses with scores. LangSmith speeds up the process of collecting and incorporating human feedback with annotation queues.

Heuristic evaluators
> These are hardcoded functions and assertions that perform computations to determine a score. You can use reference-free heuristics (for example, checking whether output is valid JSON) or reference-based heuristics such as accuracy. Reference-based evaluation compares an output to a predefined ground truth, whereas reference-free evaluation assesses qualitative characteristics without a ground truth. Custom heuristic evaluators are useful for code-generation tasks such as schema checking and unit testing with hardcoded evaluation logic.

LLM-as-a-judge evaluators
> This evaluator integrates human grading rules into an LLM prompt to evaluate whether the output is correct relative to the reference answer supplied from the dataset output. As you iterate in preproduction, you'll need to audit the scores and tune the LLM-as-a-judge to produce reliable scores.

To get started with evaluation, start simple with heuristic evaluators. Then implement human evaluators before moving on to LLM-as-a-judge to automate your human review. This enables you to add depth and scale once your criteria are well-defined.

 When using LLM-as-a-judge evaluators, use straightforward prompts that can easily be replicated and understood by a human. For example, avoid asking an LLM to produce scores on a range of 0 to 10 with vague distinctions between scores.

Figure 10-10 illustrates LLM-as-a-judge evaluator in the context of a RAG use case. Note that the reference answer is the ground truth.

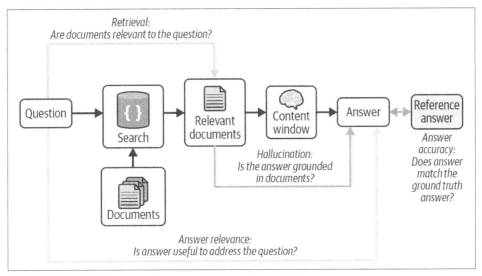

Figure 10-10. LLM-as-a-judge evaluator used in a RAG use case

Improving LLM-as-a-judge evaluators performance

Using an LLM-as-a-judge is an effective method to grade natural language outputs from LLM applications. This involves passing the generated output to a separate LLM for judgment and evaluation. But how can you trust the results of LLM-as-a-judge evaluation?

Often, rounds of prompt engineering are required to improve accuracy, which is cumbersome and time-consuming. Fortunately, LangSmith provides a *few-shot* prompt solution whereby human corrections to LLM-as-a-judge outputs are stored as few-shot examples, which are then fed back into the prompt in future iterations.

By utilizing few-shot learning, the LLM can improve accuracy and align outputs with human preferences by providing examples of correct behavior. This is especially useful when it's difficult to construct instructions on how the LLM should behave or be formatted.

The few-shot evaluator follows these steps:

1. The LLM evaluator provides feedback on generated outputs, assessing factors such as correctness, relevance, or other criteria.

2. It adds human corrections to modify or correct the LLM evaluator's feedback in LangSmith. This is where human preferences and judgment are captured.

3. These corrections are stored as few-shot examples in LangSmith, with an option to leave explanations for corrections.

4. The few-shot examples are incorporated into future prompts as subsequent evaluation runs.

Over time, the few-shot evaluator will become increasingly aligned with human preferences. This self-improving mechanism reduces the need for time-consuming prompt engineering, while improving the accuracy and relevance of LLM-as-a-judge evaluations.

Here's how to easily set up the LLM-as-a-judge evaluator in LangSmith for offline evaluation. First, navigate to the "Datasets and Testing" section in the sidebar and select the dataset you want to configure the evaluator for. Click the Add Auto-Evaluator button at the top right of the dashboard to add an evaluator to the dataset. This will open a modal you can use to configure the evaluator.

Select the LLM-as-a-judge option and give your evaluator a name. You will now have the option to set an inline prompt or load a prompt from the prompt hub that will be used to evaluate the results of the runs in the experiment. For the sake of this example, choose the Create Few-Shot Evaluator option, as shown in Figure 10-11.

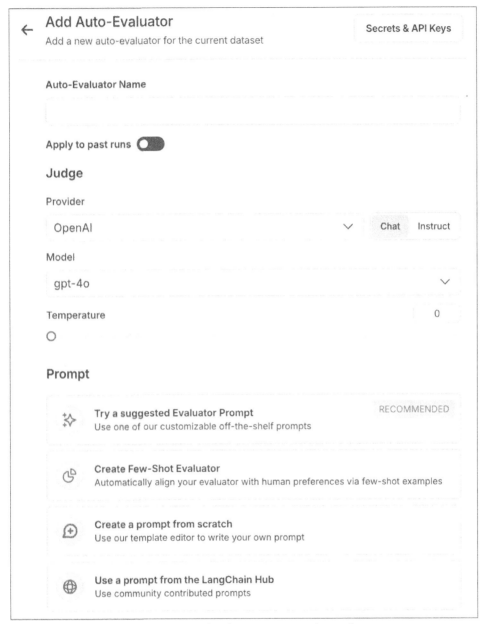

Figure 10-11. LangSmith UI options for the LLM-as-a-judge evaluator

This option will create a dataset that holds few-shot examples that will autopopulate when you make corrections on the evaluator feedback. The examples in this dataset will be inserted in the system prompt message.

You can also specify the scoring criteria in the Schema field and toggle between primitive types—for example, integer and Boolean (see Figure 10-12).

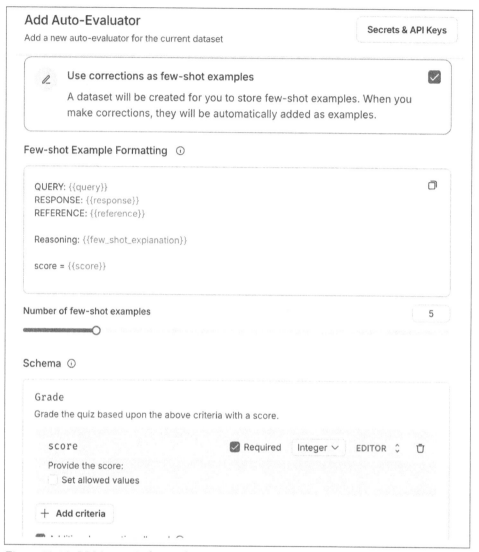

Figure 10-12. LLM-as-a-judge evaluator scoring criteria

Save the evaluator and navigate back to the dataset details page. Moving forward, each subsequent experiment run from the dataset will be evaluated by the evaluator you configured.

Pairwise evaluation

Ranking LLM outputs by preference can be less cognitively demanding for human or LLM-as-a-judge evaluators. For example, assessing which output is more informative, specific, or safe. Pairwise evaluation compares two outputs simultaneously from different versions of an application to determine which version better meets evaluation criteria.

LangSmith natively supports running and visualizing pairwise LLM app generations, highlighting preference for one generation over another based on guidelines set by the pairwise evaluator. LangSmith's pairwise evaluation enables you to do the following:

- Define a custom pairwise LLM-as-a-judge evaluator using any desired criteria
- Compare two LLM generations using this evaluator

As per the LangSmith docs (*https://oreil.ly/ruFvy*), you can use custom pairwise evaluators in the LangSmith SDK and visualize the results of pairwise evaluations in the LangSmith UI.

After creating an evaluation experiment, you can navigate to the Pairwise Experiments tab in the Datasets & Experiments section. The UI enables you to dive into each pairwise experiment, showing which LLM generation is preferred based upon our criteria. If you click the RANKED_PREFERENCE score under each answer, you can dive deeper into each evaluation trace (see Figure 10-13).

Figure 10-13. Pairwise experiment UI evaluation trace

Regression Testing

In traditional software development, tests are expected to pass 100% based on functional requirements. This ensures stable behavior once the test is validated. In contrast, however, AI models' output performances can vary significantly due to model *drift* (degradation due to changes in data distribution or updates to the model). As a result, testing AI applications may not always lead to a perfect score on the evaluation dataset.

This has several implications. First, it's important to track results and performance of your tests over time to prevent regression of your app's performance. *Regression* testing ensures that the latest updates or changes of the LLM model of your app do not *regress* (perform worse) relative to the baseline.

Second, it's crucial to compare the individual data points between two or more experimental runs to see where the model got it right or wrong.

LangSmith's comparison view has native support for regression testing, allowing you to quickly see examples that have changed relative to the baseline. Runs that regressed or improved are highlighted differently in the LangSmith dashboard (see Figure 10-14).

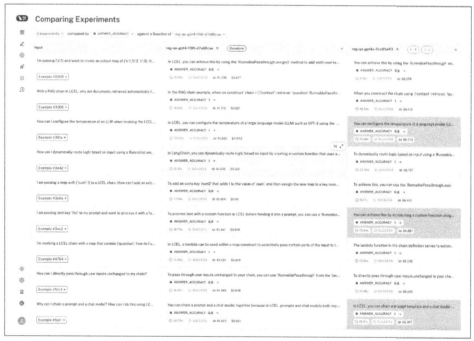

Figure 10-14. LangSmith's experiments comparison view

In LangSmith's Comparing Experiments dashboard, you can do the following:

- Compare multiple experiments and runs associated with a dataset. Aggregate stats of runs is useful for migrating models or prompts, which may result in performance improvements or regression on specific examples.
- Set a baseline run and compare it against prior app versions to detect unexpected regressions. If a regression occurs, you can isolate both the app version and the specific examples that contain performance changes.
- Drill into data points that behaved differently between compared experiments and runs.

This regression testing is crucial to ensure that your application maintains high performance over time regardless of updates and LLM changes.

Now that we've covered various preproduction testing strategies, let's explore a specific use case.

Evaluating an Agent's End-to-End Performance

Although agents show a lot of promise in executing autonomous tasks and workflows, testing an agent's performance can be challenging. In previous chapters, you learned how agents use tool calling with planning and memory to generate responses. In particular, tool calling enables the model to respond to a given prompt by generating a tool to invoke and the input arguments required to execute the tool.

Since agents use an LLM to decide the control flow of the application, each agent run can have significantly different outcomes. For example, different tools might be called, agents might get stuck in a loop, or the number of steps from start to finish can vary significantly.

Ideally, agents should be tested at three different levels of granularity:

Response
> The agent's final response to focus on the end-to-end performance. The inputs are a prompt and an optional list of tools, whereas the output is the final agent response.

Single step
> Any single, important step of the agent to drill into specific tool calls or decisions. In this case, the output is a tool call.

Trajectory
> The full trajectory of the agent. In this case, the output is the list of tool calls.

Figure 10-15 illustrates these levels:

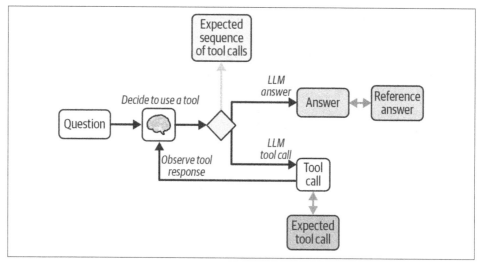

Figure 10-15. An example of an agentic app's flow

Let's dive deeper into each of these three agent-testing granularities.

Testing an agent's final response

In order to assess the overall performance of an agent on a task, you can treat the agent as a black box and define success based on whether or not it completes the task.

Testing for the agent's final response typically involves the following:

Inputs
    User input and (optionally) predefined tools

Output
    Agent's final response

Evaluator
    LLM-as-a-judge

To implement this in a programmatic manner, first create a dataset that includes questions and expected answers from the agent:

Python

```
from langsmith import Client

client = Client()

# Create a dataset
examples = [
```

```python
    ("Which country's customers spent the most? And how much did they spend?",
        """The country whose customers spent the most is the USA, with a total
        expenditure of $523.06"""),
    ("What was the most purchased track of 2013?",
        "The most purchased track of 2013 was Hot Girl."),
    ("How many albums does the artist Led Zeppelin have?",
        "Led Zeppelin has 14 albums"),
    ("What is the total price for the album "Big Ones"?",
        "The total price for the album 'Big Ones' is 14.85"),
    ("Which sales agent made the most in sales in 2009?",
        "Steve Johnson made the most sales in 2009"),
]


dataset_name = "SQL Agent Response"
if not client.has_dataset(dataset_name=dataset_name):
    dataset = client.create_dataset(dataset_name=dataset_name)
    inputs, outputs = zip(
        *[({"input": text}, {"output": label}) for text, label in examples]
    )
    client.create_examples(inputs=inputs, outputs=outputs, dataset_id=dataset.id)

## chain
def predict_sql_agent_answer(example: dict):
    """Use this for answer evaluation"""
    msg = {"messages": ("user", example["input"])}
    messages = graph.invoke(msg, config)
    return {"response": messages['messages'][-1].content}
```

JavaScript

```javascript
import { Client } from 'langsmith';

const client = new Client();

// Create a dataset
const examples = [
  ["Which country's customers spent the most? And how much did they spend?",
    `The country whose customers spent the most is the USA, with a total
    expenditure of $523.06`],
  ["What was the most purchased track of 2013?",
    "The most purchased track of 2013 was Hot Girl."],
  ["How many albums does the artist Led Zeppelin have?",
    "Led Zeppelin has 14 albums"],
  ["What is the total price for the album 'Big Ones'?",
    "The total price for the album 'Big Ones' is 14.85"],
  ["Which sales agent made the most in sales in 2009?",
    "Steve Johnson made the most sales in 2009"],
];

const datasetName = "SQL Agent Response";

async function createDataset() {
  const hasDataset = await client.hasDataset({ datasetName });
```

```
  if (!hasDataset) {
    const dataset = await client.createDataset(datasetName);
    const inputs = examples.map(([text]) => ({ input: text }));
    const outputs = examples.map(([, label]) => ({ output: label }));

    await client.createExamples({ inputs, outputs, datasetId: dataset.id });
  }
}

createDataset();

// Chain function
async function predictSqlAgentAnswer(example) {
  // Use this for answer evaluation
  const msg = { messages: [{ role: "user", content: example.input }] };
  const output = await graph.invoke(msg, config);
  return { response: output.messages[output.messages.length - 1].content };
}
```

Next, as discussed earlier, we can utilize the LLM to compare the generated answer with the reference answer:

Python

```python
from langchain import hub
from langchain_openai import ChatOpenAI
from langsmith.evaluation import evaluate

# Grade prompt
grade_prompt_answer_accuracy = hub.pull("langchain-ai/rag-answer-vs-reference")

def answer_evaluator(run, example) -> dict:
    """
    A simple evaluator for RAG answer accuracy
    """

    # Get question, ground truth answer, RAG chain answer
    input_question = example.inputs["input"]
    reference = example.outputs["output"]
    prediction = run.outputs["response"]

    # LLM grader
    llm = ChatOpenAI(model="gpt-4o", temperature=0)

    # Structured prompt
    answer_grader = grade_prompt_answer_accuracy | llm

    # Run evaluator
    score = answer_grader.invoke({"question": input_question,
                                  "correct_answer": reference,
                                  "student_answer": prediction})
    score = score["Score"]
```

```
                return {"key": "answer_v_reference_score", "score": score}


        ## Run evaluation
        experiment_results = evaluate(
            predict_sql_agent_answer,
            data=dataset_name,
            evaluators=[answer_evaluator],
            num_repetitions=3,
        )
```

JavaScript

```javascript
import { pull } from "langchain/hub";
import { ChatOpenAI } from "langchain_openai";
import { evaluate } from "langsmith/evaluation";

async function answerEvaluator(run, example) {
  /**
   * A simple evaluator for RAG answer accuracy
   */

  // Get question, ground truth answer, RAG chain answer
  const inputQuestion = example.inputs["input"];
  const reference = example.outputs["output"];
  const prediction = run.outputs["response"];

  // LLM grader
  const llm = new ChatOpenAI({ model: "gpt-4o", temperature: 0 });

  // Grade prompt
  const gradePromptAnswerAccuracy = pull(
    "langchain-ai/rag-answer-vs-reference"
  );

  // Structured prompt
  const answerGrader = gradePromptAnswerAccuracy.pipe(llm);

  // Run evaluator
  const scoreResult = await answerGrader.invoke({
    question: inputQuestion,
    correct_answer: reference,
    student_answer: prediction
  });

  const score = scoreResult["Score"];

  return { key: "answer_v_reference_score", score: score };
}

// Run evaluation
const experimentResults = evaluate(predictSqlAgentAnswer, {
```

```
        data: datasetName,
        evaluators: [answerEvaluator],
        numRepetitions: 3,
    });
```

Testing a single step of an agent

Testing an agent's individual action or decision enables you to identify and analyze
specifically where your application is underperforming. Testing for a single step of an
agent involves the following:

Inputs
> User input to a single step (for example, user prompt, set of tools). This can also
> include previously completed steps.

Output
> LLM response from the inputs step, which often contains tool calls indicating
> what action the agent should take next.

Evaluator
> Binary score for correct tool selection and heuristic assessment of the tool input's
> accuracy.

The following example checks a specific tool call using a custom evaluator:

Python

```python
from langsmith.schemas import Example, Run

def predict_assistant(example: dict):
    """Invoke assistant for single tool call evaluation"""
    msg = [ ("user", example["input"]) ]
    result = assistant_runnable.invoke({"messages":msg})
    return {"response": result}


def check_specific_tool_call(root_run: Run, example: Example) -> dict:
    """
    Check if the first tool call in the response matches the expected tool call.
    """
    # Expected tool call
    expected_tool_call = 'sql_db_list_tables'

    # Run
    response = root_run.outputs["response"]

    # Get tool call
    try:
        tool_call = getattr(response, 'tool_calls', [])[0]['name']
    except (IndexError, KeyError):
        tool_call = None
```

```python
        score = 1 if tool_call == expected_tool_call else 0
        return {"score": score, "key": "single_tool_call"}

    experiment_results = evaluate(
        predict_assistant,
        data=dataset_name,
        evaluators=[check_specific_tool_call],
        num_repetitions=3,
        metadata={"version": metadata},
    )
```

JavaScript

```javascript
import {evaluate} from 'langsmith/evaluation';

// Predict Assistant
function predictAssistant(example) {
    /**
     * Invoke assistant for single tool call evaluation
     */
    const msg = [{ role: "user", content: example.input }];
    const result = assistantRunnable.invoke({ messages: msg });
    return { response: result };
}

// Check Specific Tool Call
function checkSpecificToolCall(rootRun, example) {
    /**
     * Check if the first tool call in the response matches the expected
     * tool call.
     */

    // Expected tool call
    const expectedToolCall = "sql_db_list_tables";

    // Run
    const response = rootRun.outputs.response;

    // Get tool call
    let toolCall;
    try {
        toolCall = response.tool_calls?.[0]?.name;
    } catch (error) {
        toolCall = null;
    }

    const score = toolCall === expectedToolCall ? 1 : 0;
    return { score, key: "single_tool_call" };
}

// Experiment Results
const experimentResults = evaluate(predictAssistant, {
```

```
        data: datasetName,
        evaluators: [checkSpecificToolCall],
        numRepetitions: 3,
    });
```

The preceding code block implements these distinct components:

- Invoke the assistant, `assistant_runnable`, with a prompt and check if the resulting tool call is as expected.

- Utilize a specialized agent where the tools are hardcoded rather than passed with the dataset input.

- Specify the reference tool call for the step that we are evaluating for `expected_tool_call`.

Testing an agent's trajectory

It's important to look back on the steps an agent took in order to assess whether or not the trajectory lined up with expectations of the agent—that is, the number of steps or sequence of steps taken.

Testing an agent's trajectory involves the following:

Inputs
   User input and (optionally) predefined tools.

Output
   Expected sequence of tool calls or a list of tool calls in any order.

Evaluator
   Function over the steps taken. To test the outputs, you can look at an exact match binary score or metrics that focus on the number of incorrect steps. You'd need to evaluate the full agent's trajectory against a reference trajectory and then compile as a set of messages to pass into the LLM-as-a-judge.

The following example assesses the trajectory of tool calls using custom evaluators:

Python

```python
def predict_sql_agent_messages(example: dict):
    """Use this for answer evaluation"""
    msg = {"messages": ("user", example["input"])}
    messages = graph.invoke(msg, config)
    return {"response": messages}


def find_tool_calls(messages):
    """
    Find all tool calls in the messages returned
    """

    tool_calls = [
```

```
            tc['name']
            for m in messages['messages'] for tc in getattr(m, 'tool_calls', [])
    ]
    return tool_calls

def contains_all_tool_calls_any_order(
    root_run: Run, example: Example
) -> dict:
    """
    Check if all expected tools are called in any order.
    """
    expected = [
        'sql_db_list_tables',
        'sql_db_schema',
        'sql_db_query_checker',
        'sql_db_query',
        'check_result'
    ]
    messages = root_run.outputs["response"]
    tool_calls = find_tool_calls(messages)
    # Optionally, log the tool calls -
    #print("Here are my tool calls:")
    #print(tool_calls)
    if set(expected) <= set(tool_calls):
        score = 1
    else:
        score = 0
    return {"score": int(score), "key": "multi_tool_call_any_order"}

def contains_all_tool_calls_in_order(root_run: Run, example: Example) -> dict:
    """
    Check if all expected tools are called in exact order.
    """
    messages = root_run.outputs["response"]
    tool_calls = find_tool_calls(messages)
    # Optionally, log the tool calls -
    #print("Here are my tool calls:")
    #print(tool_calls)
    it = iter(tool_calls)
    expected = [
        'sql_db_list_tables',
        'sql_db_schema',
        'sql_db_query_checker',
        'sql_db_query',
        'check_result'
    ]
    if all(elem in it for elem in expected):
        score = 1
    else:
        score = 0
    return {"score": int(score), "key": "multi_tool_call_in_order"}
```

```python
def contains_all_tool_calls_in_order_exact_match(
    root_run: Run, example: Example
) -> dict:
    """
    Check if all expected tools are called in exact order and without any
        additional tool calls.
    """
    expected = [
        'sql_db_list_tables',
        'sql_db_schema',
        'sql_db_query_checker',
        'sql_db_query',
        'check_result'
    ]
    messages = root_run.outputs["response"]
    tool_calls = find_tool_calls(messages)
    # Optionally, log the tool calls -
    #print("Here are my tool calls:")
    #print(tool_calls)
    if tool_calls == expected:
        score = 1
    else:
        score = 0

    return {"score": int(score), "key": "multi_tool_call_in_exact_order"}

experiment_results = evaluate(
    predict_sql_agent_messages,
    data=dataset_name,
    evaluators=[
        contains_all_tool_calls_any_order,
        contains_all_tool_calls_in_order,
        contains_all_tool_calls_in_order_exact_match
    ],
    num_repetitions=3,
)
```

JavaScript

```javascript
import {evaluate} from 'langsmith/evaluation';

// Predict SQL Agent Messages
function predictSqlAgentMessages(example) {
  /**
   * Use this for answer evaluation
   */
  const msg = { messages: [{ role: "user", content: example.input }] };
  // Replace with your graph and config
  const messages = graph.invoke(msg, config);
  return { response: messages };
}

// Find Tool Calls
```

```
function findToolCalls({messages}) {
  /**
   * Find all tool calls in the messages returned
   */
  return messages.flatMap(m => m.tool_calls?.map(tc => tc.name) || []);
}

// Contains All Tool Calls (Any Order)
function containsAllToolCallsAnyOrder(rootRun, example) {
  /**
   * Check if all expected tools are called in any order.
   */
  const expected = [
    "sql_db_list_tables",
    "sql_db_schema",
    "sql_db_query_checker",
    "sql_db_query",
    "check_result"
  ];
  const messages = rootRun.outputs.response;
  const toolCalls = findToolCalls(messages);

  const score = expected.every(tool => toolCalls.includes(tool)) ? 1 : 0;
  return { score, key: "multi_tool_call_any_order" };
}

// Contains All Tool Calls (In Order)
function containsAllToolCallsInOrder(rootRun, example) {
  /**
   * Check if all expected tools are called in exact order.
   */
  const messages = rootRun.outputs.response;
  const toolCalls = findToolCalls(messages);

  const expected = [
    "sql_db_list_tables",
    "sql_db_schema",
    "sql_db_query_checker",
    "sql_db_query",
    "check_result"
  ];

  const score = expected.every(tool => {
    let found = false;
    for (let call of toolCalls) {
      if (call === tool) {
          found = true;
          break;
      }
    }
    return found;
  }) ? 1 : 0;
```

```
    return { score, key: "multi_tool_call_in_order" };
}

// Contains All Tool Calls (Exact Order, Exact Match)
function containsAllToolCallsInOrderExactMatch(rootRun, example) {
  /**
   * Check if all expected tools are called in exact order and without any
   * additional tool calls.
   */
  const expected = [
    "sql_db_list_tables",
    "sql_db_schema",
    "sql_db_query_checker",
    "sql_db_query",
    "check_result"
  ];
  const messages = rootRun.outputs.response;
  const toolCalls = findToolCalls(messages);

  const score = JSON.stringify(toolCalls) === JSON.stringify(expected)
    ? 1
    : 0;
  return { score, key: "multi_tool_call_in_exact_order" };
}

// Experiment Results
const experimentResults = evaluate(predictSqlAgentMessages, {
  data: datasetName,
  evaluators: [
    containsAllToolCallsAnyOrder,
    containsAllToolCallsInOrder,
    containsAllToolCallsInOrderExactMatch
  ],
  numRepetitions: 3,
});
```

This implementation example includes the following:

- Invoking a precompiled LangGraph agent graph.invoke with a prompt
- Utilizing a specialized agent where the tools are hardcoded rather than passed with the dataset input
- Extracting of the list of tools called using the function find_tool_calls
- Checking if all expected tools are called in any order using the function contains_all_tool_calls_any_order or called in order using contains_all_tool_calls_in_order
- Checking whether all expected tools are called in the exact order using contains_all_tool_calls_in_order_exact_match

---

All three of these agent evaluation methods can be observed and debugged in LangSmith's experimentation UI (see Figure 10-16).

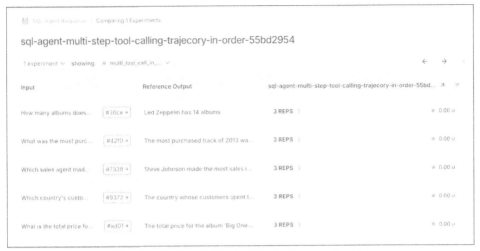

Figure 10-16. Example of an agent evaluation test in the LangSmith UI

In general, these tests are a solid starting point to help mitigate an agent's cost and unreliability due to LLM invocations and variability in tool calling.

Production

Although testing in the preproduction phase is useful, certain bugs and edge cases may not emerge until your LLM application interacts with live users. These issues can affect latency, as well as the relevancy and accuracy of outputs. In addition, observability and the process of *online evaluation* can help ensure that there are guardrails for LLM inputs or outputs. These guardrails can provide much-needed protection from prompt injection and toxicity.

The first step in this process is to set up LangSmith's tracing feature.

Tracing

A *trace* is a series of steps that your application takes to go from input to output. LangSmith makes it easy to visualize, debug, and test each trace generated from your app.

Once you've installed the relevant LangChain and LLM dependencies, all you need to do is configure the tracing environment variables based on your LangSmith account credentials:

```
export LANGCHAIN_TRACING_V2=true
export LANGCHAIN_API_KEY=<your-api-key>
```

```
# The below examples use the OpenAI API, though you can use other LLM providers

export OPENAI_API_KEY=<your-openai-api-key>
```

After the environment variables are set, no other code is required to enable tracing. Traces will be automatically logged to their specific project in the "Tracing projects" section of the LangSmith dashboard. The metrics provided include trace volume, success and failure rates, latency, token count and cost, and more—as shown in Figure 10-17.

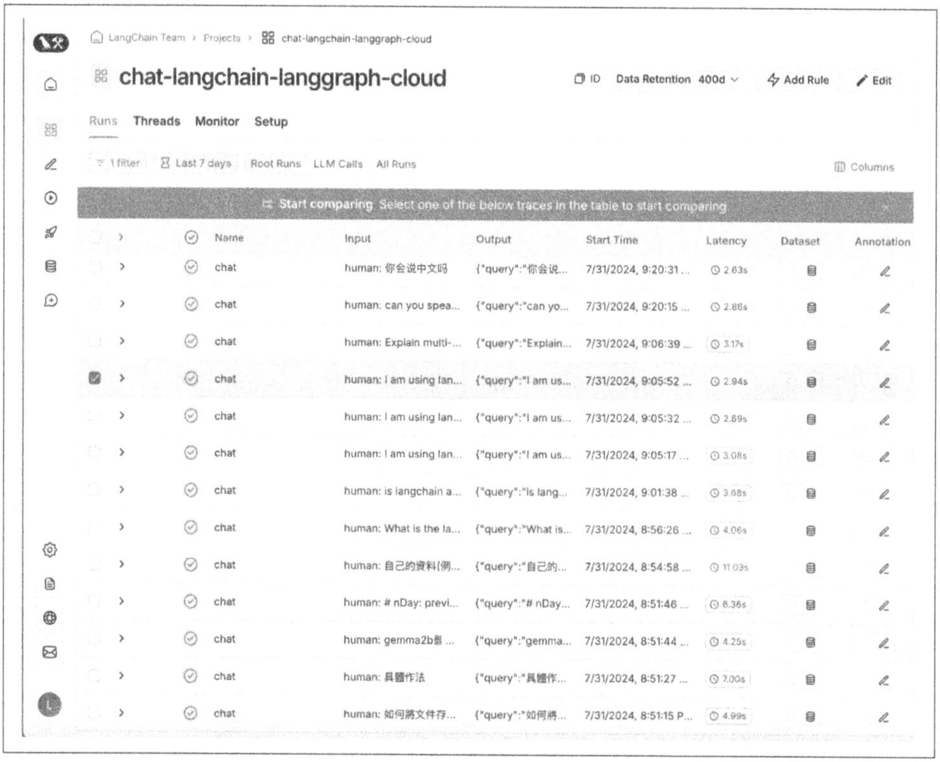

Figure 10-17. An example of LangSmith's trace performance metrics

You can review a variety of strategies to implement tracing based on your needs.

Collect Feedback in Production

Unlike the preproduction phase, evaluators for production testing don't have grounded reference responses for the LLM to compare against. Instead, evaluators need to score performance in real time as your application processes user inputs. This reference-free, real-time evaluation is often referred to as *online evaluation*.

There are at least two types of feedback you can collect in production to improve app performance:

Feedback from users
> You can directly collect user feedback explicitly or implicitly. For example, giving users the ability to click a like and dislike button or provide detailed feedback based on the application's output is an effective way to track user satisfaction. In LangSmith, you can attach user feedback to any trace or intermediate run (that is, span) of a trace, including annotating traces inline or reviewing runs together in an annotation queue.

Feedback from LLM-as-a judge evaluators
> As discussed previously, these evaluators can be implemented directly on traces to identify hallucination and toxic responses.

The earlier preproduction section already discussed how to set up LangSmith's auto evaluation in the Datasets & Experiments section of the dashboard.

Classification and Tagging

In order to implement effective guardrails against toxicity or gather insights on user sentiment analysis, we need to build an effective system for labeling user inputs and generated outputs.

This system is largely dependent on whether or not you have a dataset that contains reference labels. If you don't have preset labels, you can use the LLM-as-a-judge evaluator to assist in performing classification and tagging based upon specified criteria.

If, however, ground truth classification labels are provided, then a custom heuristic evaluator can be used to score the chain's output relative to the ground truth class labels.

Monitoring and Fixing Errors

Once your application is in production, LangSmith's tracing will catch errors and edge cases. You can add these errors into your test dataset for offline evaluation in order to prevent recurrences of the same issues.

Another useful strategy is to release your app in phases to a small group of beta users before a larger audience can access its features. This will enable you to uncover crucial bugs, develop a solid evaluation dataset with ground truth references, and assess the general performance of the app including cost, latency, and quality of outputs.

Summary

As discussed in this chapter, robust testing is crucial to ensure that your LLM application is accurate, reliable, fast, toxic-free, and cost-efficient. The three key stages of LLM app development create a data cycle that helps to ensure high performance throughout the lifetime of the application.

During the design phase, in-app error handling enables self-correction before the error reaches the user. Preproduction testing ensures each of your app's updates avoids regression in performance metrics. Finally, production monitoring gathers real-time insights and application errors that inform the subsequent design process and the cycle repeats.

Ultimately, this process of testing, evaluation, monitoring, and continuous improvement, will help you fix issues and iterate faster, and most importantly, deliver a product that users can trust to consistently deliver their desired results.

## CHAPTER 11

Building with LLMs

One of the biggest open questions in the world of LLMs today is how to best put them in the hands of end users. In some ways, LLMs are actually a more intuitive interface for computing than what came before them. They are much more forgiving of typos, slips of the tongue, and the general imprecision of humans, when compared to traditional computer applications. On the other hand, the very ability to handle inputs that are "slightly off" comes with a tendency to sometimes produce results that are also "slightly off"—which is also very much unlike any previous computing tendencies.

In fact, computers were designed to reliably repeat the same set of instructions with the same results every time. Over the past few decades, that principle of reliability has permeated the design of human-computer interfaces (variously called HCI, UX, and UI) to the extent that a lot of the usual constructs end up being subpar for use in applications that rely heavily on LLMs.

Let's take an example: Figma is a software application used by designers to create faithful renderings of designs for websites, mobile applications, book or magazine covers—the list goes on. As is the case with pretty much all productivity software (software for the creation of some kind of long-form content), its interface is a combination of the following:

- A palette of tools and prebuilt *primitives* (fundamental building blocks), in this case lines, shapes, selection and paint tools, and many more
- A canvas, where the user inserts these building blocks and organizes them into their creation: a website page, a mobile app screen, and so on

This interface is built upon the premise that the capabilities of the software are known ahead of time, which is in fact true in the case of Figma. All building blocks and tools were coded by a software engineer ahead of time. Therefore, they were known to exist at the time the interface was designed. It sounds almost silly to point that out, but the same is not strictly true of software that makes heavy use of LLMs.

Look at a word processor (e.g., Microsoft Word or Google Docs). This is a software application for the creation of long-form text content of some kind, such as a blog post, article, book chapter, and the like. The interface at our disposal here is also made up of a familiar combination:

- A palette of tools and prebuilt *primitives*: in the case of a word processor, the primitives available are tables, lists, headings, image placeholders, and so forth, and the tools are spellcheck, commenting, and so on.

- A *canvas*: in this case, it's literally a blank page, where the user types words and may include some of the elements just mentioned.

How would this situation change if we were to build an LLM-native word processor? This chapter explores three possible answers to this question, which are broadly applicable to any LLM application. For each of the patterns we explore, we'll go over what key concepts you'd need to implement it successfully. We don't mean to imply that these are the only ones, it will be a while until the dust settles on this particular question.

Let's look at each of these patterns, starting with the easiest to add to an existing app.

Interactive Chatbots

This is arguably the easiest lift to add to an existing software application. At its most basic conception, this idea just bolts on an AI sidekick—to bounce ideas off of—while all work still happens in the existing user interface of the application. An example here is GitHub Copilot Chat, which can be used in a sidebar inside the VSCode code editor.

An upgrade to this pattern is to add some communication points between the AI sidekick extension and the main application. For example, in VSCode, the assistant can "see" the content of the file currently being edited or whatever portion of that code the user has selected. And in the other direction, the assistant can insert or edit text in that open editor, arriving at some basic form of collaboration between the user and the LLM.

Streaming chat as we're describing here is currently the prototypical application of LLMs. It's almost always the first thing app developers learn to build on their LLM journey, and it's almost always the first thing companies reach for when adding LLMs to their existing applications. Maybe this will remain the case for years to come, but another possible outcome could be for streaming chat to become the command line of the LLM era—that is, the closest to direct programming access, becoming a niche interface, just as it did for computers.

To build the most basic chatbot you should use these components:

A chat model
Their dialogue tuning lends itself well to multiturn interactions with a user. Refer to the Preface for more on dialogue tuning.

Conversation history
A useful chatbot needs to be able to "get past hello." That is, if the chatbot can't remember the previous user inputs, it will be much harder to have meaningful conversations with it, which implicitly refer to previous messages.

To go beyond the basics, you'd probably add the following:

Streaming output
The best chatbot experiences currently stream LLM output token by token (or in larger chunks, like sentences or paragraphs) directly to the user, which alleviates the latency inherent to LLMs today.

Tool calling
To give the chatbot the ability to interact with the main canvas and tools of the application, you can expose them as tools the model can decide to call on—for instance, a "get selected text" tool and an "insert text at end of doc" tool.

Human-in-the-loop
As soon as you give the chatbot tools that can change what's in the application canvas, you create the need to give back some control to the user—for example, letting the user confirm, or even edit, before new text is inserted.

Collaborative Editing with LLMs

Most productivity software has some form of collaborative editing built in, which we can classify into one of these buckets (or somewhere in between):

Save and send
> This is the most basic version, which only supports one user editing the document at a time, before "passing the buck" to another user (for example, sending the file over email) and repeating the process until done. The most obvious example is the Microsoft Office suite of apps: Excel, Word, PowerPoint.

Version control
> This is an evolution of save and send that supports multiple editors working simultaneously on their own (and unaware of each other's changes) by providing tools to combine their work afterward: merge strategies (how to combine unrelated changes) and conflict resolution (how to combine incompatible changes). The most popular example today is Git/GitHub, used by software engineers to collaborate on software projects.

Real-time collaboration
> This enables multiple editors to work on the same document at the same time, while seeing each other's changes. This is arguably the most natural form of software-enabled collaboration, evidenced by the popularity of Google Docs and Google Sheets among technical and nontechnical computer users.

This pattern of LLM user experience consists of employing an LLM agent as one of those "users" contributing to this shared document. This can take many forms, including the following:

- An always-on "copilot" giving you suggestions on how to complete the next sentence

- An asynchronous "drafter," which you task with, for example, going off and researching the topic in question and returning later with a section you can incorporate in your final document

To build this, you'd likely need the following:

Shared state
> The LLM agent and the human users should be on the same footing in terms of access and understanding of the state of the document—that is, they would be able to parse the state of the document and produce edits to that state in a compatible format.

Task manager

Producing a useful edit to the document will invariably be a multistep process, which can take time and fail halfway. This creates the need for reliable scheduling and orchestration of long-running jobs, with queueing, error recovery, and control over running tasks.

Merging forks

Users will continue to edit the document after tasking the LLM agent, so LLM outputs will need to be merged with the users' work, either manually by the user (an experience like Git) or automatically (through conflict resolution algorithms such as CRDT and operational transformation (OT), employed by applications such as Google Docs).

Concurrency

The fact that the human user and the LLM agent are working on the same thing at the same time requires the ability to handle interruptions, cancellations, reroutings (do this instead), and queueing (do this as well).

Undo/redo stack

This is a ubiquitous pattern in productivity software, which inevitably is needed here too. Users change their minds and want to go back to an earlier state of the document, and the LLM application needs to be capable of following them there.

Intermediate output

Merging user and LLM outputs is made a lot easier when those outputs are gradual and arrive piecemeal as soon as they're produced, in much the same way that a person writes a 10-paragraph page one sentence at a time.

Ambient Computing

A very useful UX pattern has been the always-on background software that pipes up when something "interesting" has happened that deserves your attention. You can find this in many places today. A few examples are:

- You can set an alert in your brokerage app to notify you when some stock goes below a certain price.
- You can ask Google to notify you when new search results are found matching some search query.
- You can define alerts for your computer infrastructure to notify you when something is outside the regular pattern of behavior.

The main obstacle to deploying this pattern more widely may be coming up with a reliable definition of *interesting* ahead of time that is both of the following:

Useful
It will notify you when you think it should.

Practical
Most users won't want to spend massive amounts of time ahead precreating endless rules for alerts.

The reasoning capabilities of LLMs can unlock new applications of this pattern of *ambient computing* that are simultaneously more useful (they identify more of what you'd find interesting) and less work to set up (their reasoning can replace a lot or all of the manual setup of rules).

The big difference between *collaborative* and *ambient* is concurrency:

Collaborative
You and the LLM are usually (or sometimes) doing work at the same time and feeding off each other's work.

Ambient
The LLM is continuously doing some kind of work in the background while you, the user, are presumably doing something else entirely.

To build this, you need:

Triggers
The LLM agent needs to receive (or poll periodically for) new information from the environment. This is in fact what motivates ambient computing: a preexisting source of periodic or continuous new information that needs to be processed.

Long-term memory
It would not be possible to detect new interesting events without consulting a database of previously received information.

Reflection (or learning)
Understanding what is *interesting* (what deserves human input) likely requires learning from each previous interesting event after it happens. This is usually called a *reflection step*, in which the LLM produces an update to its long-term memory, possibly modifying its internal "rules" for detecting future interesting events.

Summarize output

An agent working in the background is likely to produce much more output than the human user would like to see. This requires that the agent architecture be modified to produce summaries of the work done and surface to the user only what is new or noteworthy.

Task manager

Having an LLM agent working continuously in the background requires employing some system for managing the work, queuing new runs, and handling and recovering from error.

Summary

LLMs have the potential to change not only how we build software (*https://oreil.ly/ RqnCm*), but also the very software we build. This new capability that we developers have at our disposal to generate new content will not only enhance many existing apps, but it can make new things possible that we haven't dreamed of yet.

There's no shortcut here. You really do need to build something (s)crappy, speak to users, and rinse and repeat until something new and unexpected comes out the other side.

With this last chapter, and the book as a whole, we have tried to give you the knowledge we think can help you build something uniquely good with LLMs. We want to thank you for coming on this journey with us and wish you the best of luck in your career and future.

Index

L

LangChain (see also LangGraph; large language models; LLM applications; retrieval-augmented generation)
  assembling LLM applications, 16-22, 115-118
  beginnings of, x
  benefits of, ix-x, xx, 1-3
  documentation for, 2
  getting specific formats out of LLMs, 13-16
  interfaces provided, 4
  making LLM prompts reusable, 7-13
  setting up, 3
  using LLMs in, 4-7
LangChain Expression Language (LCEL)
  imperative versus declarative composition, 17
  optimized execution plan using, 20
LangGraph (see also cognitive architectures; LangChain; LangSmith)
  adding memory to chatbots, 105-107
  basics of, 98-101
  building chatbot memory systems, 96-98
  building LangGraph agents, 139-143
  configuration file, 204
  control flow illustration, 197
  creating a StateGraph, 101-105
  installing, 101
  intermediate output, 176
  modifying chat history, 107-114
  purpose of, 98
  self-corrective RAG, 217-223
  stream modes supported in, 178
  streaming LLM output token-by-token, 178
  subgraphs, 161-165
LangGraph Platform API
  data models, 201
  deployment using, 198
  features, 202-204
LangGraph Studio, 210-212
LangSmith (see also LangChain; LangGraph)
  account creation, 199
  agent evaluation example, 247
  comparison view/regression testing, 234
  dataset creation, 224
  deployment from LangSmith UI, 207-209
  few-shot prompting, 229-232
  pairwise evaluation, 233
  trace results in, 222

  tracing, 248
language models, xi
large language model (llm) dataset, 225
large language models (LLMs) (see also structured output)
  alternative providers for, 2
  ambient computing with, 255
  benefits and drawbacks of, 251
  brief primer on, xi-xiii
  building with, 251-257
  Claude and Bard, x
  collaborative editing with, 254-255
  deployment example, 192
  getting specific formats out of LLMs, 13-16
  limitations of knowledge corpus, 23
  LLM-based embeddings, 27
  versus machine learning, x
  for multilingual output, xi
  open source LLMs, xv, xxi
  OpenAI's GPT-3, xi
  OpenAI's GPT-3.5, ix
  relevant content for LLMs, 24, 59-68
  types of, xiii-xv
  using in LangChain, 4-7
latency, 172, 176, 253
LCEL (see LangChain Expression Language)
Llama, xv, xxi
llm (large language model) dataset, 225
LLM applications (see also deployment; evaluation metrics; testing)
  agentic, 135
  assembling, 16-22, 115-118
  benefits of LangChain for building, 1-3
  challenge in building good applications, 1
  common features of, 115
  key stages of app development, 216
  major LLM architectures, 117
  multiactor applications, 98
  multitasking LLMs, 186-188
  patterns and key concepts for successful, 173-188
  security considerations, 213
  trade-off between agency and reliability, 116, 171-173
LLM call architecture, 118-121
LLM-as-a-judge evaluators, 228
LLM-driven loop, 136
LLMs (see large language models)
logical routing, 81-84

About the Authors

Mayo Oshin is a tech entrepreneur, AI advisor, and angel investor. Mayo was an early developer contributor and advocate for the open source LangChain library and an early pioneer in the popular AI "chat" with data movement (5+ million people reached through his thought-leadership ideas so far).

Mayo has consulted with, advised, and trained hundreds of engineers and product managers at various leading institutions, including Amazon, LinkedIn, Evercore, Visa, and BCG.

You can learn more about him at his website, *mayooshin.com*, and get his latest ideas on AI and technology on X (*https://x.com/mayowaoshin*).

Nuno Campos is a founding software engineer at LangChain, Inc. Nuno has a decade of experience as a Python and JavaScript software engineer, architect and open source maintainer. He has worked for various tech startups in software engineering and data science roles. He holds an MSc in Finance.

Colophon

The animals on the cover of *Learning LangChain* are European tree frogs (*Hyla arborea*).

They are primarily found in mainland Europe, typically close to vegetation. Their green skin can adjust its color from green to grey or brown, depending on a variety of factors. This ability helps to camouflage them from predators. They also use their sticky tongues (for meals, i.e., insects) and the sticky pads on their feet (for movement) to navigate life in their habitat.

During mating season, European tree frogs congregate close to ponds so that they can lay eggs near water for the soon-to-be tadpoles. The males perform a mating call that is striking for its volume, particularly when many frogs are gathered in one place. The females then lay clumps of 800 to 1,000 eggs. About 10 to 14 days later, the tadpoles hatch, and the cycle of life begins anew.

Many of the animals on O'Reilly covers are endangered; all of them are important to the world.

The cover illustration is by Karen Montgomery, based on an antique line engraving from *Meyers Kleines Lexicon*. The series design is by Edie Freedman, Ellie Volckhausen, and Karen Montgomery. The cover fonts are Gilroy Semibold and Guardian Sans. The text font is Adobe Minion Pro; the heading font is Adobe Myriad Condensed; and the code font is Dalton Maag's Ubuntu Mono.

O'REILLY®

Learn from experts.
Become one yourself.

60,000+ titles | Live events with experts | Role-based courses
Interactive learning | Certification preparation

**Try the O'Reilly learning platform
free for 10 days.**

www.ingramcontent.com/pod-product-compliance
Lightning Source LLC
Jackson TN
JSHW061120160825
89471JS00009B/258